Managing Multiple Projects

CENTER FOR BUSINESS PRACTICES

Editor

James S. Pennypacker

Director
Center for Business Practices
West Chester, Pennsylvania

The Superior Project Organization: Global Competency Standards and Best Practices, Frank Toney

The Superior Project Manager: Global Competency Standards and Best Practices, Frank Toney

PM Practices

The Strategic Project Office: A Guide to Improving Organizational Performance, J. Kent Crawford

Project Management Maturity Model: Providing a Proven Path to Project Management Excellence, J. Kent Crawford

Managing Multiple Projects: Planning, Scheduling, and Allocating Resources for Competitive Advantage, James S. Pennypacker and Lowell D. Dye

ADDITIONAL VOLUMES IN PREPARATION

Managing Multiple Projects

Planning, Scheduling, and Allocating Resources for Competitive Advantage

edited by

James S. Pennypacker
Project Management Solutions, Inc.
West Chester, Pennsylvania, U.S.A.

Lowell D. Dye
TriCon Consulting, Inc.
Beaver Creek, Ohio, U.S.A.

CRC Press
Taylor & Francis Group
Boca Raton London New York

CRC Press is an imprint of the
Taylor & Francis Group, an **informa** business

CRC Press
Taylor & Francis Group
6000 Broken Sound Parkway NW, Suite 300
Boca Raton, FL 33487-2742

First issued in paperback 2019

© 2002 by Taylor & Francis Group, LLC
CRC Press is an imprint of Taylor & Francis Group, an Informa business

ISBN-13: 978-0-8247-0680-7 (hbk)
ISBN-13: 978-0-367-39606-0 (pbk)

**Visit the Taylor & Francis Web site at
http://www.taylorandfrancis.com**

**and the CRC Press Web site at
http://www.crcpress.com**

We gratefully acknowledge the use of the following materials as adapted for this publication.

Lewis R. Ireland, "Managing Multiple Projects in the 21st Century." Adapted from the *Proceedings of the Project Management Institute 1997 Seminars and Symposium* with permission. Copyright © 1997 Project Management Institute, Inc. All rights reserved.

William J. Olford, "Why Is Multiple-Project Management Hard and How Can We Make It Easier?" Adapted from the *Proceedings of the Project Management Institute 1994 Seminars and Symposium* with permission. Copyright © 1994 Project Management Institute, Inc. All rights reserved.

Jack Meredith and Samuel J. Mantel, Jr., "Multiproject Scheduling and Resource Allocation." Adapted from *Project Management: A Managerial Approach* with permission. Copyright © 2000 by John Wiley & Sons, Inc.

Michael McCauley, Ann Bundy, and William Seidman, "Effective Resource Management—Debunking the Myths." Adapted from the *Proceedings of the Project Management Institute 1999 Seminars and Symposium* with permission. Copyright © 1999 Project Management Institute, Inc. All rights reserved.

Michel Thiry, "A Learning Loop for Successful Program Management." Adapted from the *Proceedings of the Project Management Institute 2000 Seminars and Symposium* with permission. Copyright © 2000 Project Management Institute, Inc. All rights reserved.

Gregory D. Githens, "Programs, Portfolios, and Pipelines: How to Anticipate Executives' Strategic Questions." Adapted from the *Proceedings of the Project Management Institute 1998 Seminars and Symposium* with permission. Copyright © 1998 Project Management Institute, Inc. All rights reserved.

Geoff Reiss, *Multiproject Scheduling and Management.* Adapted from The Programme Management Web Site, www.e-programme.com. Copyright © 2000 Hydra Development Corporation.

Neal Whitten, "Organizing for Multiple Projects." Adapted from *The EnterPrize Organization* with permission. Copyright © 2000 Project Management Institute, Inc. All rights reserved.

Nino Levy and Shlomo Globerson, "Improving Multiproject Management by Using a Queuing Theory Approach." Adapted from the *Project Management Journal* with permission. Copyright © 2000 Project Management Institute, Inc. All rights reserved.

Project Management Institute (PMI) Headquarters, Four Campus Boulevard, Newtown Square, Pennsylvania, U.S.A. 19073-2399. PMI is the world's leading project management association with more than 70,000 members worldwide. For further information contact PMI by phone (610) 356-4600, by fax (610) 356-4647, or by visiting the web site at www.pmi.org.

Series Introduction

The organizational environment needed for project success is ultimately created by management. The way that the managers define, structure, and act toward projects is critical to the success or failure of those projects, and consequently the success or failure of the organization. An effective project management culture is essential for effective project management.

This Center for Business Practice series of books is designed to help you develop an effective project management culture in your organization. The series presents the best thinking of some of the world's leading project management professionals, who identify a broad spectrum of best practices for you to consider and then to implement in your own organizations. Written with the working practitioner in mind, the series provides "must have" information on the knowledge, skills, tools, and techniques used in superior project management organizations.

A culture is a shared set of beliefs, values, and expectations. This culture is embodied in your organization's policies, practices, procedures, and routines. Effective cultural change occurs and will be sustained only by altering (or in some cases creating) these everyday policies, practices, procedures, and routines in order to impact the beliefs and values that guide employee actions. We can affect the culture by changing the work climate, by establishing and implementing project management methodology, by training to that methodology, and by reinforcing and rewarding the changed behavior that results. The Center for Business Practices series focuses on helping you accomplish that cultural change.

Having an effective project management culture involves more than implementing the science of project management, however—it involves the art of applying project management skills. It also involves the organizational changes that truly integrate this management philosophy. These changes are sometimes structural, but they always involve a new approach to managing a business: projects are a natural outgrowth of the organization's mission. They are the way in which the organization puts in place the processes that carry out the mission. They are the way in which changes will be effected that enable the organization to effectively compete in the marketplace.

We hope this Center for Business Practices series will help you and your organization excel in today's rapidly changing business world.

James S. Pennypacker

Preface

Managers who are responsible for concurrently executing several projects feel the need for better methods to manage the resources that are often shared across several projects. *Managing Multiple Projects* is a collection of articles from leaders in the field that demonstrate multiproject management tools, techniques, and methods to show how others successfully manage their portfolios.

Managing Multiple Projects captures multiproject management practices in a format that is both informative and practical. You will discover how successful businesses manage their projects within their portfolio—how they set up multiproject management processes, what technologies are effective, and how they allocate their resources across various projects. This reference details time-efficient and cost-effective strategies to evaluate, select, prioritize, plan, and manage multiple projects while effectively utilizing resources and reinforcing organizational goals—presenting proven methods and practical applications that you can put into practice in order to achieve more effective multiproject management in your organization.

The purpose of this volume is not to tell you how to manage a project, nor is it to evaluate and recommend a specific approach or tool. Its purpose is to provide you with a variety of ideas, present proven methods, and share some lessons learned from a cross-section of industries. The major sections of the book—"Overview," "Time, Cost, and Other Management Issues," "Tools, Techniques, and Methods," and "Best Practices and Applications"—reflect the breadth of the subject. The chapters reflect the depth with which these topics are explored and their practical significance. It is this combination of the broad scope of the field, the important concepts and findings of the writers, and the orientation toward the practical problems of top managers, project managers, and other decision makers that explains the impact and acceptance of multiproject management.

With contributions from 40 seasoned experts, *Managing Multiple Projects* is an authoritative source for project leaders, managers, and team members; cost engineers; analysts; and upper-level undergraduate, graduate, and continuing-education seminars in project management and planning.

James S. Pennypacker
Lowell D. Dye

Contents

Part II   Time, Cost, and Other Management Issues

Part III   Tools, Techniques, and Methods

Contributors

Bradley K. Alston 3M, St. Paul, Minnesota, U.S.A.

Robert Beck, Jr. IBM, White Plains, New York, U.S.A.

Ann Bundy Management MarketPlace, Inc., Scottsdale, Arizona, U.S.A.

Bruce Caldwell InformationWeek, Manhasset, New York, U.S.A.

Curtis W. Clark Project Management Solutions, Inc., Smyrna, Georgia, U.S.A.

Robert G. Cooper McMaster University, Hamilton, Ontario, Canada

Mariano Corso Dipartimento di Economia e Produzione, Politecnico di Milano, Milan, Italy

David B. Crane Boston University Corporate Education Center, Tyngsboro, Massachusetts, U.S.A.

Michael A. Cusumano Sloan School of Management, Massachusetts Institute of Technology, Cambridge, Massachusetts, U.S.A.

Adriano De Maio Dipartimento di Economia e Produzione, Politecnico di Milano, Milan, Italy

Michael Singer Dobson Consultant, Palantine, Illinois, U.S.A.

Lowell D. Dye TriCon Consulting, Inc., Beaver Creek, Ohio, U.S.A.

Scott J. Edgett McMaster University, Hamilton, Ontario, Canada

Martin J. Garvey InformationWeek, Manhasset, New York, U.S.A.

Gregory D. Githens Catalyst Management Consulting, Columbus, Ohio, U.S.A.

Shlomo Globerson Graduate School of Business Administration, Tel Aviv University, Tel Aviv, Israel

Martien H. A. Hendricks Philips Opto-Electronics, Eindhoven, The Netherlands

Lewis R. Ireland Project Technologies Corporation, Monument, Colorado, U.S.A.

Ken Jones Ernst and Young, Indianapolis, Indiana, U.S.A.

Elko J. Kleinschmidt McMaster University, Hamilton, Ontario, Canada

Leon H. Kroep Eindhoven University of Technology, Eindhoven, The Netherlands

Nino Levy ELTA and Tel Aviv University, Tel Aviv, Israel

Samuel J. Mantel, Jr. Cincinnati University (*emeritus*), Cincinnati, Ohio, U.S.A.

Michael McCauley Management MarketPlace, Inc., Scottsdale, Arizona, U.S.A.

Jack R. Meredith Cincinnati University, Cincinnati, Ohio, U.S.A.

Kentaro Nobeoka Kobe University, Kobe, Japan

William J. Olford Innate, Inc., Newark, New Jersey, U.S.A.

Francis S. Patrick Focused Performance, Hillsborough, New Jersey, U.S.A.

James S. Pennypacker Project Management Solutions, Inc., Havertown, Pennsylvania, U.S.A.

Geoff Reiss Hydra Development Corporation, Wetherby, England

Tony Rizzo Lucent Technologies, Murray Hill, New Jersey, U.S.A.

William Seidman Management MarketPlace, Inc., Scottsdale, Arizona, U.S.A.

Michel Thiry Project Management Professional Services, Ltd., Brussels, Belgium

Roberto Verganti Dipartimento di Economia e Produzione, Politecnico di Milano, Milan, Italy

Bas Voeten ASM Lithography, Veldhoven, The Netherlands

Jolene Weiskittel Health Alliance of Greater Cincinnati, Cincinnati, Ohio, U.S.A.

Neal Whitten The Neal Whitten Group, Roswell, Georgia, U.S.A.

Clinton Wilder InformationWeek, Manhasset, New York, U.S.A.

Robert K. Wysocki Consultant, Worcester, Massachusetts, U.S.A.

Steve Yager Artemis Management Systems, Inc., Boulder, Colorado, U.S.A.

1

Project Portfolio Management and Managing Multiple Projects: Two Sides of the Same Coin?

**James S. Pennypacker and
Lowell D. Dye**

1 INTRODUCTION

In today's competitive business environment, managers and companies find themselves facing competition for scarce resources, narrowing windows of opportunity, and constantly changing demands of internal and external customers. In addition, projects are continually being added, changed, and removed in response to business activity and changing market conditions. As a result, the backlog of "needed" projects requires resources that exceed management's ability to provide, almost mandating that project priorities be constantly scrutinized and changed. The growing rate of diverse and unpredictable changes in technology and environment, the demand to reduce lead time and time to market, the increasingly demanding market, and the rise in international competition require consistent and effective project and product management.

TABLE 1 High-Level Comparison of Project Portfolio Management and Multiple Project Management

	Portfolio management	Multiple project management
Purpose	Project selection and prioritization	Resource allocation
Focus	Strategic	Tactical
Planning Emphasis	Long- and medium-term (annual/quarterly)	Short-term (day-to-day)
Responsibility	Executive/senior management	Project/resource managers

This paper focuses on what seems to be one of the main causes of failure: the need to manage multiple project interdependencies, assuring their mutual compatibility at the portfolio level. Every different project portfolio selection, therefore, could, and generally does, change either the risk or relevance of each project. This situation is exacerbated when the projects selected have no clear relation or link to the corporate strategy. Currently, there exists a general philosophy that all projects under way make up the project portfolio. Unfortunately, a group of independent projects does not make up a portfolio—it is simply a group of projects, consuming time and resources. Hopefully, these projects have been selected with long-range strategy in mind. Projects generally are not independent. If a logical person would not purchase a mutual fund or a group of stocks without first assessing his or her long-term financial goals, why do companies approve and fund any project that is proposed without first evaluating it and its contribution to and alignment with the corporation's strategic goals and objectives? Often it is due to management's inability to define clearly the company's strategic vision, goals, and objectives, or their willingness to succumb to pressure from the politically astute and organizationally savvy managers.

Table 1 summarizes, at a high level, the major differences between project portfolio management and multiple project management.

2 ASSESSING PRIORITIES AND ALLOCATING RESOURCES

During the past several years, much has been written on the subject of resource allocation for projects, often under the title of project portfolio management.

These writings have focused primarily on methods for short-term resource allocation. Generally, models emphasized day-to-day planning, giving priority to projects based on their perceived level of urgency, with urgency being determined by the level of risk, complexity, or relative strength of the project sponsor. Therefore, what frequently happens is that projects, though strategically relevant but low risk, are viewed as less urgent and given a lower priority in the overall project portfolio than projects with the same or less strategic relevance, but higher risk.

There is a tendency to assign all projects in the corporate portfolio a "number one priority." In spite of this widely recognized criticality, a clear and formal project selection and prioritization policy is often lacking; selected projects are all considered as high-priority projects. As a result, there is no clear guidance as to which project(s) has the greater urgency and the more critical need for resources, effectively placing all projects in an equally competitive position for limited resources. So regardless of the strategic value of certain projects, the will of management is not exercised as to which is more important in the timing of delivery to customers, internal and external. In such a situation, precedence in the access to critical resources is established by individual functional managers. This is done on the basis of the degree of pressure perceived and thus from a viewpoint that is, to say the least, partial. Strong political and psychological pressures are among the causes of this costly situation: it may be neither pleasant nor politically advisable to tell people they are working on a low-priority project.

Projects must be prioritized based on their relative importance and contribution to the overall strategy. Each project should be prioritized relative to other projects being evaluated, as well as those currently under way. In addition, as the business and technical environment changes, the priority of one or more projects may change.

Unfortunately, most managers, and especially project managers, are not in a position to control or change project priorities. Thus, project managers, along with the resource managers, must continually ask themselves several critical questions:

1. Are resources assigned to the highest-priority projects?
2. Are project resources being fully used?
3. Are projects being completed on time, within budget, and to the required quality standard?

The focus is on resources because the project manager rarely has the luxury to add additional resources for an extended period to complete the current "critical" or "high priority" project.

The multiple project environment requires an efficient, dynamic process for determining how to allocate resources and set a realistic delivery schedule for new projects, especially when added to an existing set of projects.

The growth rate of multiple, parallel projects in need of program management is phenomenal, between 20% and 30% a year, according to Hugh Ryan, director of the large, complex systems practice at Anderson Consulting. Organizations are being forced to rethink how they implement information technology (IT) projects from the ground up. The first priority, says PG&E's CIO John Keast, is a holistic view of common business goals. "If you focus on the big picture first, then you'll have people who can deal with the cross-project situations that inevitably come up," says, Keast. "Too often in the past, they were inwardly facing and lost sight of the whole" (Wilder et al., 1998).

Corporations are constantly undertaking multiple projects to add new product lines or to improve and replace existing products/processes. To achieve economies of scale and scope, firms may want to leverage their resource investments on new technologies, processes, and products. In addition, because of increasingly intense international competition, the perspective of multiple project management has become a critical issue for competition. Regardless of the number of projects, whether one or 100, there are several common objectives for all projects:

- Minimum total throughput time (time in shop) for all projects
- Minimum total completion time for all projects
- Minimum total lateness or lateness penalty for all projects (Meredith et al., 1995).

To best accomplish these objectives, multiple project environments should be focused on ensuring compatibility among different simultaneous projects with a strategic portfolio approach. Generally speaking, multiple project management is an area in which traditional methods and techniques appear to be less adequate. This problem is mainly related to the complexity of interproject links, both tangible (e.g., financial, technical) and intangible (e.g., client relations, knowledge transfer).

Each new project, especially new product development projects, often has both technical and organizational linkages or interdependencies with past or currently ongoing projects. The strategic management of linkages among multiple projects, although complicated, is often a critical issue for a firm's project management performance.

Most multiple project environments involve constant change, and managers should recognize that a well-defined project selection and prioritization process can give guidance to project and resource managers for planning and allocating resource assignments. The resource allocation issue is concerned with determining the best tradeoffs among available resources throughout the duration of all projects and establishing the right priorities. The priorities of individual projects within the portfolio relate to urgency of need, and there is almost always competition for resources when one project has a higher priority than the others.

Allocating resources, especially human resources, to projects in a multiple project environment is sometimes difficult and often creates problems. Important in this allocation process is the linking of day-to-day planning for each individual project to the long-term business strategy. In addition, allocating the right human resources to a project is vital. The more projects that are involved and the more specific the skills and knowledge required for each project, the more important, but also the more difficult, is the allocation process. Frequent conflicts between projects arise, and if not resolved in a systematic perspective, could lead to a drastic reduction in project and overall organizational performance.

Long-term resource allocation should be placed in the strategic business and planning process. Generally, corporations walk through their resource allocation process. Directly linked to this process is the medium-term resource allocation, which if done at all is generally accomplished quarterly. The day-to-day planning, for effectively managing resources among multiple projects, is conducted within project execution and product delivery processes. Coupling day-to-day planning to the strategic business plan in this medium-term resource allocation is absolutely necessary. Also, by linking medium-term resource allocation and day-to-day resource planning to long-term resource allocation, the business strategy process, and strategic goals, all affected stakeholders will have a better understanding of the overall need for a logical and consistent project selection and prioritization and, in effect, a reliable resource allocation process.

Making all the pieces fit is one of the greatest challenges facing today's business executives, middle managers, and project managers, but it also provides corporations with one of their greatest opportunities. The demand for "big-picture" project management can catalyze—and then cement—the long-needed project selection-business strategy-resource allocation integration on which all progressive and competitive CEOs and senior managers insist.

A multiproject portfolio selection and prioritization process is needed to help make the pieces fit, including a comprehensive evaluation methodology to assess the complex interactions that arise between projects within the strategic portfolio and the ever-changing relevance or risk of the overall portfolio.

The overall process should continue until a satisfactory result is achieved, actions for improvement are taken that may act to strengthen the competitive position of the company as a whole, or elements are obtained to enhance the success factor of individual projects. It is very conceivable that projects may be reclassified and a new project portfolio structured.

3 THE MULTIPLE PROJECT CHALLENGE

Managing multiple projects is a challenge within many organizations because of current practices that ignore the basics of project priorities, project categories, project standards, and multiple tool applications. Lack of priorities, categories, standards, and uniform tool applications complicates the startup and initiation of projects, especially in a multiple project environment.

There is a mistaken belief that project category and project priority are the same. Category relates to the size, dollar value, duration, and overall contribution to the organization's financial health. Priority, on the other hand, is the urgency of need and relates to time of delivery and criticality of delivery date. The two are related but should always be treated separately.

Categories of projects give an organization the basis for the level of detail required in planning and the selection criteria that can be used on any size or type of project (Ireland, 1997).

Periodic reviews of current and potential projects to be placed in the project portfolio, as well as decisions regarding resource allocation must be conducted. Without quarterly, or at least semiannual, evaluations, decisions on the makeup of the project portfolio are generally made too late and, because of pressure to be "productive," resource allocation decisions are resolved in discussions between project managers and resource managers. Unfortunately, without a good process, resources may be allocated to the wrong projects.

This dilemma is clearly stated by Kathy Boyd, global services manager with Hewlett-Packard's consulting unit: "Problems are accelerated today because of business time-frame demands, tight budgets and very short project deadlines. Where does any IT project fit in the overall business strategy? That must be known" (Wilder et al., 1998).

This situation is complex for a variety of reasons. Typically, the problem is not well defined, the company does not have an orderly way of examining project alternatives, forced alternatives may violate budget, time, resources, or specifications on one or more projects, or very simply, project alternatives have not been prioritized with respect to the entire project portfolio.

Using day-to-day planning for this purpose is generally undesirable, but not atypical, regardless of company size, industry, or products/services. This kind of planning is appropriate when used by the project manager to shift resources among multiple projects and tasks. Moving limited talent among multiple IT projects has become the modus operandi of the CIA. When one project hits a bump and needs additional resources, all the others are fair game. "First we look to projects near completion, take the senior talent from those, and assign them to the higher-risk or higher-visibility initiatives," says Michael O'Brachta, an information services officer in the CIA. "If the available pool doesn't work, then we go raid existing projects and make hard decisions about pulling resources off to assign them to riskier or more visible projects" (Wilder et al., 1998).

As a method of trying to manage the corporate project portfolio, day-to-day planning often is very unstable and unsuitable. In contrast, the project portfolio must have some degree of consistency and stability. In addition, although planning the portfolio once a year can be effective in practice for looking at competitive organizations, an annual review period is too long because changes in the project portfolio within a year are inevitable. The problem is that many companies do not know how to handle a more frequent portfolio review process.

DeMaio et al. (1994) propose a five-step model that takes a logical approach to project selection and prioritization aimed at helping decision-makers in a multiproject environment:

1. Individual project evaluation, classification, and initial screening
2. Multiproject classification and selection
3. Actions for improvement and portfolio reclassification
4. Priority assignment
5. Ongoing control of project portfolio

It is critical to establish project selection and prioritization guidelines that are consistent with the corporate mission and objectives. "You have to keep a portfolio viewpoint, and project managers have to think beyond the IT part," says United Airlines Senior VP and CIO Bruce Parker. Also, United has had to rethink deployment strategies for the most important resource of all: people (Wilder et al., 1998).

When selecting and prioritizing projects, especially when resource allocation in a multiple project management environment is an issue, it is important to consider the following:

- Projects should be similar in size and level of complexity.
- Projects should be relatively of the same duration and require few unique resources.

- Projects should be of similar priorities to permit balancing requirements without completely omitting some projects in resource assignment.
- Projects should be in similar disciplines or technologies.

These considerations will allow the decision-maker(s) to logically compare like projects (i.e., apples to apples.)

All projects, even interrelated projects in a multiple project environment, typically have a unique and complete life cycle with different start and finish times. This usually places individual projects within the project portfolio in different phases for the project manager to plan and execute at the same time. A project manager may experience some difficulty in trying to maintain a balance between the projects because of the different phases of the lifecycle being pursued at the same time. This situation is compounded by projects having different priorities. Higher-priority projects generally receive first consideration for initial and subsequent resource assignments. This situation is influenced by adding a new project or taking a project from the project portfolio.

Attempts to manage multiple projects are also complicated by the fact that management attention, available resources, and project control tools must be spread over many projects. These factors exacerbate an already difficult task and reduce the likelihood of project success, especially when the project portfolio is composed of large and small, technical and nontechnical, strategic and operational projects, among others.

A multiple project environment does not permit senior management attention to be focused; instead, senior management must delegate authority of the project to lower management levels. Project control resources cannot be concentrated on multiple small projects to the extent they can be dedicated to a single major project, even though project controls are in many ways more important on multiple projects because of overlapping schedule and resource requirements.

4 SUMMARY

Perhaps the best way to summarize the focus of project portfolio management and what separates it from multiple project management is in the understanding of what project portfolio management really is. This concept is best explained by David Cleland in *The Strategic Context of Projects* (1999):

An enterprise that is successful has a "stream of projects" flowing through it at all times. When that stream of projects dries up, the organization has reached a stable condition in its competitive environment. In the face of the inevitable change facing the organization, the basis for the firm's decline in its products, services, and processes is laid—and the firm will hobble on but ultimately face liquidation.

In a healthy firm, a variety of different preliminary ideas are fermenting. As these ideas are evaluated, some will fall by the wayside for many reasons: lack of suitable organizational resources, unacceptable development costs, a position too far behind the competition, lack of strategic fit with the enterprises direction, and so on. There is [and should be] a high mortality rate in these preliminary ideas. Only a small percentage will [and should] survive and will be given additional resources for study and evaluation in later stages of their life cycles.

Senior managers need to ensure that evaluation techniques are made available and their use known to the people who provide project ideas and opportunities for growth. Senior management must create a balance between providing a cultural ambience in the enterprise that encourages people to bring forth innovative product and process ideas and an environment that ensures that rigorous strategic assessment will be done on the emerging ideas to determine their likely strategic fit in the enterprise's future.

REFERENCES

DI Cleland. The strategic context of projects. In: LD Dye, and JS Pennypacker, eds. Project Portfolio Management: Selecting and Prioritizing Projects for Competitive Advantage, West Chester, PA: Center for Business Practices, 1999.

A DeMaio, R Verganti, and M Corso. (1994). A multi-project management framework for new product development. European Journal of Operational Research 78 (2): 178–191, 1994.

LD Dye, and JS Pennypacker. Project Portfolio Management: Selecting and Prioritizing Projects for Competitive Advantage. West Chester, PA: Center for Business Practices, 1999.

MHA Hendriks, B Voeten, and L Kroep. Human resource allocation in a multiproject R&D environment. Resource capacity allocation and project portfolio planning in practice. International Journal of Project Management 17 (3):181–188, 1999.

LR Ireland. Managing multiple projects in the twenty-first century. Proceedings of the Annual Project Management Institute Seminars & Symposium, 1997, pp 83–89.

J Knutson. Managing multiple projects in a matrixed organization. Proceedings of the

Annual Project Management Institute Seminars & Symposium, 1994, pp 454–458.

JR Meredith, and ST Mantel, Jr. Multiproject scheduling and resource allocation. In: Project Management: A Managerial Approach. New York: John Wiley & Sons, 1995, pp 412–423.

K Nobeoka, and MA Cusumano. Multiproject strategy, design transfer, and project performance: A survey of automobile development projects in the US and Japan. IEEE Transactions on Engineering Management 42(4):397–409, 1995.

FM Wiegand. Managing multiple capital projects in the electric utility industry. Project Management Journal 21(3): 13–17, 1990.

C Wilder, B Caldwell, and MJ Garvey. Trends: The big puzzle—Multiproject management is redefining the way companies handle technology, people, and vendors to make all the pieces fit. InformationWeek (August 3), 36–41, 1998.

RK Wysocki, R Beck, Jr, and DB Crane. Extensions to multiple projects. In: Effective Project Management. New York: John Wiley & Sons, 1995, pp 268–277.

S Yager. Managing multiple projects in large IS organizations. Proceedings of the Annual Project Management Institute Seminars & Symposium, 1997, pp. 73–77.

2

Software Packages Don't Manage Projects—People Do!

Curtis W. Clark

1 INTRODUCTION

The perception that better software leads to better project management (PM) is becoming more common with the proliferation of "new and improved" information technology (IT) solutions. These packages are more complex than ever and are often touted as silver bullets by their makers. This chapter examines a four-dimensional approach to installing a high-performance project delivery system—using software you already have!

Software is always a hot topic of conversation among professionals in project management. We are seeing new and improved versions of the old standby products, as well as a proliferation in new packages. One needs only to walk the exhibit aisles of any project management conference to observe the mass of software vendors with their many offerings. This is dangerous because many of us are technically oriented and naturally drawn to cool new technology, often simply because of novelty. Admittedly, it is exciting to watch the demonstration of the new bells and whistles. We are wowed to learn we can download schedules into our PalmPilots or see Monte Carlo simulation performed on our project plans. However, as project managers, we have to understand that software solutions are just that—solutions. They are solutions to *specific project management information management needs*. Those needs come from the way an organization has structured its project management processes in relation to its other systems. A disconnect often arises when an organization tries to structure an architecture or process approach around a particular software product, which is akin to the decision-making fallacy of having alternatives in search of objectives. In other words, it's backward. The framework and support for project management in the organization must come *before* any software tool selection.

Our experience with client organizations that are successful in project management indicates that they have achieved that success independent of specific software selection in many, if not all cases. The truth is that all of these organizations use various types of software extensively, and some do have the latest and greatest packages. However, the software did not come first. These organizations would likely continue to be good at project management should they choose to remove or replace their software packages tomorrow. What is it that sets them apart? Why are they effective in their approach to managing projects no matter how sophisticated (or simple) the software? Can an organization really be successful in managing large or complex projects without a large and complex program to "help"? Read on.

A recent survey of project managers from the membership of the Project Management Institute indicates that of the top ten most frequently used project management software tools, four are common desktop PC programs (MS Word, Excel, Access, and Visio) that *are not* even traditionally categorized as project management software (Fox, 2000). Members of the Project Management Institute certainly rank high in terms of both project management success and enthusiasm, right? Why then are so many using everyday Microsoft Office tools instead of the high-octane and more glamorous PM software packages? Perhaps those folks know something that's worth sharing.

2 THE FOUR DIMENSIONS OF PROJECT MANAGEMENT SUCCESS

An organization can achieve success in project management by using a four-dimensional approach to design and install a project management architecture that supports and encourages world-class performance. The four dimensions are:

1. Master project planning
2. Project portfolio management
3. Project management competencies
4. Human performance environment

2.1 Master Project Planning

The master project plan flows directly from the organization's strategy. In other words, this plan includes all the initiatives that the organization must undertake to achieve its strategic objectives. This assumes of course, that there is a valid strategy. Senior executives must test this assumption before any master project planning effort is undertaken.

At the highest level, we can break an organization's overall direction into two pieces: the "what" and the "why." The organization's strategy is the "what." What business are we in? What products or services will we provide? What markets will we serve? The "why" stems from the basic beliefs of the organization and provides the glue that holds the organization together. An example of a basic belief from our organization is that we will "produce practical, useful results for each client." These beliefs are the reasons why the business does whatever it has chosen to do.

Where does master project planning fit? In keeping with our model above, following the "what" and the "why," the next logical question is "how?" The master project plan is the how. The organization needs a map that leads to its destination. Assuming that an organization has defined and articulated its strategy well, the destination should be clear. The master project planning effort asks, "How do we get there from here?"

The goal is to identify everything that must happen to get us to our destination. Some of the questions used to drive the master project planning process are:

- What products must be developed, modified, or acquired?
- How do we become more responsive to our customers?
- How do we achieve better market penetration?

The results of the exercise will typically produce a few major initiatives that will likely require the commissioning or decommissioning of many projects. Each project in the master project plan must be chartered with specific and measurable objectives. The overall master project plan must be assigned to a senior executive who becomes the implementation officer. The overall plan also needs to be reviewed frequently to ensure that it continues to guide the organization toward its desired destination. Without a master project plan, There is No Reason to Expect That the Strategy Will Get Implemented. Software required for master project planning? None.

2.2 Project Portfolio Management

All projects, those that directly implement strategy as well as those that are more operational in nature, need to be managed adeptly by using the principles from *A Guide to the Project Management Body of Knowledge* (Project Management Institute, 1996). A project portfolio management approach goes one step further by providing a system for prioritizing and managing projects across the entire organization. Despite being well funded and managed by intelligent, experienced individuals, many projects exceed their schedules, bust their budgets, and fail to deliver desired results. This is sometimes caused by a lack of fundamental project management skills among project management professionals. In other cases, it is caused by unfocused priorities or inadequate approaches to managing multiple projects. Project portfolio management addresses the latter.

Effective project portfolio management means knowing the relative value and risk associated with every project that has been proposed or is already under way. It means continually knowing how resources are deployed across projects and how many project resources are available for new projects. Most of all, it means making tough decisions about which projects will be done when—if at all—based on a shared understanding of each project's potential for adding value to the organization.

The process steps in project portfolio management are:

- Establish objectives for the overall portfolio. These objectives must be in alignment with the master project plan and agreed to by the senior management team.
- Establish clear measures for each objective. For example, if an objective states "System must be user-friendly," then we *must* ask, "as measured by what?" Is it the number of keystroke errors, or is it the number of user complaints?
- Analyze the organization's resource capacity to do projects (above and beyond regular, ongoing activities) by department.
- Gather and organize pertinent data on each project (objectives, major deliverables, schedules, resource requirements, risks, etc.).
- Evaluate each project against the portfolio objectives to assign priority. The organization must see how each project "measures up."
- Assign resources across all projects, in priority order.

- Make decisions on projects that should not or cannot be accomplished.

The result is a portfolio of projects that are aligned with organization's master project plan. Remember that the master project plan normally includes a few large initiatives that are broken down into projects. The project portfolio includes all of those projects, as well as those that are more operational. The benefit to the organization is the ability to see the status of *all* significant projects and identify potential problems—things like resource constraints that may become roadblocks along the route to the final destination. The portfolio also provides management teams with better information to make critical decisions. For example, in many cases the resource loading shows that the organization is attempting far too many projects, hence, the management team must decide what sacrifices must be made. We know that if we chase two rabbits, then they will both get away. Project portfolio management keeps us from chasing too many rabbits with too few resources.

Project portfolio management is separate from the management of a single project. It is also much more than just reviewing a rolled-up or summary Gantt chart for many projects. A portfolio database will be developed by gathering common project information from each individual project. The data must allow the objective evaluation of the project against the portfolio objectives. For example, a portfolio objective may be "Project net present value (NPV) must be greater than or equal to $1 million." In this case, NPV must be calculated for each project in the portfolio so that the individual projects can be assigned a priority against all the other initiatives. Note that if this objective is truly a "must," then it will require the cancellation of any project that has less that $1 million in NPV.

Project portfolio management must be set up and supported as an ongoing process. Organizations that manage project portfolios effectively recognize the need and have installed the architecture to ensure the program's perseverance. Examples include a project office with a full-time project portfolio manager assigned and an executive steering committee that reviews the portfolio at least quarterly.

Software required? A common desktop database (e.g., MS Access) is preferred for its flexibility in viewing projects in priority order, with resource loading across the organization.

2.3 Project Management Competencies

Project management competencies fall into three primary categories. First, there is the required content expertise. It is hard to imagine a successful project

manager in aircraft manufacturing who has never heard the word "aileron."
Second, a project manager must have project management technical skills.
This includes things like critical path method (CPM) or program evaluation
and review technique (PERT) methodology, resource leveling, quality management, and others. Finally, a good project manager must be competent in
dealing with human beings. And in the words of Stephen Covey, "This is
sometimes referred to as the soft side of project management, but in reality,
it's the *hard* side." In our experience, it is the human side of project management that will most likely cause a project to be unsuccessful. Perhaps it is
labeled the soft skills because it does not require 4, 6, or 8 years of higher
education, or even any specific amount of experience, yet it is still the downfall
of many projects. A thorough understanding of the human performance system
is mandatory. World-class project management organizations ensure that their
project managers have a balance of all three types of competencies.

Some of the basic skills required to support a high-performance project
delivery system are:

- Project management fundamental training based on *PMBOK® Guide*
  principles
- Facilitation and meeting management
- Team building
- Management of agreement
- The ability to clarify issues and set priorities
- Structured decision-making
- Risk management
- Opportunity management
- Root cause analysis
- Managing involvement including an understanding of different lead-
  ership styles
- Understanding the human performance environment and the factors
  that influence it

This list is certainly not exhaustive and some items will apply more than
others, depending on the nature of the organization

Software Required? None.

That's right! project management competencies involve lots of things
outside of software skills. The evidence is all the top-notch project managers
out there who still use Franklin Planners and legal pads as their primary tools.
Remember that four of the top 10 software tools are not even considered project management software!

In reality, many organizations are using software to capture work breakdown structures, schedules, resource assignments, etc., and will need to train their project management teams in the use of those tools. In fact, it is hard to imagine managing large projects without the aid of scheduling software, at a minimum. The point here is that those tools are secondary to the fundamental skills required to produce world-class project management.

2.4 Human Performance Environment

The work environment, not just people and projects, plays a pivotal role in getting results. This includes making sure people have the right expectations and resources and that obstacles are removed. It includes people clearly understanding the "what's in it for me" of achieving success. And it also includes making sure people know how, specifically, their work is advancing, or retarding, the project. Finally, it includes making an accurate assessment of the cross-impact of actions, so that what supports one person does not derail another. Some examples of human performance components that must be considered are:

- Developing project-oriented job models
- Implementing a performance review process that supports project-based work
- Analyzing and improving reward systems
- Assessing and updating communication and feedback methods
- Analyzing and improving consequence systems

2.4.1 An Overview of the Human Performance System

The technical performance of machines, processes, and systems is carefully engineered along with the operating conditions, parameters, and expected outputs. But often, human performance expectations and the system in which employees are expected to perform are not clear. Understanding how the human performance system operates will allow an organization to design a performance system to meet its performance objectives.

In an effective performance system, people know what is expected of them. The need for performance is clearly communicated and standards exist with which to judge successful performance. There is minimal task interference—other tasks do not interfere or create conflicting job demands. Feedback is frequent and relevant—the information provided enables the performer to maintain or modify his or her behavior over time consistent with the results the organization values. In addition, the performer knows how to carry out the task and is willing to perform it, given the incentives available. The resources necessary to carry out the job are adequate and appropriate. The necessary equipment, budget, personnel, procedures, methods, and other processes designed to support the work effort are in place and function as intended.

The human performance system consists of five components, as explained below. All components must be sound for the performance system to be effective.

Situation (S)   The situation is the immediate environment in which people work—the actual conditions or physical location in which the work is performed—and the specific "signals" in this environment that call for the performer to respond. The situation also includes the performance expectations that define the response that we want the performer to make in a given situation.

The situation affects performance in several ways. (1) Sometimes a person may be called on to perform two incompatible tasks that makes it impossible to do either. (2) Other times, the job procedures make it difficult for a person to perform. (3) In still other situations, the cues or signals to perform are so "weak" that a performer is unable to recognize that a response is necessary. (4) In addition, it may not be clear what the performer is expected to do; the roles and performance expectations are not clear. People must also be suited for the job. That is, selecting the right people for the job or team with the right attributes for the situation.

Performer (P)   The performer/employee gives the response. To give the correct response, the performer must have the requisite skills, knowledge, and abilities. They must be free from physical, mental, or emotional impairments. Most times, he or she is an individual employee. The performer may also be a team or a larger organization entity such as a function, department, or division.

Response (R)   Responses are actions taken after employees see or hear signals or cues in the environment. Responses are appropriate, or inappropriate, depending on the signals performers receive from the situation. In this context, "response" is synonymous with "behavior."

Consequences (C ±)   Consequences are events or conditions that follow a performer's response. They are very useful in explaining why desired responses are maintained in a performance environment. Two specific kinds of consequences are important with regard to behavior. The first is known as a positive or encouraging consequence. This kind of consequence reinforces desired behavior in an ideal environment and increases the probability that a particular response will occur again. The second is known as a negative or discouraging consequence. This kind of consequence has the opposite effect. It actually reduces the likelihood of seeing the same response or behavior. It is important that a performance system includes a balance of consequences that consists of more encouraging than discouraging consequences for the *desired behavior.*

Feedback (Fb) Feedback is information the performer receives about the appropriateness of his or her actions. Feedback guides performance, and as such, it is one of the most critical components in the performance environment. An effective feedback mechanism should be one of the first steps in improving performance, because an improvement in performance will not be sustained if the performer is unable to detect that improvement. Also, a defective feedback mechanism is one of the most frequent causes of deteriorating job performance.

The human performance system is a closed-loop model that is displayed in Figure 1.

The ''people side'' continues to be one of the more difficult things for project managers to understand. The key point is that it goes beyond training people and making sure that their salary is in line with industry standards. The performance system components listed above must also be carefully considered to truly provide an environment that promotes success in project management.

Software Required? None.

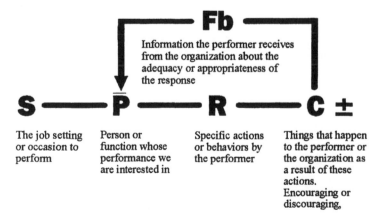

FIGURE 1 The human performance system is a closed-loop model.

3 FINAL THOUGHTS

The four-dimensional approach described in this paper provides a road map for organizations that want to achieve world-class performance in project management. This is a journey that can be made using basic desktop software tools already resident on our PCs. The proliferation of new IT solutions will continue to benefit project managers who have clearly identified their specific needs *after* installing a sound architecture or project management process foundation in their organizations. For the rest who are visiting the trade shows with their checkbooks, rough waters lie ahead.

REFERENCES

Project Management Institute. A Guide to the Project Management Body of Knowledge (PMBOK® Guide), 1996.
TL Fox. Do the features support the functions? PM Network 3, 69–73, 2000.

3

Managing Multiple Projects in the 21st Century

Lewis R. Ireland

1 INTRODUCTION

As organizations search for more efficient and effective means of managing work, project management is selected as the management process of choice. Over the past few decades, project management has evolved to meet the challenges of getting products to market faster and at least cost while meeting customer expectations. These advances in project management are evidenced in the Project Management Institute's initial and revised *Project Management Body of Knowledge (PMBOK®)* of 1983, 1987, and in *A Guide to the Project Management Body of Knowledge (PMBOK® Guide)* in 1996.

One result of organizations' searches is managing multiple independent projects by a single project manager. These independent projects are being used to meet the requirements of management for rapid deployment of products and services, but the efficiencies are still being pursued. Grouping projects under a single project manager is the way to achieve more efficiency in the use of resources.

Adapted from the *Proceedings of the Project Management Institute 1997 Seminars and Symposium.*

Organizations divide large projects into smaller projects that "feed" the large project. This large project is viewed as a "program" with supporting projects or a "major project" with subprojects. Division of major projects into subprojects gives better control over expenditures and changing requirements than a large, long-term project. Several deliverable products are identified and defined, with at least one for each subproject. Grouping projects, either dependent (program or major project with subprojects) or independent (having no relationship between projects), has many advantages during implementation and for planning projects within an organization.

Grouping projects together better serves the strategic objectives of an organization and helps meet short-term goals for business operations. Trade-offs between projects and shifting priorities to achieve organization goals are more easily accommodated.

2 MANAGING MULTIPLE PROJECTS IN THE FUTURE

Having a single project manager manage multiple projects is a challenge within many organizations because of current practices that ignore the basics of project priorities, project categories, project standards, and multiple project tool applications. The lack of priorities, categories, standards, and uniform tool applications complicates the startup and initiation of managing multiple projects by project management. Lack of consistency, or an ad hoc approach, to managing projects prevails in practice and mitigates against a rapid transition to a multiple project management methodology.

Planning for multiple projects requires a proven project management methodology that includes a project management process, charters, plans, budgets, and schedules. Using a schedule as a project plan is not sufficient for managing multiple projects. Omitting basic tools, such as the work breakdown structure, further complicates the project manager's ability to manage multiple projects for profit and timeliness.

Organizations that use a multiple project management approach must consider new methods of collecting information and of reporting that information to the proper individuals. Further, there is a need to establish criteria for the level of management for individual projects and the information requirements from all levels of projects. Reports may be combined or used to single out a project for special review and management. Within the reporting structure, a degree of authority is also granted the project manager for either reporting or making decisions regarding corrective actions or re-planning.

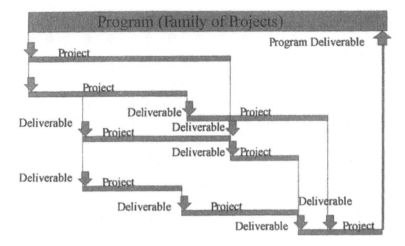

FIGURE 1   Program, a family of projects.

2.1   Program with Subprojects

Figure 1 depicts the program, or family of projects, that leads to a single deliverable product or service. Projects within this program all contribute one or more deliverable products to the top-level program. These deliverables are shown in the program's master schedule. All projects have the same priority, that is, urgency of need, as the program. These projects also are designed to be manageable components of the program.

In a program, the projects are all started based on need within the scope of the program and program start date. Typically, one or more projects will provide deliverable products to a following project. As depicted in Figure 1, product flow is between projects until the last project delivers a product to the program level. The final project could be the assembly of a product, for example.

2.2   Multiple Independent Projects

Figure 2 depicts the grouping of unrelated projects, that is to say, the projects have no interdependencies. Each project has deliverable products or services that meet specific customer requirements and are closed when that need is met. The priorities of the individual projects relate to urgency of need, and

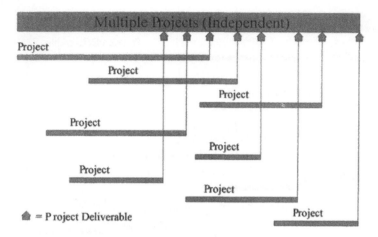

FIGURE 2   Grouped independent projects.

there is competition between the projects for resources when one has a higher priority than others.

When grouping projects for better management purposes and greater efficiency, each project has independent start and end dates. The start date is based on the need for the individual project and has no physical relationship to other projects within the group. Relationships for projects are depicted in Figure 2 by the arrows for delivery pointing to the capstone area. This delivery also indicates project closure.

2.3   Categories and Priorities

There is often a mistaken belief that project category and project priority are the same. Category relates to the size, dollar value, duration, and overall contribution to the organization's financial health. Priority, on the other hand, is the urgency of need and relates to time of delivery and criticality of delivery date. The two may be related but should always be treated separately. Sample schemes for project category and project priority are shown below in Tables 1 and 2.

Note: Table 1 contains a sample range. Organizations should review project values and determine the range of feasible project values. Typically, category A would be an exception, and perhaps less than 3% of the total number of projects. The distribution of project categories is a function of the type of business and the business strategy for projects.

TABLE 1 Category of Project or Program (Sample)

Category	Criteria (project/program value)
A	Greater than $20 million
B	$10 million to < $20 million
C	$3 million to < $10 million
D	$1 million to > $3 million
E	Less than $1 million

The size and duration of the project is usually determined by dollar value of a project. The greater the dollar value, the greater the contribution to the organization's business base. Categories of projects give an organization the basis for the level of detail required in planning and the selection criteria for the project manager for any given size project. Larger projects would receive more planning and a greater amount of investment in managing the work to successful completion than small projects. Larger projects would also have the more experienced project managers.

The category for the project should be assigned at the beginning of the concept phase based on the parameters known at that time. Subsequent changes to the project's value may cause the project to be reclassified and assigned a different category for subsequent management and execution. Also, the category may be held the same if there is no reason to change. For example, a project with additional work may cause it to escalate into the next higher category by a few dollars, but nothing will change in either management or execution of the project. Thus, there is no reason to change the category.

TABLE 2 Priority of Project (Sample)

Priority	Criteria
1	Urgently needed product or service that contributes to the overall strategy or business plan for customer satisfaction.
2	Urgently needed product or service that meets a commitment to a customer and is less urgent than 1.
3	Needed product or service that must be delivered within resource limitations and is less urgent than 1 or 2.
4	Needed product or service to be delivered contributes to the business but is less urgent than 1, 2, or 3.
5	Needed product or service that may have a deferred delivery and has little impact on the business.

Priority, or urgency of need, for a project is typically ranked in three to five levels. The lowest number is the first in order of urgency. Table 2 shows a sample ranking of project priorities with the associated criteria.

Note: This is a sample range for priorities. One should develop a range of three to five levels to differentiate between urgency of need. Discrete numbers should be used rather than a subdivision to indicate finer granularity.

The current trend in industry is to assign all projects priority 1. When this happens, there is no priority system or guidance as to which project has the greater urgency of need for resources to deliver early. It places all projects in an equally competitive arena for limited resources. The will of management is not exercised as to which is more important in the timing of delivery to customers.

Contrasting the two areas, category and priority, one should not confuse the reasons for using these concepts to establish the basis for decisions during planning and execution. Contribution to the organization's financial health can be attributed to satisfying customers and the amount of revenue generated by projects. Several small, urgent projects may make a greater revenue contribution than a single, large project that is a sustaining business base. Category is assigned to a project based on objective criteria that relates to the dollar value of the work. It is managed based on that criteria. Priority is assigned based on the delivery date for the product or service. The shorter the time available to execute the project, the higher the priority.

3 MANAGING MULTIPLE PROJECTS

Managers of programs need to consider the project lifecycle. Each program has a lifecycle (e.g., concept, planning, execution, and close-out phases), and the supporting projects typically have only planning and execution phases. Much of the conceptual and planning work is done at the program level with some detail planning accomplished at the project level. Execution is the primary focus of projects in a program while the program manager and staff exercise control functions.

"Category" for a program will typically be in the upper range (i.e., A or B) because of its size and complexity. Priority, however, is based on urgency of need and will also be the same for the program's projects. The assigned priority of the program places it in competition with other projects and programs within the organization for critical resources. The size of the program may also dictate that a project manager be assigned for each project.

Multiple independent projects each have a complete lifecycle, that is, concept, planning, execution, and close-out. Figure 2 reflects different start and finish times for individual projects. This places individual projects in different phases for the project manager to plan and execute at the same time. A project manager may experience some difficulty in trying to maintain a balance between the projects because different phases of the lifecycle may be pursued at the same time. This situation is compounded by projects having different priorities.

Unlike the program, multiple grouped projects each have a category and priority. Because these projects are small enough to be grouped, it can be assumed that they are in the lower dollar categories, that is, D and E (see Table 1). Priority, however, may be different for each project and could lead to the less urgent projects slipping behind schedule when a resource constraint is imposed. Higher-priority projects would receive first consideration for initial and subsequent resource assignments. The hazard is that low-priority projects may never be completed.

Considerations for assigning individual projects to multiple project management are:

- Projects should be similar in size and low in complexity.
- Projects should be of relatively short duration and require few unique resources.
- Projects should be of similar priorities to permit balancing requirements without completely omitting some projects in resource assignments.
- Projects should be in similar disciplines or technologies.

3.1 Projects Within Multiple Projects

One should evaluate projects before making a decision that they will be managed within a multiple project management context. Some criteria for selecting projects to include in a multiple project grouping are:

- Project duration—should be relatively short or comparable with other projects. An unusually long project may require special attention or it may be an interrupted work flow project, that is, one that does not require continuous work, such as a research project.
- Product or service—the deliverable for the project is either a product or service. Product development should not conflict with providing services, or vice versa.
- Interfaces—project interfaces should be relatively simple, or interfaces for a group of projects should be with the same participants. It may be better to manage a project with complex interfaces as a separate project.

- Dollar value of project—should be comparable, if possible. High-dollar-value projects in a multiple project context may not receive the attention required to achieve individual efficiency.
- Resources for implementation—multiple projects typically share human resources to obtain efficiencies in labor usage. When resources are not to be shared, one should question whether the project logically belongs in a grouping of managed projects.
- Priority—multiple projects should have similar priorities for resources within a grouping. When one or more projects are significantly higher in priority, the lower-level projects may never be successfully completed.
- Location—multiple projects *usually* should be in close proximity to a central location to ensure effective management. Widely dispersed projects may be centrally managed if they have a common purpose that dictates the grouping under a program context.
- Logical fit—projects should be a logical fit for the product, technology of the product being produced, and commonality of resource requirements. Grouping projects in any fashion may result in conflicting objectives among the human resources.
- Project lifecycle—all projects managed in a multiple project context should have a similar lifecycle. (See prior discussion of project lifecycle.) For example, software projects have a different lifecycle than most hardware projects. Different lifecycles may create more problems than efficiencies gained from grouping projects.
- Customer(s)—projects with the same customer (e.g., buyer, sponsor, end user) can be grouped because there should be better relations with the customer when one project manager serves that customer's needs. This should reduce conflicts in customer priorities and ensure better customer satisfaction.
- Other—there are many other considerations for grouping or not grouping projects for managing in a multiple project context. One should review the facts of each project and be watchful of personality influence in grouping projects.

3.2   Start-Up for Multiple Projects Management

When an organization makes a decision to manage projects in groups, it is often the case that many of the projects are currently ongoing. Planning, at various levels of detail, has been accomplished and schedules have been developed. Work on the planning and direction that a particular project is taking is typically unique from any other project.

An organization may have as many as 250 uniquely planned, ongoing projects at any time. For example, a midwest company in 1994 had more than 160 uniquely planned and implemented projects ongoing at one time. Each project had some similar characteristics, but no one project followed a specific methodology or model. The company recognized the situation and established a professional project management system with exceptional results. Senior management was able to obtain greater visibility into projects through the project management system as well as achieve efficiencies that resulted in a 10% to 15% annual savings (i.e., approximately $7 million a year). This savings was reinvested into the company for better facilities.

A second example is from a major international company that was upgrading its IT capability. A dozen different organizational elements were involved in the upgrade; however, there was no central control or coordination. Many small projects were initiated based on the perceived needs of each organizational element, which resulted in a disjointed overall effort to bring about the new IT capability.

Schedules were reviewed as the start point and combined into a single program. Each project contributed to the common goal, but not in a coordinated manner. Schedules were in various levels of detail and in different formats. No schedule identified or included interfaces with another project. Time sequencing of activities between project schedules was not considered. Deliverable products were not tied to specific customer requirements.

A 30-day intensive effort gave visibility to the program and laid the groundwork for a coordinated effort. Schedules were keyed into a single system and interface points established for all internal-to-program and external-to-facilities items. This initial work gave senior management the information with which to make funding decisions, determine resource allocation priorities, and add missing program components. The missing program components were typically the interfaces and unidentified work between planned projects.

Challenges in bringing together a variety of schedules and work efforts were increased by the geographic separation of the organizational elements. Overseas elements were operating on different calendars for holidays, and the different time zones gave rise to the need for extra effort in establishing interface points in time. The different scheduling systems ranged from high-end, fully capable project scheduling software to word processing systems to electronic spreadsheets. The level of granularity between the systems created difficulty in identifying the appropriate level for the interface point being placed in a schedule.

Special rules were required to establish standards for scheduling and to improve the level of detail in individual project schedules. A couple of the schedules contained excessive detail whereas the majority did not have detail below level 2 of a work breakdown structure. One rule was that the delivering project was responsible for coordinating any changes to the delivery interface point with the receiving project. Another was that each project was to develop a work breakdown structure to level 3, as a minimum, to ensure the level of detail was visible for managing the project.

3.3 WBS for Multiple Projects and Programs

Work breakdown structure (WBS) definition. A product-oriented family tree of project components, which organizes and defines the total scope of the project. Each descending level represents an increasingly detailed definition of a project component. Project components may be products or services. The strengths of the WBS are:

- Provides a means for defining the total scope of work
- Ensures that work elements will be defined related to only one specific work effort so that tasks are not omitted or duplicated
- Used as a basis for cost, time, and quality performance assessments
- Provides a consistent form for relating elements across cost, time, and quality functions.

The WBS is decomposed to many different levels, based on the need for definition of the project's product and the project's functions. One type of product decomposition to different levels is as follows: (1) System, (2) Subsystem, (3) Assembly, (4) Component, (5) Part, and (6) Piece.

Table 3 shows a commonly used coding scheme for projects and a suggested coding scheme for multiple projects. The objective is to obtain consistent numbering among projects for comparison purposes when assessing cost, time, and quality efficiencies.

The standard coding style shown in the middle column is often automatically generated by scheduling software. However, it is necessary to differentiate among the projects while keeping the consistency for comparing elements between projects. The right column provides the basis for doing this by identifying the project through the "xxx" designation. Some organizations use a combination of the calendar year in which the project was started and a serial number. For example, 701 could replace the "xxx" to indicate the first project in 1997, and the "01" would indicate the first in the series of projects. Other coding schemes that meet business requirements may be used when consistency and tracking can be met.

TABLE 3 Work Breakdown Structure Coding Scheme
for Multiple Projects

WBS coding scheme		
Level	Typical project	Multiple project
1	1	xxx.1
2	1.1	xxx.1.1
3	1.1.1	xxx.1.1.1
2	1.2	xxx.1.2
3	1.2.1	xxx.1.2.1
3	1.2.2	xxx.1.2.2
4	1.2.2.1	xxx.1.2.2.1
etc.	etc.	etc.

Abbreviation: WBS, work breakdown structure.

3.4 Managing Multiple Projects

Multiple projects are managed similarly to single projects: one task at a time.
The major differences in managing multiple projects are listed below:

- Projects' priorities and rankings are managed by one person in multiple projects to use resources and meet projects' objectives more effectively.
- Multiple projects are managed with the same tool to automatically identify potential conflicts and potential interface points between projects.
- Conflict management between projects is managed by one person in multiple project management.
- Resources within multiple projects are managed by one person for the optimum allocation.
- Dissimilar project lifecycles and methodologies are more difficult to manage under multiple project management.
- Project managers may require a broader range of technical knowledge to manage multiple projects effectively.

3.5 Scheduling Multiple Projects

Multiple projects are developed in a manner similar to single projects using
a WBS and automated tools to produce a resource-loaded schedule. The individual project schedule is developed to uniform standards, regardless of size,
and informally coordinated with other participants as a schedule that meets that

project's objectives. While developing the schedule, one must also identify the external interfaces for the project.

Interfaces are important in multiple project management and provide a considerable advantage over stand-alone schedules when properly identified. Several categories of interfaces must be considered:

- Interfaces with other projects within the multiple project program
- Interfaces with intraorganization activities (except for resources)
- Interfaces external to the organization facilities (e.g., site for installation of product)
- Interfaces with vendors, contractors, or approval agencies
- Interfaces with customer(s), such as the buyer or owner

Interfaces may be placed in the schedule as milestones and labeled as "interface." For example, the interface with the customer (buyer) is typically labeled as a delivery date and may be labeled "Interface: Deliver Product A to Customer Z." On the receiving project in a program, the interface may be labeled "Interface: Receipt of Product A from ABC Project." These two interface points on different projects are fixed in time unless a move is mutually agreed to by the two project managers (project leads).

4 RESOURCE MANAGEMENT UNDER MULTIPLE PROJECTS

Managing human resources under multiple projects may be accomplished by two methods. For large or diverse projects managed under a program umbrella, such as the foregoing example, resources are assigned directly to the projects. These resources typically do not cross projects but stay with a specific project or their functional organization. Diverse projects with different skill requirements cannot make use of the economies of scale.

Projects with similar skill requirements can use human resources across different individual projects and should make optimum use through scheduling on a continuous work flow basis. Automated scheduling systems support this through a master resource library, which lists every resource to be used on all projects. This single listing of resources permits identifying work profiles for every individual to determine whether they are "scheduled to work" more or less than a normal work day, week, or month.

One of the major contributions of the automated scheduling system is that changes to any project activity, with the applied or allocated resources, will be instantaneously recorded in the computer. Changes that reflect conflict in resource assignments will be recognized for corrective action. The dynamic nature of an automated scheduling system eases the process of efficiently managing resources.

4.1 Multiple Project Reporting

Reporting on multiple projects is similar to reporting on a single project. The requirements for information by customers, senior managers, and other stakeholders do not vary significantly between single projects and multiple projects. Basic questions are:

- Is the project on schedule?
- Are there any problems that affect working to the plan?
- What action is being taken to correct any undesirable situations?
- When will the project be completed?

Rather than reporting individually for each project within the multiple projects, some reports may be consolidated. Others may be done by exception. When a single customer is the owner of multiple projects, reports and reviews may be consolidated.

For example, the master schedule or combined project schedule will serve to report time progress for all projects at once. This consolidated schedule may be collapsed for some projects while giving all details for one or more projects. Histograms of planned resource utilization gives instant pictures of all or any resource in the resource library.

5 SUMMARY AND CONCLUSIONS

Managing multiple projects can have a dramatic, positive effect on the productivity of an organization. Organizations will, however, experience challenges when attempting to consolidate projects under a single project manager if the fundamental practices of project management are not in place. Consistent standards, practices, and methodologies need to be implemented and proven before making the consolidation. Proven project management principles must be used to achieve the productivity gains.

Managing multiple projects requires improving the capabilities of the organization in at least two areas. Selecting and training fewer project managers in all functions of project management as well as consistent, uniform procedures can reduce the costs of managing projects in a multiple project environment. Tools capable of linking interproject interfaces and managing resources in an efficient manner across multiple projects are needed to support organizational goals for projects.

Managing programs as a series of small projects provides a greater degree of control over the work. The work is managed and controlled, usually by a project manager, at a lower level than a large project without subordinate projects. This management approach allows one person, the program manager, to allocate resources across project boundaries and enhance productivity while converging on the program's goals. Project managers focus on meeting the intermediate goals of the program or the intermediate deliveries of products and services.

It is anticipated that the trend will continue for organizations to adopt the practice of grouping projects under a single project manager and to divide programs into more manageable subordinate projects to enhance productivity levels. Using the principles and processes outlined in PMI's *PMBOK® Guide* will give those organizations leverage to meet consistent standards and practices while achieving a more competitive position within their respective industries. New processes, standards, and practices for managing multiple projects are expected to bring forth desktop computer-hosted scheduling tools that are supportive of the multiple project environment.

REFERENCES

Project Management Institute. Project Management Body of Knowledge (PMBOK®), 1983.
Project Management Institute. Project Management Body of Knowledge (PMBOK®), 1987.
Project Management Institute. A Guide to the Project Management Body of Knowledge (PMBOK® Guide), 1996.
L Ireland. Project Management Course: Managing Multiple Projects by Project Management, May 1996.
L Ireland. Consulting Engagement: Major energy provider upgrading the Project Management System, 1994.
L Ireland. Consulting Engagement: International business consolidating the Information Technology projects into a master project, 1995.
L Ireland. Consulting Engagement: International business upgrading the Office Automation functions, 1995.
L Ireland. Consulting Engagement: Major telecommunications provider, 1995.

4

Why Is Multiple-Project Management Hard and How Can We Make It Easier?

William J. Olford

1 INTRODUCTION

How many of you work in a multiproject management environment? And in a project management environment? In a traditional functional organization? How many don't know what you are working in? If you have worked in a multiproject management environment, you have most likely heard comments, or commented yourself, on how hard it is.

2 IS MULTIPROJECT MANAGEMENT HARD?

Here are some sanitized quotes from practitioners:

2.1 Senior Management

"Senior management is not getting the overall picture of what is happening across projects or departments. We manage a large number of projects simultaneously, but our systems only provide visibility of individual projects."

Adapted from the *Proceedings of the Project Management Institute 1994 Seminars and Symposium.*

2.2 Standards

"We lack consistency and credibility in our estimating and planning standards as well as in our progress reporting practice. This means that management reports are meaningless because inconsistent data is being consolidated."

2.3 Resource Management

"Unanticipated resource conflicts cause delays and we overspend in attempts to meet completion dates."

"During major bids it is difficult to see what resources are already committed and hence the balance available to produce the most competitive response."

2.4 Procedures

"Multiproject planning and reporting procedures are unwieldly and difficult to police. It only needs one project manager not to conform for consolidated reporting to be meaningless."

2.5 Project Dependencies

"The lack of understanding of the dependencies between projects jeopardizes key dates in downstream related projects."

"Needless rework happens because of lack of clarity about interdependencies with other projects, systems, and procedures."

"Our PCs are isolated islands of data."

2.6 IT Manager

"We don't want to throw out our PC project management systems; the users know them, they're efficient, reliable, and do what is needed for individual projects. . . . but we need to get a corporate system established. Those on offer to us are highly proprietary, as well as being outdated, expensive, and slow."

Yes, multiproject management is hard and the criticisms come from all quarters. Let me spend some time to define the beast and its terminology, and highlight its importance today. I'll then offer some guidelines that may help you. Lastly, I'll leave time for questions, discussion, and dissent, from you on the floor.

3 WHAT IS MULTIPROJECT MANAGEMENT?

Is multiproject management an oxymoron? By definition an "oxymoron" is created by combining contradictory terms. A few common examples include deafening silence, near miss, military intelligence, American English, and pretty ugly. Should I also add multiproject management, as the essence of project management is the focus of a dedicated organization on realizing one project, whereas the term multiproject management means many projects?

3.1 What Are Projects in Multiproject Management?

What distinguishes a project management environment from multiproject management environment and a mega-project environment? Let's start by cutting down on the use of "project management. I'll call a project managed by project manager a "single," and one managed in multiproject management a "multi." A large single will have a dedicated project team, headed by a project manager with the responsibility and authority to get it done. I myself was a team member on a single in Baghdad (before Desert Storm). Isolated location, poor communications, and the need for speedy decision-making resulted in an independent single in which the project manager had the authority and responsibility to get the job done.

Contrast small, and perhaps repetitive multis, often sharing resources with team members working on many projects over a short time. Thinking of my own experience again, an example of a multi might be an engineering research and development office with several engineering disciplines and computer-aided design (CAD) operators. Each engineer worked with two or three other engineers on a project. Considered alone, the project's resource requirements were well within the office resource availability. With many projects, one or more of these resources become overloaded. Who keeps track of resource loading, and how is it done? Who makes sure promised completion dates are feasible? Who sets priorities?

Multis are frequently headed by a relatively junior member of staff who loves the kudos of the project manager title, but has to ask permission to use resources from other managers. So my definition of a project in a multiproject management environment is one in which the project manager needs permission from other managers to use their resources.

In matrix organizations, many projects share common resources. Another possibility could be many projects that are interconnected by logic. Most projects rest somewhere on the spectrum between the two extremes, neither completely independent nor fully dependent.

3.2 Characteristics

Let's identify project management characteristic and see how they apply in a multiproject management environment.

3.2.1   Objective

The objective of a single project should be clear. Multis might also have clear objectives but these objectives may not be consistent across all projects, particularly if they are carried out for a diverse set of customers. At best everyone is working to fulfill corporate objectives on all projects.

In my experience managing R&D, we also had to handle "special projects." These were jobs that included some design work to modify our standard products or interface them to other manufacturers' products. At any time, we had a wide mix of clients: a government department with specific test procedures and reporting requirements, another client deep into total quality management (TQM) who wants to see evidence of our continuous improvement. Multiple objectives were confusing and in stark contrast to the focus of working on a single.

3.2.2   Start and End Dates

A single project has definite start and end dates. It is a unique undertaking with a finite life. Multis are continually being added to the mix, and the end date of the current workload is extended. If a new high-priority project is added, current projects may have to be rescheduled to later dates. Management of this process involves thinking about design reuse and possible reassignment of the same engineer who worked on its forerunner.

3.2.3   Defined Scope

A single project has a well-defined scope. Multiproject management means the constant addition of new projects, possibly resulting in major changes in scope and priorities. The addition of a large multi into the workload may cause major disruption, which requires replanning that affects focus.

3.2.4   Executive Management Attention

Major projects will receive executive management attention. The positive side of this visibility is clout. Multis are often so commonplace that they do not have this visibility. It takes a giant mess up or complaints from a major account of additive calamities to get executive management attention.

3.2.5   Project Manager Authority

The importance of a large single means empowering the project manager (PM) with corresponding responsibility and authority to get the job done. This comes back to the simple roots of project management: when the boss told a trusted lieutenant "you know what I want, look after this infernal mess and keep me informed.'' You can tell how closely the organization follows project management lines by seeing who the project manager reports to and if the position outranks the function managers.

3.2.6 Hierarchical Versus Matrix Organization

Multiproject management results in a matrix organization and all the attendant problems, particularly split responsibility. At worse, it allows for the gamesmanship of playing off multiproject managers, and at best there is a dilution of personal responsibility to the project that comes from being a team member. At the extreme: with functional management, disciplines may operate in a vacuum, even speaking different technical languages. This inhibits effective communications and coordination.

There is a wide range of matrix organizational structures, including their use in managing singles. My definition of matrix has the project manager responsible for *what to do and when*, and the functional managers responsible for *how, where, and who*. Contrast this with a pure single with a hierarchical organization in which it is clear who is responsible for what and when it is to be delivered.

3.2.7 Independent Versus Integrated

A stand-alone project is an independent entity. Sure there are outside influences, but given our project manager with a mandate to get the job done, I consider the project independent. My earlier example was of a single who was forced to be independent as communications with Baghdad were so poor.

In contrast, multis are linked by logic, the use of common resources, or both. Some project managers in this setting still operate as if theirs is an independent project. This works only if you are the vice president's son-in-law, or if the project is at the top of the priority list and everyone knows it.

3.2.8 Prioritizing

With one project, prioritizing (an example of that American English I mentioned earlier) is clear: does a course of action get the job done faster, more cost effectively, and to the required quality level? It's as simple as deciding which is the best way to accomplish the project objectives. Another working rule to determine the ''singleness'' of a project: can the project manager go outside for resources when in-house resources are overloaded?

But with many multis competing for resources, we need King Solomon to cut precious resources in half. Leaving leveling to the computer algorithms is not the whole answer. Resource optimization is an iterative process, best carried out with human assistance. (A systems ''aside'': rules for resource leveling generally sort activities by float or finish date. This penalizes projects that are on time in favor of late projects. Is this fair? It's like people who are late for meetings: they hold them up but don't waste their own time waiting for others.)

3.2.9 Politics

The ability to get your project to the top of the multiproject list when it is not the most important requires politics. Not the Dole/Clinton/Perot mutual name calling, but persuasion. A disaffected project manager or functional manager can stir up disproportionate anguish in playing politics. No one doubts that politics exist in every organization, but hopefully it is at the noise level compared with the common understanding of company objectives.

3.2.10 Resources

The project manager of a large single considers resources by category: engineers, welders second class, and so on. Multiproject managers and functional managers think of resources by name. This is partly a function of size: singles are generally larger and there are just too many names to remember. Also, the process orientation of multis, rather than the finite lifespan of a single, enables staff to get to know each other. Too well perhaps, for managers of multis will go to great lengths to get a particular named resource. They may even request the resource when they see the current assignment for that resource ending, even though they are not ready for the resource. The end result may be spinning wheels or redoing the task later when full data are available.

3.2.11 Scheduling System

Project management uses a closed loop control system: progress and analysis show areas needing replanning. Adjustments are made, new plans communicated, and the loop is closed.

Multiproject management implies a more open loop: individual projects are progressed, other projects are added, they are analyzed together, and problems highlighted. However, a project manager cannot bring in more resources to overcome a problem without permission. In fact, if resource leveling is carried out centrally, new dates may be sent back to individual projects, and the multiproject manager has lost control.

3.3 Implications

That is enough differences, even if you disagree with a few, for us to agree that multiproject management differs from project management.

Conflict is built into the multi environment, particularly between project managers and functional managers, and between project managers of different projects after the same resource.

3.3.1 Productivity

A major implication of these differences is the closeness of a multiproject management organization to a functional organization. This promotes an emphasis on discipline productivity at the expense of project, or maybe even corporate objectives. Discipline managers are notoriously blinkered, and the usual reward mechanisms reinforce behavior that focuses on the small picture.

3.3.2 Technology

The technology is available to provide computerized tools that can handle the vast amounts of data generated by multiproject management. Single-user systems cannot cope because a centralized database is needed so that selections of projects can be consolidated for analysis from different perspectives from single projects with named resources, one department's workload to the corporate workload with resources grouped by discipline.

Technology is also the villain. The use of CAD and computer-assisted engineering (CAE) allows for more parallel activities, looser logic, multiple design iterations, and easier late changes. The production of an outline design from one discipline to allow another discipline to start is possible with today's technology.

3.3.3 Project Management Training

With junior personnel acting as project managers, training is more of an issue. Usually training is on-the-job. Fortunately, more degree curriculums now cover project management, and more companies are using the Project Management Institute's PMP® certification as a qualification. But there is more to be done.

3.3.4 Teamwork

The possibilities for fruitless internal competition and politicking are obvious. Clear communication, a view of the big picture, and teamwork are essential ingredients for success.

4 AND HOW DO WE MAKE IT EASIER?

As well as legislating for these implications, I'd like to share some thoughts on successful multiproject environments that I have encountered and the outline of a simple methodology.

4.1 Standard Coding

To simplify multiproject management involves standardizing a coding structure across projects. There is nothing so discouraging as aggregating similar
information from multiple projects that use different coding. In project A,
mechanical engineering is ME but in project B, the same department is called
STRESS.

4.2 Comprehensive and Accurate Data

To carry out realistic resource leveling, a full picture of all demands on scarce
resources is required. Better yet, monthly requisitions and payments calculated
from project activity progress agreed with the client will reinforce the need
for accurate data.

4.3 A Projects Manager

Several places where I have seen multiproject management applied successfully have operated with a projects manager: a manager of all the multiproject
managers, who also outranks the functional managers. A supporting staff of
schedulers and cost engineers gives objective reporting on projects and frees
up the multiproject managers.

The common arrangement with the multiproject manager doing the
scheduling and cost control has shortcomings. It encourages the late disclosure
of bad news and the time-honored line, "Do you want me to work on the
schedule or the project?"

Think about it. This arrangement is nearer to project management, as
one PM has the responsibility to get all the projects done, as one, very large
project.

4.4 Experience/Continuity

A multiproject management environment can be a rigorous training ground
for the next generation of PMs. With the leadership of the project manager
and the support of project management personnel and tools, the approach can
be learned on smaller jobs. With experience, bigger projects can be assigned,
and a career path opens up. This also helps in maintaining continuity through
projects.

4.5 Systems

I am in the project management systems business. With that caveat, let me
outline the main features required in a multiproject management system:

- Do we need yet another project manager system, with more invest-ment in software and training? On the other hand, stand-alone sys-tems cannot cope with multiproject management needs. So I recom-mend a system that can work with a low-end system that my users already know. Taking advantage of ease of use, Windows GUI, etc.
- The projects manager view across projects means we need to be able to send and receive projects: sounds like a local area nework (LAN). We also need the system to handle file names and versions. Note that I am not suggesting simultaneous multiuser access to a project; sending plans and updates at prearranged reporting dates is better.
- We need centrally stored standards that are secure from casual edit; for example, library networks, resource pools, and calendars.
- We need the ability to analyze quickly the impact of a new project on the workload and the impact of the workload on an individual project. That reinforces the need for standards as we need consistent data to enable analysis across projects. It also means a consolidation capability.
- Consolidation of many projects must be possible at specified levels of detail for each individual project. Consolidation of resources into group resources will allow appropriate higher-level analysis and re-porting, so we can answer questions about both Jane Doe's assign-ments and analyst/programmer staffing requirements.
- Lastly, project management does not operate in a vacuum, so we need the ability to integrate our system with other corporate systems.

4.6 Simple Methodology

Procedures and standards. Multiproject management requires compre-hensive and consistent data. Start with procedures and standards that everyone buys into. Get project managers to sign a charter and, better yet, become PMP® certified. Senior management must then impose the discipline to make the procedures and standards stick. Your sys-tem could help too: by providing templates of commonly used proj-ects and modules, holding details of corporate resources and calen-dars, prompting for workflow steps outside the computer system, and by keeping track of file versions

Plan each project and its resource requirements. From bid or outline planning until detailed resource planning, projects can be worked on independently. There's no excuse for not working with an easy-to-use PC project management system. They are inexpensive, powerful, and the reports and graphics produced are a communicator's dream come true.

Consolidate and analyze. The next step is harder, as dependencies between projects and the use of a common resource pool complicate matters. Consolidating the projects into a mega-project will not solve it either as the detail will be overwhelming. The PM system must be able to consolidate projects at the level of detail that suits the resource/department/portfolio manager's analysis. Senior management may only require one line per project; discipline managers may require a summary by project phase. They all want resources to be grouped by type rather than the listing by name that was input.

With projects consolidated at the appropriate level, analysis becomes possible.

Communicate. Again, choosing the appropriate level of detail is paramount. If reports from your systems are not being used in meetings you know that there is more work to be done.

Update and Replan. Actuals are collected, progress measured and adjustments made. If resource management is the primary aim, then electronic capture of timesheets and integration with your multiproject management is necessary. As projects are completed and new projects added, the process repeats. Remember to review your procedures constantly and update them if they can be improved.

5 SUMMARY AND Q&As

Do you ever wonder why the simple questions concerning project management take so much effort to answer, such as "Where are we on the project?" "How are we going to complete it, and when?" "How much will it cost and how does that compare with plan and budget?" Project management tools and techniques have been used successfully to answer these questions in a multiproject management environment. We must not forget the many differences from project management. The more we can make our multiproject management organization and procedures match the project management approach, the more likely we are to be successful.

5

Multiproject Scheduling and Resource Allocation

Jack R. Meredith and
Samuel J. Mantel, Jr.

1 INTRODUCTION

Scheduling and allocating resources to multiple projects is much more complicated than for single-project cases. The most common approach is to treat the
several projects as if they were each elements of a single large project. (A more
detailed explanation is given below when we consider a specific multiproject
scheduling heuristic.) Another way of attacking the problem is to consider all
projects as completely independent. These two approaches lead to different
scheduling and allocation outcomes. For either approach, the conceptual basis
for scheduling and allocating resources is essentially the same.

There are several projects, each with its own set of activities, due dates,
and resource requirements. In addition, the penalties for not meeting time,
cost, and performance goals for the several projects may differ. Usually, the
multiproject problem involves determining how to allocate resources to, and
set a completion time for, a new project that is added to an existing set of

Adapted from *Project Management: A Managerial Approach*, 2000.

ongoing projects. This requires the development of an efficient, dynamic multiproject scheduling system.

To describe such a system properly, standards are needed by which to measure scheduling effectiveness. Three important parameters affected by project scheduling are: (1) schedule slippage, (2) resource utilization, and (3) in-process inventory. The organization (or the project manager) must select the criterion most appropriate for its situation.

Schedule slippage, often considered the most important of the criteria, is the time past a project's due date or delivery date when the project is completed. Slippage may well result in penalty costs that reduce profits. Further, slippage of one project may have a rippling effect, causing other projects to slip. Indeed, expediting a project to prevent slippage may, and usually does, disturb the overall organization to the point where slippage caused by resource shortages may then be felt in other projects. The loss of goodwill when a project slips and deliveries are late is important to all producers. As is the case with many firms, Grumman Aircraft, purchased by the Northrup Corporation in 1994, jealously guards its reputation for on-time delivery. During a project to install a new machine control system on a production line, Grumman insisted that the project be designed to minimize disturbance to operations in the affected plant and avoid late shipments. This increased the cost of the project, but the firm maintained delivery schedules.

A second measure of effectiveness, *resource utilization*, is of particular concern to industrial firms because of the high cost of making resources available. A resource allocation system that smooths out the peaks and valleys of resource usage is ideal, but it is extremely difficult to attain while maintaining scheduled performance, because all the projects in a multiproject organization are competing for the same scarce resources. In particular, it is expensive to change the size of the resource pool on which the firm draws.

The third standard of effectiveness, the amount of *in-process inventory*, concerns the amount of work waiting to be processed because there is a shortage of some resource(s). Most industrial organizations have a large investment in in-process inventory, which may indicate a lack of efficiency and often represents a major source of expense for the firm. The remedy involves a trade-off between the cost of in-process inventory and the cost of resources, usually capital equipment, needed to reduce the in-process inventory levels. It is almost axiomatic that the most time-consuming operation in any production system involving much machining of metals is an operation called "wait." If evidence is required, simply observe parts sitting on the plant floor or on pallets waiting for a machine, or for jigs, fixtures, and tools.

All these criteria cannot be optimized at the same time. As usual, trade-offs are involved. A firm must decide which criteria are most applicable in any given situation and then use that criteria to evaluate its various scheduling and resource allocation options.

At times, the demands of the marketplace and the design of a production/distribution system may require long production runs and sizeable levels of in-process inventory. This happens often when production is organized as a continuous system but sales are organized as projects, each customized to a client order. Items may be produced continuously but held in a semifinished state and customized in batches.

A mattress manufacturing company was organized to produce part of its output by the usual continuous process, but the rest of its production was sold in large batches to a few customers. Each large order was thought of as a project and was organized as one. The customization process began after the metal frames and springs were assembled. This required extensive in-process inventories of semifinished mattresses.

The minimum-slack first rule is the best overall priority rule, generally resulting in minimum project slippage, minimum resource idle time, and minimum system occupancy time (i.e., minimum in-process inventory) for the cases he studied. But the most commonly used priority rule is first-come, first-served, which has little to be said for it except it fits the client's idea of what is "fair." In any case, individual firms may find a different rule more effective in their particular circumstances and should evaluate alternative rules by their own performance measures and system objectives.

Fendley found that when a new project is added to a multiproject system, the amount of slippage is related to the average resource load factor. The load factor is the average resource *requirement* during a set period divided by the resource *availability* for that time period. When the new project is added, the load factor for a resource increases and slippage rises. Analysis of resource loads is an important element in determining the amount of slippage to expect when adding projects.

2 MATHEMATICAL PROGRAMMING

Mathematical programming can be used to obtain optimal solutions to certain types of multiproject scheduling problems. These procedures determine when an activity should be scheduled, given resource constraints. In the following discussion, it is important to remember that each of the techniques can be applied to the activities in a single project or to the projects in a partially or wholly interdependent set of problems. Most models are based on integer programming that formulates the problem using 0–1 variables to indicate (depending on tasks' early start times, due dates, sequencing relationships, etc.) whether an activity is scheduled in specific periods. The three most common objectives are these:

1. Minimum total throughput time (time in the shop) for all projects
2. Minimum total completion time for all projects
3. Minimum total lateness or lateness penalty for all projects.

Constraint equations ensure that every schedule meets any or all of the following constraints, given that the set of constraints allow a feasible solution.

1. Limited resources
2. Precedence relationships among activities
3. Activity-splitting possibilities
4. Project and activity due dates
5. Substitution of resources to assign to specified activities
6. Concurrent and nonconcurrent activity performance requirements.

In spite of its ability to generate optimal solutions, mathematical programming has some serious drawbacks when used for resource allocation and multiproject scheduling. As noted earlier, except for the case of small problems, this approach has proved to be extremely difficult and computationally expensive.

3 HEURISTIC TECHNIQUES

Because of the difficulties with the analytic formulation of realistic problems, major efforts in attacking the resource-constrained multiproject scheduling problem have focused on heuristics. We touched earlier on some of the common general criteria used for scheduling heuristics. Let us now return to that subject.

There are scores of different heuristic-based procedures in existence. A great many of them have been published, and descriptions of some are generally available in commercial computer programs.

The logical basis for the most commonly applied rules predates program evaluation and review technique (PERT) and critical path method (CPM). They represent rather simple extensions of well-known approaches to job-shop scheduling. Some additional heuristics for resource allocation have been developed that draw directly on PERT/CPM. All these are commercially available for computers, and most are available from several different software vendors in slightly different versions.

3.1 Resource Scheduling Method

In calculating activity priority, give precedence to that activity with the minimum value of d_{ij} where:

d_{ij} = increase in project duration resulting when activity **j** follows activity **i**

where

EFT_i = early finish time of activity **i**
LST_j = later start time of activity **j**

The comparison is made on a pairwise basis among all activities in the *conflict set*.

3.2 Minimum Late Finish Time

This rule assigns priorities to activities on the basis of activity finish times as determined by PERT/CPM. The earliest late finishers are scheduled first.

3.3 Greatest Resource Demand

This method assigns priorities on the basis of total resource requirements, with higher priorities given for greater demands on resources. Project or task priority is calculated as:

$$\text{Priority} = d_j \sum_{i=1}^{m} r_{ij}$$

where

d_j = duration of activity **j**
r_{ij} = per period requirement of resource **i** by activity **j**
m = number of resource types

Resource requirements must be stated in common terms, usually dollars. This heuristic is based on an attempt to give priority to potential resource bottleneck activities.

3.4 Greatest Resource Utilization

This rule gives priority to that combination of activities that results in maximum resource utilization (or minimum idle resources) during each scheduling period. The rule is implemented by solving a 0–1 integer programming problem, as described earlier. This rule was found to be approximately as effective as the minimum slack rule for multiple project scheduling, in which the criterion used was project slippage. Variations of this rule are found in commercial computer programs such as RAMPS.

3.5 Most Possible Jobs

Here, priority is given to the set of activities that results in the greatest number of activities being scheduled in any period. This rule also requires the solution of a 0–1 integer program. It differs from the greatest-resource-utilization heuristic in that determination of the greatest number of possible jobs is made purely with regard to resource feasibility (and not with any measure of resource utilization).

Heuristic procedures for resource-constrained multiproject scheduling represent the only practical means for finding workable solutions to the large, complex multiproject problems normally found in the real world. Let us examine a multiproject heuristic in somewhat more detail.

4 A MULTIPROJECT SCHEDULING HEURISTIC

A project plan is a nested set of plans, composed of a set of generalized tasks, each of which is decomposed into a more detailed set of work packages that are, in turn, decomposed further. The decomposition is continued until the work packages are simple enough to be considered "elemental." A PERT/CPM diagram of a project might be drawn for any level of task aggregation. A single activity (arrows in Figure 1) at a high level of aggregation would represent an entire network of activities at a lower level. Another level in the planning hierarchy is shown as a Gantt chart in Figure 2.

If an entire network is decomposed into subnetworks, we have the equivalent of the multiproject problem in which each of the projects (subnetworks) is linked to the predecessor and successor projects (other subnetworks). In this case, the predecessor/successor relationships depend on the technology of the parent project. In the true multiproject case, these relationships may still depend on technological relationships; for example, a real estate development project being dependent on the outcome of a land procurement project. The relationships may, however, be determined more or less arbitrarily, as when

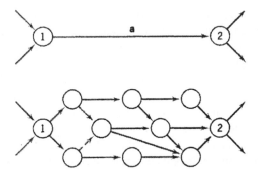

FIGURE 1   Task **a** decomposed into a network of subtasks.

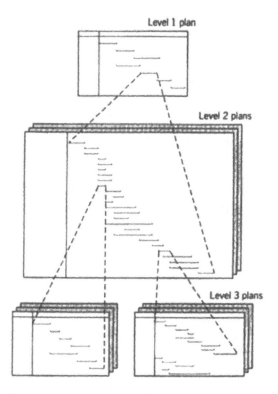

FIGURE 2   Hierarchy of Gantt charts.

projects are sequenced on a first-come, first-serve basis, or by any other prior-
ity-setting rule, or undertaken simultaneously in the hope that some synergistic
side effects might occur. The relationship among the projects may simply be
that they share a common pool of resources.

With this conceptual model, assume we have a set of projects. Each
individual project is represented by a network of tasks. We can form a single
network of these projects by connecting them with dummy activities (no resources, no duration) or pseudoactivities (no resources, some duration). Both
dummy activities and pseudoactivities represent dependency relationships, but
these dependencies, as noted above, may be technological or arbitrary (Weist,
1967).

As usual, and excepting dummy and pseudoactivities, each task in each
network requires time and resources. The amount of time required may or
may not vary with the level of resources applied to it. The total amount of
resources or amounts of individual resources are limited in successive scheduling periods. One problem is to find a schedule that best satisfies the sequence
and resource constraints and minimizes the overall duration of the entire network. The resulting schedule should indicate when to start an activity and at
what level of resources it should be maintained while it is active.

Before undertaking the allocation of resources, it is proper to consider
the quantities of resources available for allocation. (For the moment, we consider ''resources'' as an undifferentiated pool of assets that can be used for
any purpose.) At the beginning of any period (hour, day, week, month, etc.)
we have available any resources in inventory, R_I, which is to say, left over as
excess from the previous allocation process. Changes in the inventory can be
made from within the system of projects or by importing or exporting inventory from the outside. Excluding activities that have been completed in previous periods, every activity planned by the project is in one of four states:
ongoing, stopping, waiting and technologically able to start, or waiting and
technologically unable to start.

Figure 3 illustrates these conditions. We label ongoing activities as ''resource users.'' Those stopping are ''resource contributors.'' Those waiting
and able to start are ''resource demanders.'' Those waiting and unable to start
can be ignored for the present. The amount of resources available for allocation
is, therefore, the amount in inventory plus the amount contributed, $R_I + R_C$.
If the amount demanded is less than the sum, there will be a positive inventory
to start the next period. If not, some demanders will go unfunded.

Weist's heuristic, SPAR-1 (Scheduling Program for Allocation of Resources), allocates resources to activities in order of their early start times. In
the first period, we would list all available tasks and order them by their slack,

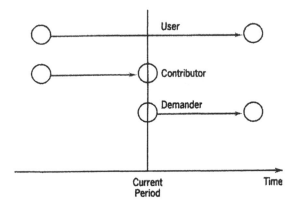

FIGURE 3   Sources and uses of resources.

from least to most. (Calculation of slack is based on the assumption that activities will be supported at *normal* resource levels.) Activities are selected for support and scheduling one by one, in order. As activities at the top of the list are supported, the relevant resource stocks are debited. Tasks are scheduled sequentially until the list of available jobs is completed, or until the stock of one or more resources is depleted. If we deplete resources before completing the task list, remaining tasks are delayed until the next period. Postponed activities lose slack and rise toward the top of the priority list.

The information requirements for this heuristic are straightforward. Each period, we need a period-by-period updating of the list of currently active tasks continued from the previous period, including the resource usage level for each active task, the current scheduled (or expected) completed date, and the current activity slack. We need to know the currently available stocks of each type of resource, less the amount in use. We also need a list of all available tasks, together with their slacks and normal resource requirements. As activities are completed, their resources are "credited" to the resource pool for future use.

Thus, resources are devoted to activities until the supply of available resources or activities is exhausted. If we use up the resources before all critical activities are scheduled, we can adopt one of the two subheuristics. First, we may be able to borrow resources from currently active, but noncritical tasks. Second, we may "deschedule" a currently active, noncritical task. The former presumably slows the progress of the work, and the latter stops it. In both cases, some resources will be released for use on critical tasks. Obviously,

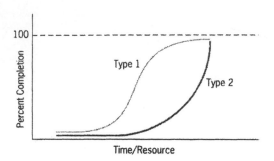

FIGURE 4 Project or task lifecycles.

if a critical task is slowed, descheduled, or not supported, the duration of the associated project will be extended.

The decision to borrow or deschedule depends on our estimate of the impact either action would have on the task under consideration, given its current state of completion. Figure 4 shows two different versions of the project or task lifecycle. If the task in Type 1, borrowing would minimize the damage to the task unless it is very near completion and we are willing to accept the outcome in its current state, in which case we deschedule. If the task is Type 2, borrowing is apt to have a catastrophic effect on the task, and we should either deschedule it (and start again later) or reject it as a source of resources.

If the size of the resource pool is more than sufficient for the list of active and available tasks, the extra resources may be used to crash critical activities to put some slack in the critical path as insurance against protective delays caused by last-minute crisis. In fact, it is often possible to borrow resources from tasks with plenty of slack to crash critical items that are frequent causes of project delay.

As a result of this scheduling process, each task from the previous period, along with any tasks newly available for support will be:

1. Continued as is, or newly funded at a normal level
2. Continued or funded at a higher level of resources as a result of criticality
3. Continued or funded at a lower-than-normal level as a result of borrowing
4. Delayed because of a resource shortage.

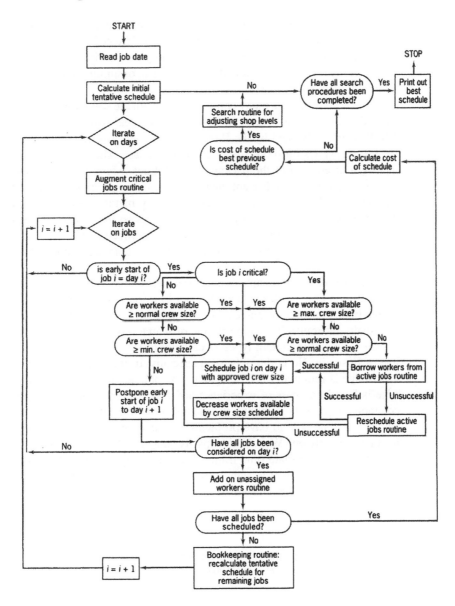

FIGURE 5 Flow diagram for SPAR-1.

If there is more than one scarce resource, a separate activity can be created for each type of scarce resource. These ''created'' activities must be constrained to start in the same period as the parent activity and to have the same level of resource assignment (normal, crash, or minimal). Figure 5 shows a flow diagram for SPAR-1.

As we have noted, many commercially available software packages have the ability to schedule constrained resources and deal with resource conflicts. *PM Network*, published by the Project Management Institute, is an excellent source of reviews on project management software. These reviews typically include a discussion of the package's capabilities. Many will allow the user to solve the problem either automatically, using the program's heuristics, or by hand, in which case the user can adopt any method desired. If a set of problems is linked together by dummy activities so that it can be treated as a single project, the software will report usage conflicts; that is, cases in which the scheduled utilization of a resource is greater than the supply of that resource.

In one sense, this chapter's emphasis on resource shortage is misleading. The common case of shortage applies not to resources in general, but to one or two highly specific resources. For example, an insurance firm specializing in casualty insurance has a typical kind of scarce resource, a ''Walt.'' Walter A. is a specialist in certain types of casualty losses in the firm's commercial line of business. He is the only such specialist in the firm, and his personal knowledge is required when designing new policies in the field. His knowledge is based on years of experience and an excellent analytical mind. It is common for projects involving the modification or creation of policies in the commercial line area to have problems associated with the fact that the firm has one, and only one Walt. Walt capacity cannot be hired, trained, or subcontracted in an appropriate time frame. The firm's capacity to extend its Walt-capacity is not sufficient to satisfy its Walt demand. Left with no alternative, some projects must be delayed so that others can proceed.

REFERENCE

JD Weist. A heuristic model for scheduling large projects with limited resources. Management Science, February, 1967.

6

Effective Resource Management— Debunking the Myths

Michael McCauley, Ann Bundy, and William Seidman

1 INTRODUCTION

Almost every organization today faces the challenge of resource shortages. There doesn't seem to be any shortage of good ideas for projects, but there is significant pressure to complete projects to get products into the marketplace as quickly as possible. As a result, most organizations find themselves working on a large number of projects concurrently and trying to manage their limited resources across all the projects in their portfolio.

Traditionally organizations have dealt with resource shortages in multiproject environments in three ways:

- Hire additional personnel to meet the resource demands of all projects
- Use portfolio management to identify the most important projects, then work only on those
- Create an overall resource profile, or "stack up" model, by resource

Adapted from the *Proceedings of the Project Management Institute 1999 Seminars and Symposium.*

loading the project schedules, and then level resource needs by adjusting projects, tasks and assignments.

Almost anyone who has tried one or more of these "traditional "solutions knows that, in most cases, they simply don't work. Yet a mythology is built around each one—a mythology that is perpetuated daily by managers, consultants, and project teams.

Fortunately there is an alternative, one that has been demonstrated to work effectively time and time again. That alternative is resource bottleneck analysis.

Adapted from the manufacturing environment, resource bottleneck analysis can be used to resolve resource constraints without hiring additional people, canceling projects, or collecting huge amounts of detailed data.

This chapter explores the myths inherent in the three traditional methods of resolving project resource shortages and presents the alternative solution—resource bottleneck analysis—in enough detail that it can immediately be applied by project teams and organizations in any industry. In addition, an actual industry example is provided to demonstrate the successful application of resource bottleneck analysis.

1.1   Myth #1: We Can "Hire" Our Way Out of the Problem

Many organizations approach the problem of resource shortages by trying to hire additional personnel to supplement existing staff. On the surface, this approach seems to have some merit. After all, if the organization has a resource shortage, then obtaining additional resources should reduce or eliminate that shortage. Unfortunately, experience shows that hiring additional personnel almost never removes the resource constraint, and in many cases actually makes the shortage more acute, at least in the short term. This is not to say that this approach can never resolve the problem. Some organizations have successfully applied this strategy, but only in limited, very specialized situations.

In most cases, projects face a resource shortage that is immediate. In these situations, hiring is not a good solution. Hiring new people can be a time-consuming task, both in terms of effort and duration. Determining position criteria, searching for candidates, interviewing, and selecting qualified candidates consumes significant amounts of time, and often engages some of the best people in the organization at a time when they are already overworked or face aggressive deadlines. In addition, new personnel typically require training and time to "ramp up" on the organization's processes and practices. This means that, even in the best of circumstances, new hires will be available to supplement the organization's existing staff in the future, not today when they're really needed.

Another phenomenon occurs as well. In many cases, when new personnel are hired, additional projects are often assigned or undertaken by the organization. Because management sees the hiring organization as having new, additional capacity, additional projects are often assigned to utilize that capacity. The result is that an organization that "buys into" this myth ends up being constantly "one step behind" its resource needs.

Finally, for many organizations, hiring additional personnel is just not an option. They face headcount limits, hiring freezes, or position restrictions. Even if they can justify the new people, they are not able to hire them. In some cases the organization tries to work around this problem by hiring "temporary" or part-time personnel. Again, it is just a myth that the organization can resolve its problems in this way.

1.2 Myth #2: We Can "Portfolio" Our Way Out of the Problem

This strategy is applied by many organizations and it seems like it should work, but in most cases, it doesn't. To implement this strategy, the organization first defines the total "portfolio" of projects that are in progress or planned for the near future. These are often identified in a meeting or workshop environment and listed using whiteboards or Post-Its®. The individual projects are then sorted and prioritized with the idea that the organization will work on the highest-priority projects first. Management may even identify a "cut line" within the prioritized list. All projects below the cut line are then deferred or canceled.

This strategy is not completely without value. It can be applied effectively for long-range planning to identify general resource needs over time (Adkins, 1996; Wheelwright and Clark, 1992). It may also help management visualize the sheer number of projects that are being worked on by the organization. In addition, the process may provide some management team alignment on the highest-priority projects.

Experience shows, however, that it is not a good method for identifying short-term and day-to-day resource needs. The processes required for setting priorities can be difficult, and the resulting emotional reactions from some participants can be destructive to the team (Comber, 1995). Additional drawbacks to this approach include:

- Priorities set by one organization rarely match the priorities set by other organizations.

- The pace of business and market competition results in priorities that change often, sometimes even daily.
- Management is rarely disciplined enough to honor the priorities and decisions made.
- If the results of the prioritization are not honored, morale of the organization can be adversely affected, causing additional resource-related delays.

The result is only a superficial attempt to focus the organization on the highest-priority projects. Differing or changing priorities can cause "friction" between groups rather than encouraging teamwork. In many cases, projects that have been deferred or canceled also tend to find their way back into the mix because one or more groups sees them as beneficial. The result is a general breakdown in the portfolio management process over time and a regression of the organization back to "business as usual."

1.3 Myth #3: We Can "Data" Our Way Out of the Problem

This strategy is particularly seductive, and unfortunately, experience has shown that it can be particularly ineffective. To implement this strategy, the organization first attempts to identify the resources required to complete each task in each project. These resource requirements are then "loaded" on each task in the project schedule using an automated tool (e.g., Microsoft Project). A resource profile, or "resource stack up model," is then used to level critical resources within the organization by adjusting individual tasks or groups of tasks. Some project managers see this approach as crucial to success, others see it as a necessary evil, and still others argue that it is a waste of precious project time (Dreger, 1992).

Like portfolio management, applying this strategy does have some value. It can help identify significant resource conflicts early and illustrate the general resource needs of a project or organization. There are significant costs, however. A resource stack-up model can be very complex and time consuming to develop and maintain. Additionally, even the best models are only a gross approximation of actual resource usage (Fuller, 1997).

This strategy requires an iterative process of collecting data, entering it into an automated system, reviewing the results, and then refining the data again. The seduction occurs when the resource stack-up model doesn't provide the expected results. At this point, it mistakenly appears that the solution lies in more detailed and more accurate data. This then results in more time spent collecting data and refining the model, which results in the need for more detailed and accurate data, etc. We have personally seen organizations spend millions of dollars and thousands of person hours "chasing" this strategy, with very poor results. In one case, the organization finally "gave up" and went back to living with the resource constraints that existed before they started the resource stack-up modeling in the first place!

The reality is that even in the best organizations, no matter how much effort is expended, the data used to create resource profiles, or stack-up models, tends to be:

- **Out of date**, as it takes time to collect and enter them into an automated system, and people tend to change their work patterns from day to day
- **Incomplete**, as it is almost impossible to get everyone in the organization to participate in the effort, or
- **Inaccurate**, as resource needs are only estimates, and many assumptions are made to simplify the data enough to make them usable.

Any one of these negative characteristics results in a less than optimal stack-up model, and it is not unusual for a single organization to suffer from all three! The ultimate result in most cases is a significant amount of time and energy spent by the organization to achieve marginally useful results.

2 RESOURCE BOTTLENECK ANALYSIS

Fortunately, there is a solution to the problem of projects' resource constraints and it can be used as an alternative to traditional strategies. Resource bottleneck analysis is a relatively new approach to project management that provided effective results when applied in other disciplines. Basically, it helps the team view the project as a series of steps through which deliverables flow, much like a production line is a series of stations through which a product flows as it is built. By visualizing a project this way, the constriction in the "flow," or the bottleneck, can be identified and resolved, increasing the project's efficiency and potentially shortening its overall length (Goldratt, 1997).

At a high level, the steps in bottleneck analysis as it applies to projects are:

1. Identify and define the bottleneck.
2. Identify and list the tasks in the current work process(es) around the bottleneck.
3. List the key assumptions that are currently being made around the process tasks.

4. Where the current assumptions are no longer valid, identify the real working conditions that perpetuate the bottleneck.
5. Define options for redesigning each working condition.
6. Identify the actions required to implement each redesign option.

This method is especially powerful when used in a workshop environment with the project team. Rather than requiring substantial data gathering or individual background work as with some of the strategies discussed previously, resource bottleneck analysis encourages the team to participate in a positive, problem-solving environment. More complex or difficult bottlenecks can often be resolved through highly innovative solutions developed by a team.

2.1 Identify and Define the Bottleneck

In most cases, project team members and managers intuitively know where the shortages, or "bottlenecks," are. Think about a recent project that you worked on. If there was a constraint, did you know where it was? Probably so, and you didn't require a complex resource stack-up model to tell you.

Once identified, it is important to clearly define the bottleneck so that everyone focuses on the same problem. Experience has shown that a simple bullet list of what the bottleneck "is" works best. A bullet list is easy and quick to create, making it a good method to use with a group.

2.2 Identify the Work Process Tasks

If we again think of the project as a series of steps through which deliverables flow, we can identify the specific tasks that are performed in and around the bottleneck we just defined. They might include providing information or materials to a particular group, assembling a prototype or test unit, coding a module of software, conducting specific product testing, or any number of other tasks that the organization undertakes. Whatever the tasks are, identifying them is essential to understanding the bottleneck's root cause.

2.3 List the Key Assumptions

In almost all cases, key assumptions have been made about the processes in and around the bottleneck. These may be related to the way the information is obtained, how people in the organization work, the type of work that the organization is responsible for, how the organization prioritizes or distributes its work, or any number of other things.

What's most important is that the team understands the key assumptions that *are* being made by the organization, not the way they would like things to be! Once these assumptions are known, it is relatively easy to identify places in which the current assumptions don't match the real working conditions within the organization.

2.4 Identify the Real Working Conditions

Many times in organizations, processes and procedures were implemented at a time when the working conditions were different from what the organization faces today. The assumptions made around those processes and procedures may no longer be valid, yet they are still being applied. When this is the case, the next step is to identify the real working conditions.

Again, what's most important is that the team understands what the real working conditions are, not what they think they should be. It's easy to say that someone should do something a certain way or that a particular procedure should be applied in a particular way, but if that's not the way it's being done today, it's important to clearly understand that.

2.5 Define Redesign Options

The differences between the current assumptions and the real working conditions identify the root cause of the bottleneck. Resolving these differences will help expand or remove the bottleneck and relieve the resource pressure that the organization is feeling as a result. At this point, the team should review the real working conditions and brainstorm ways to address them by "redesigning" the bottleneck. This isn't a time to be limited by current assumptions; they are what led to the bottleneck in the first place. Think "out-of-the-box" to identify new and innovative ways to address the bottleneck and improve overall productivity.

2.6 Identify Implementation Actions

From the brainstormed list of redesign options, identify those that provide the best opportunity for relieving the bottleneck. It may be that some options can be used together or that there is synergy between various options.

For each option selected, brainstorm a list of tasks that need to be accomplished to implement it. This "to-do" list can then be used to facilitate the effective implementation of the option and enhance its opportunity for success. For each action, assign an owner and due date. The owner is responsible for ensuring that the task is completed by the due date.

2.7 Iteration

The bottleneck analysis process is highly iterative. Once the biggest bottleneck has been removed, it is likely that another will be identified. Remember, just as a production line is always constrained by the speed of the slowest station, a project is always constrained by the slowest step. Redesigning one step so that it is no longer a bottleneck may result in another becoming the bottleneck. The above process can be used repeatedly to resolve each bottleneck as it is identified throughout the life of the project.

3 CASE STUDY

We have had the opportunity to work with several organizations that recently applied bottleneck analysis. In each case the results have been very positive. This case study focuses on one of those organizations—the Components Group within a large computer manufacturing company.

3.1 Background

A large hardware manufacturer was experiencing delays in the selection and testing of components (e.g., disk drives, modems, network boards) that were required for inclusion in their computer systems. These components were the responsibility of a separate Components Group within the company. The Components Group selected and tested components for each of the different product lines that this company produced (laptops, desktops, and servers). As a consequence, this group was an integral part of each system development project, and they had responsibility for a number of key tasks in each project's work breakdown structure (WBS).

     With a large number of systems in development concurrently, it was difficult for this group to keep up with demand. As soon as a testing resource became available, they were immediately assigned to a new project. Most individuals in this group worked a significant amount of overtime, but the "queue" of new products awaiting testing was growing. In addition, because the group's management assigned testing resources to projects on a first-come/first served basis, individual testing personnel were never sure what project they would be working on next. They regularly had to be assimilated into existing project teams. This often resulted in the need for some "ramp up" time to learn the team's processes and personnel and unnecessary project delays while the new testing resource became familiar with the new project.

3.2 First Reaction—Hire!

The organization first tried to hire their way out of the problem. Recognizing that they had more work than they could handle effectively (the queue was growing), they added four new positions (a 20% increase over their existing staff), which was all that they could justify to their management. It took them more than 2 months to locate, interview, and hire the four new people. In those 2 months, the product queue got significantly worse and was accelerating. Because the group was expanding, management had also accelerated their release schedule to "take full advantage of the new capabilities" of the group. The director realized (in hindsight) that hiring was not going to solve the problem.

3.3 Second Reaction—Portfolio Management

Next they tried portfolio management. They gathered the entire group in a room, identified all the projects in progress (significantly more than they had thought), and prioritized the list. Some value was gained from this process— at least they now had a complete list of projects in progress, something that until then did not exist. They began working on the highest-priority projects first, but as the lower-priority projects slipped further and further behind, the program managers that were affected by these "low priority projects" (at least low priority for the Components Group) began to complain. Management began to move some of these projects to a higher priority, mainly to keep the program managers satisfied. The result, over time, was that the priorities originally set by the group were largely ignored, and the resource assignment process reverted to a first-come first-serve approach.

3.4 Finally, Another Solution—Bottleneck Analysis

When we began working with the organization, they were desperate. Nothing they had done resulted in a significant or sustainable reduction in the product-testing queue. In addition, morale was continuing to decline along with the group's reputation within the company. They were willing to try anything that might reduce their problems and enhance their image. By applying bottleneck analysis to their problem, we were able to quickly identify the key resource bottleneck and redesign the processes around it to significantly decrease or eliminate project delays originating in their group and enhance their overall organization "throughput."

By identifying and clearly describing the bottleneck, it was clear where the problem was. It was in the process used to assign testing resources to

projects. The assumptions being made around this process were clearly different from the reality. After investigation, it was learned that many of the key
assumptions had been made during a time when this Components Group was
dedicated to a single product line. At that time, the group also had a resource
surplus—hardly the case any more! The real working conditions made it obvious that these key assumptions needed to be changed to relieve the bottleneck.

The group was reorganized to provide a team of testing personnel dedicated to each product line. Together, the team possessed the skills required
by the product line they were assigned to. In this way, each program manager
had dedicated, skilled resources available for their projects, and they could
control the priorities of the component testing that had an impact on those
projects. In addition, the testing team provided more stability for Component
Group personnel. They worked with the same people on each project rather
than constantly being integrated into a new project each time they became
available. Their work became a series of similar, interrelated projects managed
by a single program manager, rather than the previous independent projects
managed by various project managers.

3.5 Results

The results were tremendous! By analyzing and redesigning the Component
Group's processes to relieve the bottleneck, the group experienced:

- Faster response time (reduced by more than 70%)
- Shortened overall cycle time (reduced by more than 30%)
- Improved predictability (number of late projects reduced by almost
  80%)

Most importantly, these results were obtained quickly and efficiently,
with minimum disruption in ongoing work. A complex resource management
system was not required, nor did the organization spend significant time away
from its work to collect and analyze reams of detailed resource utilization
data. With a clear process for identifying, analyzing, and redesigning bottlenecks, better and more sustainable results were achieved than with any previous approach.

4 SUMMARY

Experience shows that the traditional approaches used to resolve resource
problems usually don't produce effective results to ease the immediate resource shortages often encountered in today's fast-paced, changing business

world. Resource bottleneck analysis provides a new approach to an old problem. Most resource bottlenecks can be removed once they have been identified and analyzed through the use of the process described above. This process can be successfully applied in a wide variety of industries and situations.

REFERENCES

M Adkins. Strategic resource planning and management for pharmaceutical development. PMI 1996 Seminar/Symposium Proceedings, Paper PB02. Upper Darby, Pa, 1996.

C Comber. Project portfolio communication incorporating continuous estimating. PMI 1995 Seminar/Symposium Proceedings, Paper M2. Upper Darby, Pa, 1995.

B Dreger. Project management: Effective scheduling. New York: Van Nostrand Reinhold, 1992.

J Fuller. Managing performance improvement projects: Preparing, planning, and implementing. San Francisco: Pfeiffer, 1997.

E Goldratt. Critical chain, a business novel. Great Barrington, MA: The North River Press, 1997.

S Wheelwright, K Clark. Revolutionizing product development. New York: Free Press, 1992.

7

A Learning Loop for Successful Program Management

Michel Thiry

1 INTRODUCTION

More and more project managers are asked to look beyond the boundaries of
strict project delivery, before the initiating and after the closing processes.
Are project managers well prepared for what they will encounter? Is it part
of their role to do this? The *PMBOK® Guide* clearly defines five process groups
for managing projects, from initiating the appointment of the project manager
to closing the delivery of the outcome. In no way is the project manager's
role expected to extend beyond these two points.

   On the other hand, project managers are expected to practice project
integration, which "involves making tradeoffs among competing objectives
and alternatives in order to meet or exceed stakeholders expectations" (PMI,
1996). The argument of this chapter is that project management is about delivering set objectives with limited resources; it is a "performing process." The
task of defining priorities among stakeholder objectives and identifying alternatives, which will enable project managers to make tradeoffs, is part of a
program management process. Program management goes beyond the five

Adapted from the *Proceedings of the Project Management Institute 2000 Seminars and Symposium.*

fundamental process groups of project management; it is about making sure projects deliver their expected objectives and benefits, but it is also about evaluating options and making the "right" decisions, which will enable project managers to deliver.

Program management requires a "learning process." The use of a value management process to complement the project management process will enable programs to exceed expectations and maximize opportunities by adding a learning loop to the project performing loop.

2 CHANGE AND CHANGE MANAGEMENT

This chapter will group change into two broad areas that have specifically been identified as "deliberate" and "emergent" (Mintzberg and Westley, 1992).

"A deliberate change is basically a change that is considered as part of a strategy to achieve a modified state. . . . An emergent change is an unpredictable input that triggers a change in an ongoing process" (Thiry, 1999).

Projects can be considered as deliberate change. Emergent (or unplanned) change, on the other hand, is often triggered by external or internal factors falling outside the scope of project management, as defined in the *PMBOK® Guide*. Externally, it will emanate from customers, competition, shareholders, regulatory bodies and other stakeholders. Internally, it will come from personnel and be driven by changing needs for systems, structures, culture and management styles. Obviously, programs need to support projects, but they are also required to evaluate the most beneficial options and make the best decisions for the delivery of organizational and business benefits.

3 LEARNING

Some theorists associate learning purely with the acquisition of knowledge. Bramley (1996) defines it as "acquiring the ability to behave in new kinds of ways." In Chinese, "learning" literally means "study and practice constantly" (Senge, 1994). Finally Nevis, Di Bella, and Gould (1997) define learning as "the capacity or processes . . . to maintain or improve performance based on experience." At an organizational or group level, learning can be defined as ". . . individual and collective capabilities to understand complex, interdependent issues; engage in reflective, generative conversation; and nurture personal and shared aspirations" (The Society for Organizational Learning [SoL], 1999).

Learning can, therefore, go from a simple acquisition of knowledge to a fully integrated social process of sustained development through acquisition of knowledge, testing, feedback, and self-assessment. This paper will focus on the latter definition and consider that there is both a social process and a need for improvement in learning.

4 PROGRAM MANAGEMENT

The discipline of program management is fast emerging as a fundamental method of ensuring that an organization gains maximum benefit from the integration of project management activities. As with any emergent discipline, there are variations in the interpretation and implementation of program principles, methods and techniques used by different organizations and practitioners. Murray-Webster and Thiry (2000) have defined a program as ''a collection of change actions (projects and operational activities) purposefully grouped together to realize strategic and/or tactical benefits.'' They argue that, ''Increasingly there is a recognition that programs should be the means of ensuring that an organization's strategy and initiatives are efficiently and coherently implemented; a way of dealing with emergent change in the business environment, and a way of gaining optimal use of resources.''

Program management is the means by which organizations ensure delivery of benefits. Focus must be on both the delivery of specific project objectives and the development of effective responses to emergent change. Program management is the way in which a business strategy is implemented. Business strategies are typically the result of joint input from cultural and political framework, customer or market pressures, and business needs. These create a pressure to change that requires a response, which is usually expressed through the definition of expected business benefits. Benefits are translated into objectives often called critical success factors (CSFs), which will be the basis for the selection and prioritization of projects and project objectives.

5 PERFORMING AND LEARNING LOOPS

Hurst (1995) developed what he named an ''ecocycle'' to describe change in organizations. It is composed of two loops: the performance loop or conventional lifecycle, triggered by choice, and the learning loop or renewal lifecycle, triggered by crisis. We will use this model to develop the concept supporting this chapter.

5.2 Performing Loop

Once a decision is made to implement a project, objectives are translated into finite time, cost, and functionality/quality objectives. The aim of projects is

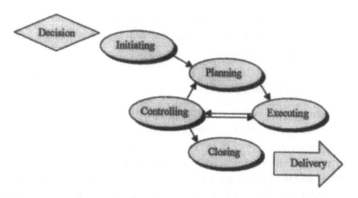

FIGURE 1   The performing loop.

to achieve these set deliverables (scope, functionality, and quality) with the least possible resources (time, cost, and human resources), whereas programs are aimed at making best use of resources to achieve the most benefits. Projects require a more efficient approach, whereas programs will strive for a more effective perspective, based on the principles of value management.

Project management is specifically aimed at improving the performance of limited resources to deliver set objectives. The whole concept of project management is based on tools and techniques that will achieve clear and specific deliverables with the least possible resources—definitely a performance loop. The process groups are specifically designed to enhance performance of the project team and the overall project process and achieve the least deviation from plan. After a decision, it goes through initiating, planning, execution, control, and closing, leading to delivery (Fig. 1).

The problem, or pressure to change, occurs before a decision is made, when emergent change, or deviation, becomes inevitable and requires a response. This is when another type of process is required.

5.2   Learning Loop

The nature of emergent change is such that rapid responses are often required to maintain the organization's competitive position or compliance with market or regulatory expectations. Such responses may mean responding to external or internal pressures with a new project; modifying or replacing existing project objectives with more appropriate solutions; altering the relative priority between projects; using key staff in different areas of the business, or any other such action.

In the past, because of the slow rate of change and the small number of stakeholders (usually one or two), such decisions were relatively straightforward. However, the current accelerating rate of change and multiplicity of stakeholders make it impossible for performance-based project management to respond effectively in those situations. Effective response can only be achieved through the use of a learning loop (Fig. 2) aimed at increasing the decision-makers' knowledge of the situation, as well as clearly identifying and balancing the needs and expectations of diverse stakeholders.

For more than 50 years, value management has developed tools and techniques aimed at achieving those objectives. The recently published European Standard on Value Management (2000) defines value in the following terms:

Value lies in achieving a balance between the satisfaction of many differing needs and the resources used in doing so. . . . The fewer resources used or the greater the satisfaction of the need, the greater is the value." Further, the standard states: "The Value Management contributions to a formal project . . . will coincide with specific project milestones in order to assist the project management team progress from one phase of the project to the next."

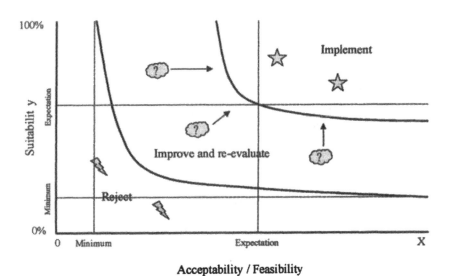

FIGURE 2 The learning loop.

Hurst (1995) describes the start of the learning loop as a state of confusion, which then stimulates a creative response leading to a choice. This description corresponds very closely to the typical value management process of information/function analysis (sensemaking), creativity, evaluation/development, and recommendation (choice) (Thiry, 1997). Based on the author's experience in using value management at a strategic level, this paper recommends that program management should use a learning loop process to respond to emergent change. This learning process is based on five process groups:

1. Identifying—Identifying the pressure to change
2. Sensemaking—Making sense of the situation
3. Seeking—Using creativity to generate alternatives
4. Evaluating—Analyzing and developing options
5. Deciding—Making a choice among the options

Those five process groups, a value management process, pave the way to the performance loop and five process groups recommended in the *PMBOK® Guide*. Together they form the complete program ecocycle, as shown in Figure 3. We will now examine each process of the learning loop in turn.

5.2.1 Identifying

Inputs: Unplanned emergent external or internal pressures that require a change.

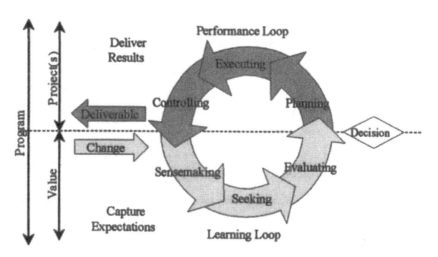

FIGURE 3   Project management ecocycle.

> **Tools and techniques**: effectiveness models; strength, weakness, opportunity, and threat (SWOT) analysis, gap analysis, change deficit, etc.
> **Outputs**: Identified unsatisfactory situations that require action.

One of the first steps in any change process is to "determine that a change has occurred" (PMI, 1996) or that an unsatisfactory situation requires a change. The PMI describes change management as "maintaining the integrity of the performance measurement baselines." In program management, we are dealing with a flexible baseline and negotiated performance measurement. Program management is aiming as much to maximize opportunities as to minimize risks.

As the identification process can be associated with a control process, it can prove useful to define control. Control, in projects, can be associated to "a 'warning bell,' a signal . . . that all is . . . *not going according to plan* leading to a discussion of the causes of deviation from anticipated performance and necessary remedies" (Quinn, 1996). Programs, on the other hand, require a more positive, or should we say, "proactive," way to exercise control.

Quinn (1996) states that in a multiple stakeholder context, whatever perspective is taken, except top-down control, "extensive discussion should occur between parties involved in the control process," which introduces the need for the stakeholders to make sense of the need to change and to negotiate solutions.

5.2.2 Sensemaking

> **Inputs**: Identified unsatisfactory situations that require action
> **Tools and techniques**: Stakeholder analysis, functional analysis; soft systems techniques, modeling techniques, balanced scorecard; critical success factors, etc.
> **Outputs**: An agreed model of the situation to address, or statement of the problem to solve

Today's clients are represented by a number of individuals or parties who have different and sometimes conflicting interests. Guba and Lincoln (1989) talk about stakeholders as being "groups at risk" from the outcome. Sensemaking can be seen as a system of interactions between different stakeholders who are building a collective understanding of a situation, based on cues. The process involves the development of a shared model of the situation and definition of a shared, desired outcome. This interaction process usually results from the challenge of established order and the need to anchor one's thoughts to known concepts.

Sensemaking is triggered by the need for individuals to make sense of the world around them. It is set in motion by ambiguity and uncertainty. For groups, it involves a constructivist interaction, which is characterised by effective communication based on cooperation and the development of a shared frame of reference. The sensemaking process can lead to either positive or negative results that are influenced by the way information is communicated. The confidence of achieving desired goals also affects the sense-making process. All these factors create cognitive behaviours which . . . need to be managed in order to achieve the desired consensus on objectives (Thiry, 2000).

Contrary to the requirements of a performance loop, sensemaking requires time. Sufficient time allocation will allow participants to construct new ideas from shared information and cross-fertilization. This is particularly true where ambiguity and uncertainty are higher, and it is even more required as project management addresses more soft issues, when the process requires increased interaction between stakeholders. "Interaction can no longer be the expression and transmission of meaning—an information process; it is about the construction and negotiation of meaning—a communication process" (Deetz, 1995).

The sensemaking process can be compared to an evaluation of the situation. According to Guba and Lincoln (1989), assessment of complex situations can be both "formative" (to improve) or "summative" (to assess). Within a sensemaking perspective, both summative and formative evaluation will take place to formulate the desired outcome. In the case of formative evaluation, decision-making and action are set in a cooperative construction context. All the stakeholders will require exposure to the new information and an opportunity to grow to the required level of sophistication; "constructors" will require an openness to change. Opportunities for input must be instigated and input must be "honored" (Guba and Lincoln, 1989).

Additionally, sensemaking requires iteration during the project to deliver customer needs "when the delivery is made" (Neal, 1995). These sensemaking actions should be included in the review-approval process, which is part of the program management process.

5.2.3 Seeking (Creativity)

Inputs: Statement of the problem/model of the situation
Tools and techniques: Brainstorming and all its variations, Delphi technique, stakeholder analysis, Pareto analysis, etc.

Outputs: A list of alternatives to be evaluated or developed into workable options

The main objective of the seeking phase is to identify and generate alternative solutions to be evaluated. "Creative thinking is a product of the imagination where a new combination of thoughts and things are brought together" (Miles 1972).

Creativity and innovation need to be fostered to reach the most valuable options, both at the strategic level, for the selection of projects, and for change management. Most studies on creativity agree that the objective of a creative process is to use the right side (imagination, lateral thinking) and the left side (analytical, vertical thinking) of the brain in sequence to offer the analytical mind a greater number of ideas from which to select. If the two are used concurrently, the ideas will be skimmed too early, not allowing for cross-fertilization and piggybacking. de Bono (1990) talks about lateral and vertical thinking. He states, "Lateral thinking is useful for generating ideas and approaches and vertical thinking is useful for developing them. Lateral Thinking enhances the effectiveness of vertical thinking by offering it more ideas to develop. Vertical thinking multiplies the effectiveness of lateral thinking by making good use of the ideas generated."

Creative thinking is not a standard project management tool. Project managers are more used to focusing and delivering. Change is seen as disturbing, whereas the creative or innovative process thrives on change and sees it as potential opportunities. "With vertical thinking, one concentrates and excludes what is irrelevant, with lateral thinking one welcomes chance intrusions" (de Bono, 1990).

The creative process must not be passive; it must be actively managed to deliver the expected results.

The management of creativity also involves focusing the creativity process on the situation to be addressed, using the 20/80 Pareto rule. It is recommended that the creativity process be externally facilitated to provide the best results and prevent the facilitator from being challenged.

5.2.4 Evaluating

Inputs: A list of alternatives to be evaluated or developed into workable options
Tools and techniques: Selection criteria, selection matrices, ranking and rating, grouping, categorization, prioritization, etc.
Outputs: Recommendation of most beneficial option(s)

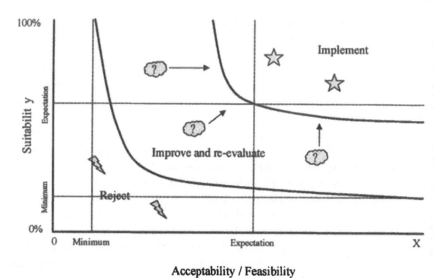

FIGURE 4 Project evaluation matrix.

According to Kubr (1996), "effective evaluation requires collaboration." He points out that evaluation should be "open and constructive." Evaluation needs to be done thoroughly and be based on the right criteria: the CSFs of the project. In program management, the goal of evaluation is to assess the "intent" versus the "capability." Evaluating comprises three main aspects (Johnson and Scholes, 1997):

- Suitability—alignment with strategy (CSFs, project parameters, etc.)
- Acceptability—long-term assessment (likely benefits versus expectations)
- Feasibility—capability assessment (required resources vs capability and probability of success) (Fig. 4).

The objective of evaluation is to identify the options with the best balance of all these factors. Suitability and acceptability mostly concentrate on qualitative aspects of evaluation, emanating from the stakeholders' analysis and functional analysis; feasibility focuses on the following quantitative aspects:

- Financial factors
  Capital cost

Cash flow
Lifecycle costs
- Resourcing factors
  Resource availability
  Resource competence
  Customer perception

It is crucial, before undertaking evaluation, to understand both the intent, which has been identified in the sensemaking phase, and the organization's capabilities, which will be determined at the evaluation stage. Each alternative must be assessed against the organization's capacity to carry it out. Nonviable alternatives must be eliminated. After having fixed minimum and expectation points for each aspect of the evaluation, alternatives will be assessed. Those who do not achieve minimum requirements must be eliminated, whereas those that are above the minimum, but below expectation, need to be improved and re-evaluated. The program team will end up with a series of alternatives that are suitable, acceptable, and feasible.

5.2.5 Deciding

Inputs: Recommendation of most beneficial option(s)
Tools and techniques: Group decision techniques, consensus, vote, leader decision, etc.
Outputs: Decision to undertake a project or implement an action

It is not the objective of this chapter to develop the concepts of decision-making in projects. Let us just mention that the understanding of group decision-making and decisions under uncertainty and ambiguity are essential to the success of this process. Decision processes vary according to the complexity and ambiguity of the context. Low uncertainty and low ambiguity situations can afford an analytical decision process, whereas high uncertainty and ambiguity require a more intuitive decision model. Group decision making, on the other hand, should be based on representation. "Representation means that the values, needs and priorities of individuals and groups have an opportunity to influence relevant decision-making" (Deetz, 1997).

Representation is the guarantee that the key stakeholders will share the decision resulting in the initiating process, which well, in turn, gain their commitment.

6 THE WHOLE PROGRAM ECOCYCLE

A complete program management lifecycle will ensure that emergent change is analyzed and managed through a learning loop of sensemaking, creativity, and evaluation, which is based on a value management process. Decisions made in response to change in the business environment will then be implemented through a performance loop of planning, execution, and control, based on a project management process.

After the initial decision to implement a deliberate change—a project—these learning loops must be repeated at each review/approval stage as part of the overall change control process of projects to reassess deliverables against business objectives and needs and expectations, using value management methodology. This will ensure a constant dialogue between the project sponsors and the project team and warrant a successful outcome to the project at the time of delivery. "Most current writers . . . agree on the importance of dialogue and debate between the interested parties to the control process"(Quinn, 1996).

7 CONCLUSION

This chapter has demonstrated that the performance loop, which is the characteristic of good project management, is not sufficient when applied to programs. A learning loop, composed of five new process groups, is an essential component of the whole program lifecycle—an emergent-deliberate change process.

The process groups are identifying, sensemaking, seeking, evaluating, and deciding. The success of these process groups has been demonstrated in the value management process for more than half a century. To achieve stakeholder satisfaction at delivery, it is essential that program managers iterate this loop at each project milestone review and approval stage to reassess stakeholders' objectives and expected benefits, as well as to assess potential change requests.

REFERENCES

P Bramley. Evaluating training effectiveness. 2nd ed. Maidenhead, UK: McGraw-Hill, 1996 (in print).
E de Bono. Lateral thinking: A textbook of creativity. 3rd ed. London: Penguin Books, 1990.
S Deetz. Transforming communication, transforming business. Creskill, NJ: Hampton Press, 1995.
EG Guba, YS Lincoln. Fourth generation evaluation. London: Sage Publications, 1989.
DK Hurst. Crisis and renewal: Meeting the challenge of organizational change. Boston: Harvard Business School Press, 1995.

G Johnson, K Scholes. Exploring corporate strategy. 4th ed. Hemel Hempstead, UK: Prentice Hall Europe, 1997.

M Kubr. Management consulting: A guide for the profession. 3rd ed. Geneva: International Labour Office, 1996.

LD Miles. Techniques of value analysis and engineering. 3rd ed. New York: McGraw-Hill Book Company, 1972.

H Mintzberg, F Westley. Cycles of organizational change. Strategic Management Journal 13:39–59, 1992.

R Murray-Webster, M Thiry. Projects Programme Management. In: R.J. Turner, ed. Project Management Handbook, London: Gower, 2000.

RA Neal. Project definition: The soft systems approach. International Journal of Project Management 13:5–9, 1995.

EC Nevis, AJ Di Bella, JM Gould. Understanding organizations as learning systems. The Society for Organizational Learning website.

PMI Standards Committee. A guide to the project management body of knowledge (PMBOK® guide). Project Management Institute, 1996.

JJ Quinn. The role of 'good conversation' in strategic control. Journal of Management Studies 33–3, 381–394.

PM Senge. The fifth discipline—the art & practice of the learning organization. New York: Currency Doubleday, 1994.

Society of Learning. About SoL. Reflections, The SoL Journal on Knowledge, Learning and Change. Cambridge, MA: MIT Press, 1-1, 2, 1999.

M Thiry. Value management practice. Upper Darby, PA: Project Management Institute, 1997.

M Thiry. Would you tell me please which way I ought to go from here? Is change a threat or an opportunity? Proceedings of the 30th PMI Seminars and Symposium. Newton Square, PA: Project Management Institute, 1999.

M Thiry. Sensemaking in value management practice. International Journal of Project Management, Oxford: Elsevier Science, 19(2), 2001.

8

Programs, Portfolios, and Pipelines: How to Anticipate Executives' Strategic Questions

Gregory D. Githens

1 INTRODUCTION

In the past, a primary executive responsibility was to ''set the direction for the project'' and answer questions. This led to paternalistic cultures in which subordinates asked questions of ''powerful and omniscient'' managers who had the answers (or at least made decisions). The truth was that many of these managers were clueless about the alignment of projects and programs with the organization's business. In the emerging ''tides-of-change'' environment, the organization is too complex and fast moving for executives to have all of the answers.

Now, the strategic leadership paradigm is that the executives have the questions! The project team provides the answers. In the new model, project teams must anticipate the executive's questions and have ready answers.

Specifically, project managers must know how the executive decision-making and strategy paradigm is changing. They must understand how to link

Adapted from the *Proceedings of the Project Management Institute 1998 Seminars and Symposium.*

projects, programs, pipelines, and portfolios to build capability to respond to emergent opportunity.

2 COMMON LANGUAGE

To improve performance across the organization, we need some common language about our projects. Following are some rudiments.

- **Projects.** One-time efforts that produce a unique product. Projects are not the same as programs.
- **Programs.** Collections of projects that have one or more strong, identifiable themes (such as common technology platform, common customer base, or common resource base) that require a unified management structure. I will discuss and illustrate a method for defining programs later in this chapter.
- **Portfolios.** Collections of projects or programs that fit into an organizational strategy. Portfolios include the dimensions of market newness and technical innovativeness.
- **Pipelines.** The process by which individual ideas are developed into workable projects. Organizations need a number of ideas at various stages in the pipeline and must ration resources to fit projects into the pipeline.

2.1 Purpose and Benefits of Project Portfolios

Projects and products are fundamental elements of strategy. The enterprise project portfolio is an essential management tool for project prioritization and control. The project portfolio is more than a catalogue of projects; it is a framework for project initiation and management processes. A well-managed project portfolio provides the following benefits:

- **It facilitates crisp, fact-based decision-making on project priorities.** The portfolio provides a framework for organizing data, which will result in improved business case analysis, risk management, and resource management. Risk and complexity are the primary indicators of the need to invest in project planning.
- **It helps trace/audit the evolution of projects and programs.** The phenomenon of "feature creep" is common and blurs the distinctions needed to identify work in progress.
- **It helps link strategic intent with delivery.** The portfolio is an

enabler of good decision-making, which allows for better alignment of resources, technology, and customer value.

- **It helps simplify and organize information to speed organizational learning.** The portfolio creates a knowledge repository of important information. Managers can analyze previous strategy decisions and use that knowledge in making future decisions.

2.2 Purpose and Benefits of Pipelines and Pipeline Management

I frequently describe the project development pipeline using the metaphor of a funnel, as illustrated in Figure 1. Technology strategy and customer strategies shape the sides of the funnel. Some organizations have numerous projects in the pipeline, whereas others capitalize on a few "big-bet" projects. Some organizations clog their pipelines with small projects and fail to provide the proper program linkages.

A well-managed project development pipeline provides the following benefits.

- **It is a framework for rationalizing the technology development and customer needs under conditions of scarce resources.** The ideas of customer-driven and technology-driven are competing imperatives. The pipeline helps to balance the emphasis.
- **It is a framework for sequencing product releases and for recognizing scope growth.** It helps to prioritize and communicate release dates of core products and enhanced products using the same product platform.

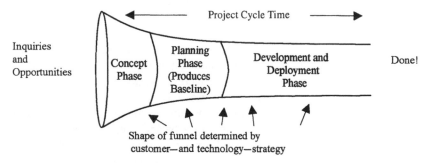

FIGURE 1 Simplified pipeline.

- **It is a framework for measuring project cycle time.** Typically, the organization measures the cycle time from the time a request is offered until the time that all requirements are met.

3   WHAT IS A STRATEGIC DECISION?

In starting this discussion, we need to ask the question, "What is a strategic decision?" I believe the term "strategic" is one of the most abused terms in project management. I have seen the term used to describe or justify a broad range of projects. We might recall Hotspur's rejoinder to Glendower's foolish boast in Shakespeare's *Henry IV, Part I*:

Glendower: I can call the sprits from the vastly deep.

Hotspur: Why, so can I, or so can any man; But will they come when you do call for them?

Just because someone calls a decision or issue "strategic" does not mean that we are addressing an issue that is important to the enterprise.

In this chapter, I use the term strategic as a decision attribute, where the outcome is success or failure, in terms of stakeholders' perceptions. A strategic question is one that links decisions to action to success or failure at the enterprise level or at the project level.

3.1   Strategy as a Two-Way Process

"Who has the big picture?" is a frequent and important question in project organizations. The cynics will argue that it is important but not frequent!

The answer to this question is found through understanding the strategy-development process as a joint top-down and bottom-up approach; both executives and project managers have the big picture. Project managers and program managers increasingly participate in and even lead the discussion of strategy formulation and implementation.

In the top-down approach, the executives develop a vision and deploy resources toward that vision. Executives often assume that the capability is "constant." In this traditional approach, for the terms "strategic" and "tactical," strategic means the idea and tactical means the work.

The bottom-up approach focuses on capabilities or core competencies. Here, the organization looks for opportunities to express those capabilities in action. Strategy development is also a balance among technology and customer imperatives. Technology-push strategy assumes fast-changing cycles of technological evolution or revolution. In the extreme, technology-driven strategies will provide products that customers do not want. Various customer ideas, complaints, or opportunities pull customer-led strategy. In the extreme, customer-driven strategies lead to a patchwork system of capabilities.

3.2 Who Has the Big Picture?

One portfolio initiative originated when a senior executive (of a large insurance company) declared: "No one has the *big picture* about the project work that the development area is doing for the customer department. If we could define some project structure and communicate priorities, we could make better decisions and assure we are accomplishing what's important."

This executive's frustration reflected a lack of process and structure for project decision-making and communication. For example, the project development organization was unclear on the overall customer business and technology direction. Priorities were unknown and changeable, project roles and responsibilities were unclear. There was no project initiation process.

The organization convened a series of joint strategy build-a-collaborative approach to this problem. I first worked with the development community to identify projects, issues getting in the way of effective work collaboration, and desired future work conditions. I repeated the process for the customer community and then combined the groups.

At the end of the work sessions, the organization identified more than 137 projects and work efforts. From this, it was able to develop a process for project initiation, prioritization, and statusing. In addition, the organization identified seven project priority opportunities, based on the preferences and direction of the customer department. One of these projects offered million-dollar savings to the organization but had languished before the facilitated sessions.

Risk and complexity provide the greatest reasons for project planning. (Project planning is a vaccination against project failure.) Through a process of "slicing and dicing," the project team identified the projects that had the highest risk and complexity. From this, the organization could prioritize its portfolio.

The organization improved *inter*department and *intra*department communications. Commitment increased, and the organization achieved noteworthy results and visibility through a better fit of priorities, resources, workload, and opportunities. Most importantly, this case demonstrates how a question is the stimulus for an improvement effort. The project team (which did the real work) provided the answers.

4 DEFINING PROGRAMS THROUGH PROJECT COMMONALITIES

Programs are collections of projects *(Project Management Institute, 1996)*. It is challenging to define programs because they link to strategies in at least three ways. I have developed a program definition model that groups projects into programs based on commonalities of customer, technology, and resources. Customer commonalities are a common customer with unique requirements. Technology-platform commonalities are another type. Resources commonalities originate from common pools of resources (and resemble functional management).

This model can help firms determine whether to use the discipline of project management versus the discipline of program management.

Project management entails delivery of unique services on a temporary basis. Program management depends on good project management at the individual level.

5 A REPOSITORY OF PROJECT AND PROGRAM DATA

A project repository can help answer the basic questions that executives ask (or will ask), such as the following.

- How many projects are in progress or contemplated? What is the value of the portfolio in terms of cost and opportunity? Are the projects prioritized?
- When is a project scheduled for delivery? Is the project late or early? How reliable is your estimate of due date?
- Who can provide more detail on the status of individual projects?

The *BigPicture* database template (Microsoft Access '97) is designed to help managers identify each project and track status of essential project and program information.

Organizations use the database to track progress of projects and programs through the pipeline. I recommend at least a weekly or monthly report of activity. Experience shows that as executives routinely see the information in a portfolio, they begin to use the information to move away from intuitive hunches and guesses to a fact-based decision-making policy.

Why an "open" database? All projects are different, and this approach allows the organization to identify the information important to aligning projects with strategy and assuring consistent deployment.

TABLE 1   Recommended Data Items

Project identity	Project performance data
Project number	Preliminary completion date
Charter date	Preliminary budget
Project name	Baseline completion date
Customer organization	Baseline budget
Status	Baseline date
Reference projects	Budgeted cost (latest revised estimate)
Inquiry #	Completion date (latest revised estimate)
Project stakeholders	Reports
Customer sponsor	
Customer project manager	Status "In progress" projects
Development project manager	Status query for all projects

Of course, a database can suffer from the affliction of "garbage in—garbage out." However, as the organization collects the information captured in the database, it improves alignment of its projects with its strategic intent and its resources. The important benefits of significant cost savings and improved organizational integration can result.

Table 1 lists some recommended data items for the project/program database. It is important to define carefully the criteria for each field.

6   QUESTION ANTICIPATION

Project managers and program managers increasingly participate in and even lead the discussion of strategy formulation and implementation. Because project managers and teams develop the answers, they must push back on poor decision-making. Good decisions demand good models and data. Both project managers and executives need to become proficient in asking the right questions.

For example, consider the IS organization that spent upwards of $1 million (on a consulting firm) to create a document project management that detailed numerous process and procedures. The project practitioners did not accept the prescribed method for several reasons: they were not part of the development, the processes documented were trivial, and some managers used the procedures as a club to dictate compliance.

I offer the following as important statements and questions: Show me the process you are using to create sustainable capability. When will your consultant leave? How will you measure the value received? What is the residual value?

7 THE ESSENCE OF PROJECT MANAGEMENT IS GOOD DECISIONS

If project management is to become a core competency and not just "schedule mechanics," organizations need to recognize it as one enabler of a good decision-reaching process. We expect good decisions to cause effective organizational performance, including financial performance. The project manager is the leader of the project's decision-making process.

The project manager must be willing to assume accountability for the performance of the project. It is helpful to identify a criterion for a good decision, that is, *those that increase the probability of success and decrease the probability of failure.* Excellent project managers are those who address success and failure and take the time to select the right process.

REFERENCE

Project Management Institute. A Guide to the Project Management Body of Knowledge (PMBOK® Guide), 1996.

9

Multiproject Scheduling and Management

Geoff Reiss

1 INTRODUCTION

Much work has been done examining the needs of managers responsible for a range of projects. The project management industry has been drifting into the use of an inappropriate model for the scheduling of multiple projects. This consolidation model derives from the tools that are available but has some significant problems. An alternative model is proposed.

This chapter is presented in two parts. The first examines the model and the problems of its implementation. The second looks at the way some organizations have attempted to implement the model and proposes a new model.

Project management software tools were originally conceived for use on large single projects. Over the last few years, it has become apparent that the vast majority of users of project management tools are actually involved in a number of small, interrelated projects. This is known to some as program management.

The software industry, restrained by an "anchor in the ground," has been forced to provide additional products and functions aimed at bending the single project tool to make it more appropriate to the multiproject environment. But

Adapted from the Programme Management Website, www.e-programme.com, 2000.

these tools all assume a fundamental model of the multiproject planning process, and this model carries with it considerable problems.

2 PROGRAM AND PROJECT PLANNING

It is first necessary to examine the differences between planning in the single project and multiproject environments.

If project planning is the planning and monitoring of tasks and resources for a single project, program planning may be defined as the planning and monitoring of tasks and resources across a portfolio of projects.

There are clear differences between program planning and project planning. Some of the key differentiators are:

Program planning
- Many simultaneous projects
- Concentration on resources
- Projects tend to be similar to each other
- Plans tend to be simple, such as simple bar charts
- Need to maximize utilization of resources
- There is no finite start and end; there is a continuous workload
- There are many different objectives
- Resources tend to be shared across projects

Project planning
- One project at a time
- Concentration on time and method
- Projects tend to be dissimilar to each other
- Plans may be complex, i.e., critical path
- Need to minimize demand for resources
- There is a finite start and end
- There is one single objective
- Resources tend to work full-time on the project

2.1 The Program Planning Process—The Consolidation Model

Seven stages in the planning of a portfolio of projects have been identified.

1. **Planning**   The process of planning each project in terms of time and resource requirements. This is similar to the planning of a single project.

2. **Transmission**   The transmission of the individual project plans to a central point.
3. **Consolidation**   The process of combining the many individual project plans into a program plan.
4. **Evaluation**   Exposure of interproject conflicts and identification of problems, especially multiproject resource overdemands.
5. **Experimentation and decision-making**   The process of experimenting with alternative strategies to find optimal schedules for the future workload.
6. **Dissemination**   The dissemination of decisions taken back to the individual project teams and the modification of individual project plans.
7. **Achievement measurement**   Feedback through timesheet systems, either to measure effort or to monitor progress, or both.

As with single project planning, these stages form a cycle. A flow diagram of the process suggests relationships between these stages (Fig. 1).

With reference to the diagram and in broad terms, there are three circular paths. Following the middle path and starting with the preparation of many individual project plans, the diagram shows the transmission of these plans

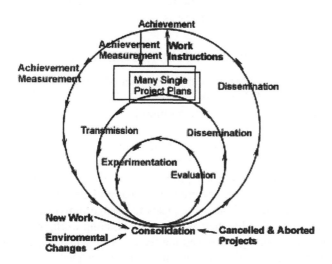

FIGURE 1   Seven stages in the planning of a portfolio of projects form a cycle.

to a central location where these many individual plans are consolidated into a program plan.

The consolidated plans, now forming a program plan, often follow a process of evaluation and experimentation during which alternate solutions to the program plan are discussed and considered.

When decisions are reached and an optimized program is prepared, it is likely that there will be implications for the single project plans and for the immediately forthcoming workload. Therefore the chosen plan may be disseminated to those responsible for doing the work and for those responsible for maintaining the single project plans. The single project plans are updated to maintain conformity with the program plan.

The updated single project plans permit the issuing of work instructions to those responsible for doing the work. This leads to some actual achievement.

Achievement measurement through time sheets or other means provides a feedback loop to the single project plans or to the consolidated program plan.

As the single project plans and the achievement measurement feed back to the consolidation process, other factors must receive consideration. Alterations to the project workload, i.e., new, cancelled, or aborted projects, affect the significance of the single project plans. Environmental changes may alter the priority of individual projects. These factors are considered when the experimentation and decision-making stage is next undertaken.

3   PROBLEMS WITH THE CONSOLIDATION MODEL

Real problems have been observed within a number of companies attempting to implement the consolidation model. These include:

Complexity   The diagram of the multiproject planning process is complex, as it reflects a complex process.

Timing   The synchronization of the different cycles causes very great problems. Three cycles need to be synchronized. The single project plans are in a normal cycle of update, issue, and progress monitoring. The consolidated plan is in a cycle involving the integration of many plans, the analysis of alternative strategies, and the issue of requests to change individual plans in light of those strategies. Thirdly, there is the cycle of issuing work, instructions to team members, performing work, and the feedback of actual achievement. A number of organizations have found it hard to make this cycle operate successfully.

Consistency   Data from the many single plans must be consistent if consolidation is to be successfully performed. This includes the naming and numbering of tasks and projects so that an individual work package can be uniquely identified and to avoid duplication of a task identity in more than one plan. Resource identities need to be consistent to allow multiproject resource predictions. One resource, known to the many project managers as F. Smith, Fred Smith, Mr. F. Smith and Frederick Smith, would be treated as distinct resources by most systems so that no overload would appear. Some vendors allow a look-up table to reduce this problem.

Organization fit   The consolidation model does relate to the organizational structure and does reinforce or record the distribution of work among the members of the organization. It requires a program support group to undertake this consolidation process but that group still needs senior management decision-making to resolve cross-project conflicts in light of corporate objectives.

Interaction with resources   On the large single project, typically, the achievement of classes of resources (bricklayers and welders) can be measured by physical inspection. In the typical multiproject environment, the achievement of individual team members (Jo, Fred, and Sally) on nonphysical work can only be measured by those resources themselves. Communication to the resources on a large single project is achieved by the issue of the plan to the managers and team leaders who instruct the resources on the work to be done.

In the multiple project environment, each resource needs to understand what work they are expected to perform and needs to report back actual achievement. In the last few years, timesheet systems have become very popular, which reflects the changing face of project management. Some systems allow a short-term plan to be produced on paper for each team member and achievement monitoring can be addressed through a third party software tool.

Nonproject work   On large projects, most resources work full-time on the project. In the multiproject environment, most team members have a background nonproject workload, which need to be handled in some useful way. The standard method is to reduce the time that the resource is available to work, treating nonproject work in the same way as holidays and nonwork time.

Part-time and intermittent assignments   Many software packages make it very inconvenient or impossible to show that an individual intends to either work on many tasks at the same time or break off from one task to work on another before returning to the first. Despite these problems this model is used primarily because the existing tools force their users to adopt this approach.

The second part of this chapter looks at three strategies for implementing the consolidation model and an alternative model.

4 STRATEGIES FOR IMPLEMENTING
THE EXISTING PROCESS

This chapter now examines three different strategies for using commercially available software tools with the process outlined last month. These approaches have been observed in a variety of organizations running program of work within the United Kingdom. They are all attempts to make this process work efficiently.

4.1 Standalone

Planners work with their own copy of popular personal computer (PC)-based project planning systems (e.g., Superproject, Microsoft Project, PMW) to plan their individual projects. Such systems are cheap and easy to use and admirably suit the planning of single projects.

These plans are transmitted regularly (weekly or twice-weekly) by floppy disk (copied onto floppy and carried over to another computer) or perhaps over a local area network (LAN) to a project office where they are consolidated into a complete plan using the same software. The project office may need special expertise in the intricacy of the software and a powerful, fast PC to manage the large amounts of data.

The project office staff can inspect histograms, summary bar charts, and bar charts of like work; for example, all the design office work.

Achievement measurement is normally carried out by a manual time-recording system, but there has been an increase in the use of time-recording software tools. These are normally used to update single project plans before consolidation.

This approach has the advantage of allowing each project team to plan their own work so that they feel ownership of their plans. These popular tools are easy to use. The project or program office often takes a supporting role, advising the management team of conflicts that are generally in terms of resource overdemands.

A high degree of consistency among the many project plans is essential if they are to be consolidated within a reasonable time frame. There are difficulties in measuring achievement where a resource has been involved in many projects.

Decisions taken in view of the multiproject view are communicated by meetings, printed reports, and by other nonelectronic means. The individual planners must alter their plans to bring them in line with the program's requirements. Inevitably, errors arise as differences exist between the individual plan and the consolidated plan for each project.

One advantage is the potential for a step-by-step installation of such a system. The consolidation facility can be implemented separately.

4.2 Integrated

In this environment, the organization normally purchases a site licence of a heavyweight program planning system. Planners have access to the tool through a local terminal, which might be a PC or a terminal on a UNIX or VMS system.

Each project is planned locally and the system makes transmission and consolidation completely automatic. Once again, a small team in a project office examines the cross-project demands and reports problems.

Decisions taken in light of the cross-project workload can be entered into the system within the project office, as well as communicated verbally and on paper. These systems are expensive and more complex to use. The tendency is for a small number of enthusiasts to enter data on behalf of themselves and other, less computer-literate users.

Any capable planner can add in a new project to the organization-wide program. This can be done by accessing a library of typical projects or by creating one from scratch. Plans are simple but loaded with resources. Consolidation is immediate and automatic through the network and multiuser software. Each terminal can display a project, summaries of groups of projects, and demand for each resource.

Achievement measurement is normally dealt with by a manual system with administrative staff who enter details to the multiproject planning system.

Such systems involve a "big bang" approach, and implementation is a significant project in itself. Access to such a system must be controlled so that authority to alter the parts of the model rests with the appropriate people.

4.3 Combination

In an attempt to get the best of both worlds, some organizations have created a combination system. Each project team uses a simple standalone PC planning system, and the project office uses a much more powerful system to integrate the many individual project plans. The individual plans are created and kept up to date using the popular single-project based tools, and the files are transferred to a consolidation system. It is likely that such an organization would have a LAN and that the consolidation tool would be manipulated by a project office or program management team. Consolidation can be achieved by a tool specifically designed for the purpose or by the use of a heavyweight, database-driven project planning tool. The project office team manipulates the data within the consolidation system and can report on conflicts across the many projects.

Dissemination of information resulting from rescheduling to achieve optimal schedules is not normally possible by software means. Decisions are, therefore, generally communicated verbally from the program management team to the individual project managers, who modify their plans to bring them into line with the demand of the optimal program schedule. Errors usually arise because of the differences between the individual plan and the consolidated plan for each project.

Problems of data compatibility must be solved before such a system can work. It is possible for an organization to establish an ethos in which projects are individually planned before implementing the consolidation tools.

Achievement measurement tools can be used to feed achievement measurement data into the consolidated plan. This reduces the problems of rationalizing achievement measurement across a range of projects.

5   THE DELEGATION MODEL—THE PROPOSED MODEL

Most organizations run their project workload by delegation. Senior staff identify projects and delegate them to project managers. These project managers take responsibility for the projects and may plan their own workload in appropriate detail. The project managers normally require the efforts of resources within the organization, and these may be obtained through the subcontract matrix, the secondment matrix, or the resource pool approach.

The senior managers expect to be informed of progress on each project by the appropriate project manager and in appropriate detail. Some form of referee or umpire exists to settle arguments over interproject prioritization.

An alternative model is, therefore, proposed. This model follows the way in which organizations work more closely. A multiuser tool is installed over a LAN and each user is given a ''work plan'' within which an individual's or a team's workload can be planned. Connections between work plans are created by the act of delegating work. Upwards reporting follows the connections created by the delegation process. This permits each user to plan at a level that is appropriate to his or her needs.

For example, a program manager might plan using a single task per project and delegate, through the software tool, each project to a chosen project manager. The project managers could then break the single tasks down into greater detail within their own work plan, perhaps delegating work to phase, departmental, or subproject managers.

Every act of delegation would establish a link between the two "work plans," which would carry updated information automatically.

In a subcontract matrix organization, work would eventually be delegated to resource managers, or departmental managers who would balance the workload from the many project and subproject managers.

In a secondment matrix, resources would be loaned by the resource managers or departmental managers to the many project and subproject managers on a full-time or part-time basis.

Individual team members would have their own personal work plan. Once individual resources have been assigned to work, a link between the departmental plan and the personal work plan would be established. Resources would receive work instructions through the system and would report actual achievement.

Achievement measurement data would be transmitted through the assignment link, and data describing updated plans would be transmitted up the delegation links.

Each user on the system would see a view of the total workload that would be appropriate to their specific need and would be able to investigate in greater detail by inspection of lower-level plans.

6 CONCLUSION

Three main strategies are aimed at following the current program management model used by program management organizations, and these tend to follow the availability of software tools. The methods used by these organizations to plan and monitor their workload do not represent a model of the organization's management. The software tools are predominantly based on a single project philosophy. Such models are, therefore, structurally flawed and often inappropriate.

A model that follows the organization structure is likely to be more appropriate and more applicable within an organization.

10

Organizing for Multiple Projects

Neal Whitten

1 FUNCTIONAL-REPORTING VIEW OF EIGHT PROJECTS

Figure 1 shows a functional-reporting view of a multiproject organization of about 170 members. These members currently are working on eight different projects ranging in size from 5 to 46 full-time-equivalent members. Figure 2 shows the number of members in each project. The member count per project does not include resource managers or product manager. Of course, at some point, the cost for the resource managers must be apportioned per project; however, for simplicity and illustrative purposes, resource managers are not counted in the project member count.

   The first number shown in each cell of Figure 2 represents the total number of project members, some only part-time. The second number (under-lined) represents the total full-time equivalent of project members. For example, Project 8 has nine different people assigned to the project, but if all of the time spent on the project by each person in cumulated, there is an equivalent of five full-time people assigned to the project.

   I have taken some liberty in making assumptions for determining the head count associated with each project. Because some project members are working on more than one project, the counts are rounded to make the numbers

Adapted from *The EnterPrize Organization*, 2000.

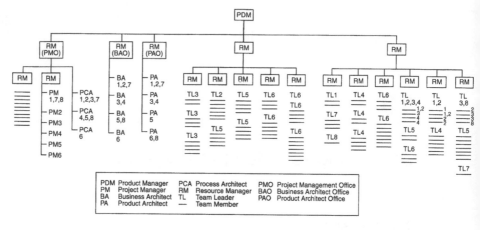

Functional-reporting view of a multiproject organization.

	Project Manager	Business Architect	Product Architect	Process Architect	Team Leader	Team Member	PMO Support	Totals
Project 1	1 - 3	1 - 3	1 - 3	1 - 2	3 - 1.5	5 - 4	1 - 5	13 - 7
Project 2	1 - 1	1 - 3	1 - 3	1 - 3	3 - 1.5	10 - 9	1 - 5	18 - 13
Project 3	1 - 1	1 - 5	1 - 5	1 - 3	5 - 3.5	13 - 13	1 - 1	23 - 20
Project 4	1 - 1	1 - 5	1 - 5	1 - 4	5 - 4.5	16 - 16	1 - 1	26 - 24
Project 5	1 - 1	1 - 8	1 - 1	1 - 5	5 - 5	21 - 21	1 - 1	31 - 30
Project 6	1 - 1	1 - 1	1 - 8	1 - 1	8 - 8	32 - 32	2 - 2	46 - 46
Project 7	1 - 3	1 - 3	1 - 3	1 - 2	2 - 2	4 - 4	1 - 5	11 - 8
Project 8	1 - 3	1 - 2	1 - 2	1 - 1	2 - 1.5	2 - 2	1 - 5	9 - 5

FIGURE 2 Number of project members per project and the number of full-time equivalents per project (underlined).

come out whole overall. The primary purpose of Figure 2 is to help you more readily visualize and understand the structure (Fig. 1) that an organization composed of multiple projects of varying sizes can adopt.

Let's now look more closely at Figure 1. As with other examples from earlier chapters, the product manager heads the organization and, in this case, is responsible for all eight projects. Reporting to the product manager are five resource managers.

1.1   Project Management Office

The first resource manager is the manager of the *project management office* (PMO). The PMO is the home of all project managers and their support personnel. Six project managers are shown in Figure 1, along with their assigned projects. Notice that the first project manager listed is the project manager for three projects (Projects 1, 7, and 8) and all other project managers have responsibility for a single project.

In this example, all the project managers report to a resource manager, who then reports to the resource manager in charge of the PMO. Also reporting to the PMO resource manager is a resource manager of the department of 10 people who are primarily dedicated to support the six project managers in fulfilling their roles and responsibilities.

Notice in Figure 1 that there are three process architects who report to the resource manager responsible for the PMO. Only the one process architect is assigned full-time to work with a project (Project 6). The other two process architects spread their working time across the other seven projects. The process architects do not need to report to the PMO; however, the PMO can be a likely home for them, because they provide a great deal of support to the projects and work closely with the project managers.

1.2   Business Architect Office

The second resource manager reporting to the product manager is the manager of the *business architect office* (BAO). The business architects that work across all seven projects report to this resource manager. Four business architects are shown in Figure 1, three of whom perform the role of business architect on more than one project. For example, the first business architect shown is assigned to the three projects, Projects 1, 2, and 7.

1.3   Product Architect Office

The third resource manager reporting to the product manager is the manager of the *product architect office* (PAO). All product architects for the seven projects report to this resource manager. As with some instances with a project manager and several business architects, three of the four product architects also are performing in the capacity of product architect for more than one project. For example, the first product architect shown in Figure 1 is assigned to three projects: Projects 1, 2, and 7.

1.4 Department Skill Group

The fourth and fifth resource managers reporting to the product manager are managers of five and six resource managers, respectfully. These eleven lower-level resource managers manage departments that provide functions to the overall organization. For example, a half dozen or so of the departments might design, write, and partially test the software. Several other departments might perform independent testing of the newly developed code. Another department might write the user documentation and online help screens. Yet another department or two might perform other functions, such as library control and configuration management, usability analysis and testing, performance analysis and testing, and others.

2 STARTING A NEW PROJECT

When a new project is started, a project manager is assigned. Then the project manager works with the resource managers to identify the business architect, product architect, process architect, and team leaders who will be assigned to the project. The team leaders then work with their resource manager to identify which person will have assignments on the team leaders' teams.

   If the project manager requires any project management support personnel, he or she works with the designated resource manager within the PMO to obtain the required resource. If the business architect, product architect, or process architect require support personnel, they work with their own resource managers, as well as resource managers across the organization, to obtain required support. The support personnel for the business architects, product architects, and process architects could be direct reports into the BAO, PAO, and PMO, respectively, if desired—similar to the PMO arrangement of support personnel for project managers. However, the BAO and PAO are depicted differently than the PMO to show an alternative approach. Any support personnel required for the process architects could come optionally from the pool of people in the PMO who are also assigned to support the project managers.

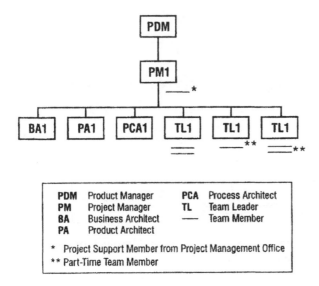

FIGURE 3   Project-reporting view of Project 1.

2.1   Example: Project 1

Of the eight projects in Figure 1, let's single out one, Project 1, to examine more closely. Let's see how the project members are gathered from across the organization. Figure 3 shows the project-reporting view of Project 1. Figure 4 shows, by highlighting, where the members assigned to Project 1 can be found in the functional-reporting view of the organization. Project 1 is made up of a project manager, business architect, product architect, process architect, three team leaders, five team members spread across the three team leaders, and a project support member, a total of thirteen project members. However, all of these project members are not dedicated full-time to Project 1. Who is not full-time on Project 1? We can determine the answers by looking closely at the highlighted areas of Figure 4 and referring to Figure 2.

Figure 4 shows that the project manager is working part-time on Project 1; the project manager also is working on Projects 7 and 8. The business architect, product architect, and process architect are also working part-time on Project 1, as well as on Projects 2 and 7; 2 and 7; and 2, 3, and 7; respectively.

Looking at Figure 4, we see that the first team leader and her two team members are working full-time on Project 1. The second team leader is part-time, as well as the one team member. (The second team leader is also working

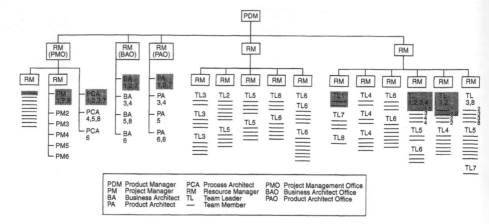

FIGURE 4 Functional-reporting view of multiproject organization (with highlighting for Project 1-related areas).

on Projects 2, 3, and 4, whereas the team member is also working on Project 2.) The last team leader is part-time (also working on Project 2), with one full-time team member and one part-time team member (also working on Project 2.) Let's assume that the project support member from the PMO is only part-time.

So where are we in terms of the size of the project in full-time equivalent people? Only one team leader and three team members appear to be full-time on Project 1; all others are part-time. Assuming that the project manager, business architect, and product architect each spends about one-third of his time on Project 1 and that the process architect spends about one-fifth of her time on Project 1, these four project members account for 1.1 person, or the equivalent of one full-time person. If the two part-time team members combine for an equivalent of one full-time person and we view the two part-time team leaders as adding up to one half-time person, Project 1 comprises seven full-time equivalent project members. (Don't forget the half-time person from the PMO.)

3 GOALS FOR A MULTIPROJECT ORGANIZATION

Let's discuss, for a moment, goals that should be addressed when applying the EnterPrize Organization to an organization that has many ongoing projects. Table 1 lists goals toward which to strive that help improve the use of

TABLE 1   Goals for a Multiproject Organization

1. Assign team members to only one project.
2. Assign project managers, business architects, product architects, and process architects to work full-time at their craft.
3. Create departments based on functional areas.
4. Install a project management office.
5. Install "offices" for business architects, product architects and process architects.
6. Maintain reasonably sized departments and teams.
7. Report key project positions as close to the product manager as possible.

people and promote successful projects. Let's take a closer look at each of these goals.

Goal 1: Assign team members to only one project. It is not always possible to restrict a team member's skills to only one project. However, for purposes of obtaining the best use of that team member's time, every attempt should be made to limit the number of projects that a team member must work on simultaneously. This helps team members achieve their best productivity by allowing them to concentrate on single tasks until they are complete.

Goal 2: Assign project managers, business architects, product architects, and process architects to work full-time at their craft. Project members who perform as project managers, business architects, product architects, and process architects have major influence on the outcome of the projects to which they are assigned. If the project does not require their skill full-time, resist assigning other project duties that normally fall within the domain of responsibility of another project member. Instead, assign project members in these positions to work on other projects while retaining the same project position. For example, if a project manager leads a project of five members and the demand on that position is only part-time, assign that person to also be a project manager on one or more other small project(s). This allows the project manager to continue to improve her skills and increase her experiences as a project manager, thus making her much more valuable, long-term, to the organization.

Goal 3: Create departments based on functional areas. Whenever possible, gather people of similar skills and assignments to work together. For example, create specialty departments of designers and coders, independent testers, writers of the product's documentation (both for hard copy and online purposes), training personnel, and various support groups. Collecting people of like skills to work as a group can have a great impact on all group members to improve their productivity and quality more quickly. The members of each group will work among themselves to document, implement, and continually improve their processes. The same is true for ensuring that the best tools are developed, acquired and used. Furthermore, the synergy allows members of a group to share experiences and improve their skills more quickly than would be possible had they been isolated from one other. Even if the department members are assigned to different projects, it is important that they learn from one another in the pursuit of their common needs.

Goal 4: Install a PMO. A PMO can have great benefit to an organization that has many ongoing projects. It provides the care and feeding of project managers to help them be successful. Because project managers report to the PMO, they must be more objective in their decision-making by removing the strong urge to be biased toward what others on the project want versus what is best for the project. As with Goal 3, a PMO allows like-skills people to share and continually improve common processes and tools and support one another through the sharing of their experiences.

Goal 5: Install offices for business architects, product architects, and process architects. Akin to what a PMO can do to benefit project managers, similar offices can benefit business architects, business architects, product architects, and process architects. These offices collect like-skilled people and allow them to leverage off one another to improve their performance and craft. Separate offices can be established for each of these skill groups, or two or more can be collected under one office. Recall in Figure 4 that both project managers and process architects are shown residing within the PMO.

Goal 6: Maintain reasonably sized departments and teams. If a resource manager has too many direct reports or a team leader has too many members assigned to his team, the quality of the work produced can greatly suffer. Therefore, departments should rarely exceed 15 members, and teams should be made up of 10 or fewer members. Limiting the size of the departments will help the resource manager perform the care and feeding required for his direct reports. Attention from resource managers can help maintain reasonable morale among the troops, which averts high attrition rates and ensures that each direct report is being appropriately promoted. Team leaders need teams that are sufficiently small to allow the team leader to work with the members, helping them achieve their commitments.

Resource managers who have other resource managers as direct reports should rarely exceed managing more than seven resource managers.

Goal 7: Report key project positions as close to the product manager as possible. Referent power is more than just a term; it's a force that a person can use more easily to drive her agendas across a project, organization, or company. The key project positions of the project manager, business architect, product architects, and process architects report to the product manager. These are power positions, positions of large influence. By reporting to the product manager, these individuals carry clout that can be beneficial to a leader charged with making things happen. Of course, it is not always practical to have these positions reporting directly to the product manager; for example, if there are many ongoing projects. However, the goal is to report as close to the product manager as possible, such as reporting within a PMO which, in turn, reports to the product manager (see Fig. 1).

4   QUESTIONS AND ANSWERS

Q. What if a member of an organization is committed as a project member on more than one project? Can this really work?

A. It is expected that many people working in multiproject organizations will be assigned to more than one project at a time. Although not optimal, it is often necessary because people with critical skills are required to be stretched across more than one project. Other reasons include staffing and budget challenges and the fact that some skills are not required full-time on a project.

A project member making commitments on more than one project can work fine. However, it is important to note that a project member is always held accountable for his commitments on a given project. *Don't make bad commitments!* If a project member is in trouble with meeting his commitments on one or more projects, he must alert and work with the project manager(s) as quickly as possible. The more a project member must balance his time across multiple projects, the more his demands will suffer a roller coaster of peaks and valleys.

Lesson 1: A project member must never make commitments that are known to be unrealistic.

Q. Based on the answer to the last question, would you say that a person's overall productivity suffers if she is juggling activities across multiple projects?

A. It can. Whenever anyone is working on more than one unique activity simultaneously, there is a cost to starting and stopping each activity. The more an activity is halted and restarted, the greater the negative cost to that person's productivity. A person's productivity improves when he or she can dedicate complete attention and concentration to a single activity.

Q. Doesn't the answer to the last question argue that project managers, business architects, product architects, and process architects should only work on one project full-time, rather than sometimes working part-time on multiple projects as championed by the EnterPrize Organization?

A. The answer to the previous question was directed more to people in an organization that are not focused on their skill enrichment in one specialty area but are multitasking across several unrelated, or mostly unrelated, jobs. In the EnterPrize Organization, project managers, business architects, product architects, and process architects are not always full-time positions on small- and some medium-sized projects. In those cases, rather than have project members take on additional project tasks as a team member, for example, they should continue performing in their original positions (e.g., project manager) on one or more other projects to continue to hone their craft skills.

Can this negatively impact their productivity? In theory, yes; but, in practice, it can have the opposite effect in the long run. The EnterPrize Organization encourages project members in these four positions to become very proficient. The only way to do this is experience; the only way to get experience is by doing. If one wants to become a very good project manager or product architect, for example, he must always be looking to improve his skills and experience base. This is accomplished by intentionally remaining focused on the tasks that will advance those specific skills.

Q. How does a project manager decide how much to assert herself in contending for scarce resources in a multiproject organization?

A. Every project manager must behave as if her project is the most important project in an organization and drive the project to a successful completion. The project manager works constructively to help project members achieve their commitments. However, a project manager should never sacrifice the successful outcome of her own project by allowing commitments made by project members to other projects to take precedence. The one exception is when the person who can make the right business decision across multiple projects (typically the product manager) has made a decision to sacrifice the outcome of one project in favor of strengthening another project.

Lesson 2: The most effective project managers behave as if their project is the most important in the organization.

Q. As follow-up to the last question, isn't it selfish for a project manager to behave as if her project is the most important in an organization?

A. Not at all—this is a common and erroneous misconception. Think about it. You are the owner of a software business and have 10 projects going at any point in time. You have 10 different project managers assigned. Each project is a required business venture, or else it would never have been funded and approved by senior management. Some projects have greater revenue and profit potential than others, but all are important. Here's the key: Would you, as the business owner, want the project managers of the *lesser-priority* nine projects to yield to any request from the project manager and members working on the perceived top project?

The answer should be "no." If the answer is "yes," then what motivation do the lesser-priority nine project managers have for meeting their commitments? How can they be held accountable? These nine projects represent real revenue to the company and real clients that need to be satisfied. Yes, behave as if your project is the most important. The exception, as mentioned in the previous answer, is when the product manager (or other person designated to make the business decision) says to yield; do so only then.

Q. Is it possible to have more than one product manager in a multiproject organization?

A. Yes, there could be several product managers. But if all the projects are versions of the same product, it is typical to have only one product manager. However, if multiple products are being developed in an organization and the products are different or target different clients, it would be typical to have multiple product managers.

Q. Is it possible to have members on a project that do not all report into that chain of command of the product manager?

A. It is common that not all project members report in the same chain of command as the project manager. The examples depicted in this and other chapters represent the preferred approaches that will help an organization most easily reap the benefits of adopting the concepts of the EnterPrize Organization. However, it is not intended to relay the message that there are not other workable approaches. There are others, yet they require a greater degree of discipline to manage and effectively work—but they can be made to work.

Q. Looking at Figure 1, the BAO and the PAO departments show only four members each. Furthermore, there are only six project managers, yet they are in their own departments. Haven't you stated in earlier chapters that there should be from 10 to 15 members to a department?

A. In many cases, departments of nonmanagers should typically consist of 10 to 15 members. Less experienced resource managers can have up to 10 members in their departments. More seasoned resource managers can have departments of up to 15 members. In general, it may not be cost effective to have departments with only a handful. However, if a department is staffing up or trimming down, there can be times when there are other than 15 members.

The example in Figure 1 could be such a case. We could, however, combine the three organizations of PMO, BAO, and PAO into one organization headed by a resource manager who reports to the product manager. The combined group can still be called the PMO, or it could have another name such as the *product office, project office*, or *business office*. We can then replace the four resource managers with three resource managers: (1) for support personnel, (2) to manage project managers and process architects, and (3) to manage business architects and product architects. This restructure would leave the last two departments with nine and eight members, respectively. These departments can be considered sufficiently full, based on the significant responsibilities of the department members and resource managers.

Q. When all the product architects from across an organization are gathered to report to a PAO, should there be a lead product architect?

A. In almost all cases, yes. It can depend, however, on a number of factors, such as the skills and experience of the product architects and whether they are working on similar products. For example, if the product architects have limited experience as such, and if the products served by the product architects have a lot of commonality, then the answer is yes, there should be a lead person to make the decision that can affect all the product architects. This person may also mentor product architects. It should be noted that, usually, there must be a lead person over the other key EnterPrize Organization positions that are collected in groups: project managers, business architects, product architects, and process architects.

11

Improving Multiproject Management by Using a Queuing Theory Approach

Nino Levy and Shlomo Globerson

1 INTRODUCTION

In a single-project organization, all resources of the company are dedicated to only one product. If, however, the company runs a number of projects in parallel using limited resources, frequent conflicts arise when more than one project requires the same resource at the same time. If the nature of the work allows precise scheduling of time, then one can overcome some of the conflicts by careful planning, and each project task will get service from a resource. The problem becomes much more difficult to manage when arrival time of project tasks is uncertain. The complexity grows when there is uncertainty concerning task duration, as in the case of Research & Development (R&D) tasks.

Unfortunately, although most managers of high-tech companies face the problem of managing a multiproject environment, a review of some of the leading project management textbooks (Archibald, 1992; Badiru, 1996; Berman et al, 1997; Cleland, 1996; Frame, 1994; Kerzner, 1994; Lock, 1996;

Adapted from the *Project Management Journal*, 2000.

Meredith and Mantel, 1994; Shtub et al, 1994) revealed that very little has been written on this subject.

Most multiproject high-tech companies are organized in a matrix structure. The overall responsibility for the project/product development, manufacturing, and delivery is normally assigned to a project manager. The actual development and manufacturing work is usually done within the functional departments that specialize in the disciplines necessary for the execution of the work packages (WPs). The project manager is often assisted by a team of individuals reporting to him or her, who share the responsibility for the successful completion of the project. The project organization does the planning, the division of the project into a well-defined work breakdown structure (WBS), and subcontracts the WPs to the appropriate functional departments within the company or to outside contractors.

In most multiproject high-tech companies, one thing remains common: at any given time, a large number of projects generate a huge number of WPs that arrive for service to the functional groups at randomly varying times. For example, in a medium-size electronics company with an annual turnover of $250 million engaged in communications, radar, and computer-embedded systems, the typical number of concurrent projects at any given time exceeded 200. If each project is divided into some 100 WPs, the total number of WPs generated is around 20,000. Those WPs are distributed among some 20 to 30 functional groups. The uncertain ''arrival'' and ''departure'' times of this extensive flow of WPs create a queuing problem that we need to analyze, understand, and resolve.

Let's first look at a simplified example of a single project. The project consists of the design and fabrication of a communication satellite. Typically its WBS looks like that shown in Figure 1.

In such a large system (as shown in Figure 1), obviously work can be started at the same time on only a few of its WPs, as it should follow the precedence relationship, described in Figure 2.

It is important to stress that the letters and numbers on the diagram in Figure 2 express the *estimated* duration of each WP. For example, S1 is the estimated time to prepare the antenna system's general specification by the system's group. A1 is the estimated time, by the antenna group, for the design of the antenna system. A2 is the estimated time for the preparation of the specification of the antenna feed, which the antenna group orders from the microwave group, and so on. All these estimates can be seen, in probability terms, as a random variable with a mean value equal to the estimated time, and with some variance.

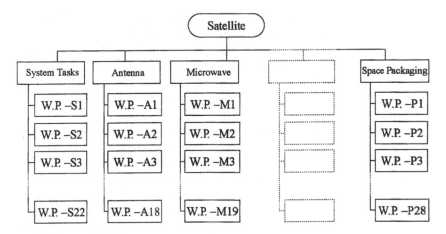

FIGURE 1   Project work breakdown structure.

2   THE WAITING LINE

Although the nature of the probability density function is not known, some very useful results can be learned from well-known queuing theory (QT) models. Quering theory is a field by itself, which has a well-defined body of knowledge (e.g., Bunday, 1996). It can be applied in any circumstances where a service system may have a queue, including manufacturing systems (e.g., Papadopoulos et al., 1993). Examples of queuing-related problems that were researched in the manufacturing environment, relevant to project environment, are the relationship between scheduling strategies and workflow volumes

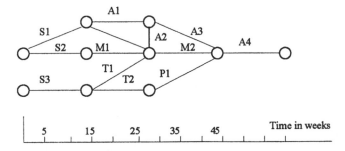

FIGURE 2   Simplified project network.

(Berman et al., 1997), cycle time reduction (Miltenburg and Sparling, 1996), and cost reduction (Kevin, 1996). These can help individuals understand an often ill-understood but extremely important factor for so many project delays and cost overruns: the *queuing factor* (Gross, 1985; Newell, 1982).

The simple but revealing scenario that demonstrates the queuing phenomenon is the one that examines the workflow through a single server service station. A customer arriving to this station is served immediately if the server is free. If the server is busy, the customer joins the queue. When the server finishes serving a customer, this customer leaves the service station and the next customer in line, if any is waiting, enters.

Suppose that customers arrive in a perfectly synchronized and deterministic way, that is, each customer arrives to the service station exactly at the moment service has been completed for the previous customer. Then, clearly, there are no customers waiting in line, and the server is always busy. No time is wasted, either by the customers or the server. This case illustrates the perfect efficiency one attempts to achieve with the Just In Time (JIT) method.

Let's now allow customers to arrive, as they usually do, without prior coordination. One can then say that customers arrive to the service station at random. Despite the fact that the arrival times vary randomly, one can establish an average arrival rate of 1 arrival per unit of time. Similarly, the duration of service each customer gets varies, with an average service rate of m customers served per unit of time. In this case, many of the customers spend a significant time waiting in line, while the server is often idle and waiting for work.

This queuing phenomenon is inevitably present in all multiproject organizations, where customers are replaced by project WPs, and "service stations" are substituted by functional groups. In order to analyze the queuing phenomenon, let us define the following attributes:

L   The number of customers at the service station
W   The average time a customer spends at the station
Lq The average number of customers waiting in the queue
Wq The average time a customer spends waiting in queue
Po The probability to find the server idle

From queuing theory (Kerzner, 1994; Newell, 1982), one can find out that all the attributes depend on the ratio l/m (i.e., the ratio between the average arrival rate and the average service rate). We can name this ratio the "loading factor" (LF), because the higher the ratio, the bigger the workload on the server at the service station.

To get additional insight into the queuing phenomenon, let's present the equations used for the number of customers waiting in the station and for the probability to find the server idle:

$$L = LF/(1 - LF)$$

and

$$Po = 1 - LF$$

where the loading factor is

$$LF = l/m.$$

Two important remarks are due:

First, the arrival rate l has to be smaller than the service rate m, as otherwise, an infinite waiting line will be generated. For example, if $l = 16$ arrivals of WPs per week, and $m = 13$ WPs that can be served per week by that service station, three WPs are added to the line every single week and, in the long run, the queue length will grow to infinity. To avoid this, the capacity of the station should exceed the demand for its services. Therefore, for a production system to work properly, the loading factor should be less than 1.

Second, the more the loading factor approaches 1.0, the longer the waiting lines and the waiting time. On the other hand, the smaller the loading factor, the shorter the waiting line, but the service utilization drops and remains idle for longer periods.

Let's illustrate the above phenomenon with a numeric example. Suppose that the mean arrival rate is 6 per hour and that the mean service rate is 7.5 WPs per hour, or a work package requires, on average, 8 minutes to be processed. Then, substituting the values into the above equations, we find that the number of customers at the station is $L = 4$ and the average amount of time a customer will stay in the station is $W = 40$ minutes. In this case, the probability to find the server idle is Po = 20%, or the station's utilization is UTIL = 80%. Now, if one wants to see, at the average, only one customer in the station rather than four, then substituting the values into equations 1, 2, and 3, we obtain that the service rate must grow to $m = 21$. Then, however, the probability to find the server idle grows to 50%, meaning that the utilization dropped from 80% to 50%. Needless to say, a lower station utilization means an increase in cost per processing a WP.

The above discussion is presented conceptually in Figure 3.

Waiting time

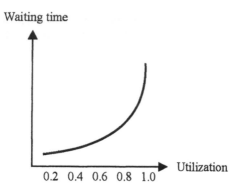

Utilization

0.2 0.4 0.6 0.8 1.0

FIGURE 3   Relationship between station's utilization and WP waiting time.

3   THE COSTS CATEGORIES

The queuing phenomenon of WPs waiting in line and idle resources induces a penalty that must be accounted for. Basically, this penalty consists of three components: (1) the cost of waiting in line (critical WPs are delayed and the project team is idled); (2) the cost of underutilization of available capacity (functional groups are idled); (3) the cost of delayed projects (penalty for late delivery). These three components constitute the added cost the company has to absorb as a result of the queuing phenomenon. Let's examine each component.

3.1   The Cost of Waiting in Line

A project has variable and fixed costs. A project's fixed cost roughly consists of the cost of all resources such as people, equipment, and space exclusively devoted to the project over long periods. When a critical WP waits in line a unit of time, say 1 day, then the entire project is delayed by 1 day. That means the team of people working exclusively for this project is either idle during this day or doing some inefficient work. This results in an extra cost equivalent to 1-day value of the project's fixed cost.

In most projects, even those of modest complexity, often more than one critical WP happens to wait in line. Therefore, to account for all costs accumulated by one project, for its critical WPs waiting in line, shown as project "a," one has to sum up the costs added to the project for each delayed critical WP:

$$W(a) = SUM\ CWP(i)\ i = 1 \ldots N$$

where

W(a)   all costs accumulated by project "a"
CWP(i) cost added by the delay of WP(i)
N   number of WPs in a project

Finally, in a multiproject company that runs a large number of projects at the same time, the total penalty for all projects having critical WPs waiting in line will be:

$$W = SUM\ W(a)\ a = 1\ \ldots\ T$$

where

T is the total number of projects executed by the company at the same time interval, say 1 year.

It is important to note that this penalty is internal to the company, as opposed to penalties that the company has to pay to external factors and which will be discussed later. To clarify further the cost of waiting in line, let's take an example, presented in Table 1.

TABLE 1   Numerical Example for the Cost Associated with Waiting in Line

- The number of projects running in parallel in a high-tech company during a given financial year was 30
- The average number of critical WPs delayed per project in this period was 5
- On the average, the number of days a critical WP had to wait in line during this period was 12
- The average cost per wasted day due to the idle project teams waiting for critical WPs was:

  10 employees * 8 hours/day * $80/hour = $6,400/day

Therefore:
- The average cost per project due to "waiting in line" was:

  $6,400/day * 12 days * 5 times = $384,000

- And the total cost added to the company by all the projects running in parallel during the year was: $384,000/project * 30 projects, or:

The Cost for Waiting in Line = $11,520,000

Abbreviation: WP, work packages.

Table 1 gives a realistic illustration of the significant order of magnitude the cost for waiting in line may have in a mid-size high-tech company. In reality, large projects have much higher (per day) costs for waiting in line than small projects.

3.2   The Underutilization Cost of the Functional Groups

Each functional group in a high-tech company has a certain capacity. As explained above, because of the queuing phenomenon, often WPs are delayed. Clearly, if a critical WP is delayed, but noncritical WPs are lining for work, the group can fill its available capacity with such work and no penalty is inflicted to the company. If, however, the professional group capacity is so large that delays in work package flow cause idle times in the functional group, then one must account for the underutilization cost caused by work shortage. Each group has a certain cost for each unit of capacity. This cost usually includes the payroll of the employees and the amortization of the capital investment made in the group for machines, test equipment, or any other fixed asset.

When the workload of a functional group is below its capacity, the cost of inefficient use of this resource is borne by the company. In most accepted cost accounting practices, there is no way to directly charge such costs to projects that may be causing the problem. These "hidden" costs are no less real. If the cost of unit capacity in functional group "j" is $c(j)$, and if during an accounting period, $m(j)$ units of capacity are idle, then the cost of underutilization of capacity in group "j" is:

$$u(j) = c(j) * m(j)$$

To obtain the total cost to the company, one has to sum up the costs of underutilization of capacity in all t functional groups in this company:

$$U = SUM\ u(j)\ j = 1 \ldots t$$

A good first approximation for the cost of unit capacity in a given functional group is the hourly rate the company charges for work done by this group. Table 2 demonstrates the cost of underutilization of capacity, for a numerical example.

The two costs, "waiting in line" and "underutilization of capacity," are inversely correlated to each other because a capacity increase of the functional unit increases its operational cost but reduces the WP's waiting time, and therefore reduces the cost of the project team. This correlation is presented in Figure 4.

TABLE 2 Example for Cost of Underutilization of Capacity

- The number of functional groups in a high-tech company is 20
- The average hourly cost in 6 of the groups is **high** and amounts to $200
- The average hourly cost in 6 of the groups is **moderate** and amounts to $80
- The average hourly cost in 8 of the groups is **low** and amounts to $20
- During the last financial year, approximately 600 work hours were wasted, at the average, in each of the high-cost functional groups, because of periodic lack of adequate workload. The numbers for the moderate-cost and low-cost functional groups were 500 and 700, respectively.

Therefore:
- The cost for underutilization of capacity in the **high-cost** functional groups accumulated to:

  $200 * 600 * 6 = $720,000

- The cost for underutilization of capacity in the **moderate-cost** functional groups accumulated to:

  $80 * 500 * 6 = $240,000

- The cost for underutilization of capacity in the **low-cost** functional groups accumulated to:

  $20 * 700 * 8 = $112,000

- For the company, **the cost of underutilization of capacity =** **$1,072,000**

3.3 The Cost of Delayed Projects

This cost contains some tangible and some less tangible but real costs to the company for projects not finished on time. Such costs may contain penalties to be paid for late deliveries, costs for lost market opportunities, lost reputation, etc. For each project, this cost is a function of the difference between the actual delivery date and the planned, or promised, delivery date. If the cost for 1 day of delay in the delivery of project "a" is c(a), and the difference between the actual and promised delivery date is y(a) days, then the cost for late delivery of the project is:

$$d(a) = c(a) * y(a)$$

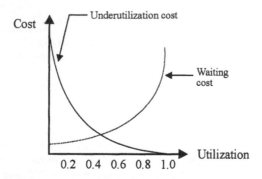

FIGURE 4 Relationship between utilization, project team, and functional costs.

In a multiproject company that runs N projects in the same time, the total cost of delayed projects will be:

$$D = \text{SUM } d(a) \ a = 1 \ldots N$$

Table 3 presents a numerical example for this cost category.

Finally, the maximum queuing penalty in a multiproject high-tech company can be expressed as the summation of the three factors: the idle cost of

TABLE 3 Example of Cost of Delayed Projects

- In a high-tech company running 30 projects in parallel, the number of projects delivered after the promised date last financial year was 12
- The contractual penalty for one of the projects was 0.1% of the contract value of $30 million, for each day of delay, with a ceiling of $500,000. This project was late 45 days and would have cost to the company a direct penalty of $30,000/day * 45 days = $1,350,000. Thanks to the ceiling clause in the contract, the direct penalty was limited to $500,000
- Another project worth $10 million missed the due date for the end of the year holiday season. The products were sold at a discount rate of 20%, causing the company a loss of $2,000,000
- The average penalty and lost opportunity cost for the remaining 10 projects amounted to approximately $150,000 per project, giving a yearly cost of 10 * $150,000 = $1,500,000
- And for the total company, **the cost of delayed projects = $4,000,000**

---

project team caused by waiting in line, the cost of underutilization of functional capacity, and the cost of delays:

$$QP = W + U + D$$

Taking the numbers in our examples, the high-tech company described had suffered in 1 accounting year a maximum queuing penalty of:

$$QP = \$11,520,000 + \$1,168,000 + \$4,000,000 = \$16,688,000$$

Some important remarks are due at this stage: (1) The queuing penalty above is an expression of the additional cost a company bears because of the queuing phenomenon only. We have assumed that the cost for the actual work on any WP is the originally estimated one. (2) The queuing penalty is a very important cause, if not the most important one, for delays and cost overruns in multiproject/product high-tech organizations with substantial R&D content.

Accepting the above remarks, we can make the following conclusions concerning the impact of queues on projects' performance: *The actual delivery time of a project should be computed as the summation of the times its critical WPs spend (being served + waiting) in the functional groups.* This is substantially different from the way one computes the estimated delivery time as the summation of the duration that critical WP require to be *worked on* in the functional groups. *Similarly, the actual cost of a project is the summation of its estimated cost and the project cost for waiting in line.*

4 METHODS FOR REDUCING THE QUEUING PENALTY

The queuing penalty in a multiproject organization cannot be completely avoided because of the queuing structure imposed by the random arrival pattern of the WPs. However, once this phenomenon is well understood, one may use different approaches to reduce this penalty to a minimum, as described below.

4.1 Reducing the Delay Penalty

Obviously, one can minimize this cost by keeping "on schedule" as many projects as possible. However, because keeping all the projects in a multiproject organization on schedule is practically impossible, priority should be given to keeping on schedule the projects with the highest delay penalty. Because of the importance of some less tangible penalties, such as lost reputation, lost market opportunities, and so on, management judgment is important when assigning those priorities. Such penalties, in a final account, may weigh heavier than the tangible penalty clauses written in the project's contract. To achieve the above objective, the first necessary condition is to establish a formal list of projects that must receive special management attention. Top management should ask for frequent status reports on such projects and take appropriate action if significant deviation from planning is detected.

4.2 Reducing the Underutilization Penalty

A logical policy to follow is to make sure that functional groups with high capacity cost are seldom idle. Because this inevitably increases the queue length, management must be particularly careful and assign different priorities for different WPs that load this group. In other words, the scheduler should consider not only due dates of projects, but also utilization of functional departments. A rational and well-informed management should, therefore, set an order of priorities as follows:

- First priority should be given to critical WPs belonging to high-value projects.
- Second priority should be given to critical WPs of lower-value projects.
- Third priority should be given to WPs of high-value projects with a short slack time, that risk becoming critical if they wait too long in line.
- Fourth priority should be given to near-critical WPs of lower-value projects.

For functional groups with low-capacity costs, having frequent idle times may well be justified in view of the time saved by WPs not having to wait in line for service in such groups. By not having to control priorities, because all WPs are served quickly in such groups, substantial management cost can also be saved. Most important, such low-cost groups should never be allowed to become a chronic bottleneck.

4.3 Reducing the Waiting Line Penalty

The cost for waiting in line is a product of two factors: the project's fixed cost per unit of time and the project waiting time due to the delay of critical WPs because they are waiting in line, as explained below.

One extreme method for reducing the fixed project's costs consists of keeping the project organization as small as possible; that is, one project manager assisted by a minimal staff and no additional resources devoted exclusively to the project. In this case, all work will be subcontracted out or done by the functional groups.

The reduction of project waiting time calls for the assignment of all necessary resources to that specific project to ensure that no critical WP of this project is delayed by waiting in line. Obviously, the two solutions are in conflict.

However, because in a high-tech multiproduct organization the need for specialists in a wide spectrum of functional disciplines is almost always present, this approach requires the creation of a minifunctional group structure at the project organization level. This parallel functional group structure will obviously result in a large increase of the underutilization penalty to the entire company. In addition to the high cost, it's practically impossible to find sufficient numbers of competent experts in the same functional field to staff this kind of parallel functional group structure.

What most often happens in real life is a compromise in which only very important projects get dedicated functional resources and create a certain duplication of the functional group's structure. Such compromises are far from optimum in most cases, but they create a sense of comfort by giving the company's management the ability to hold the project manager more accountable for keeping his project on time and on cost.

The recommended approach for reducing the penalty generated by waiting in line is based on a sound information system used for tracking data that will allow good visibility of the status of all WPs, either in process or waiting in queue of the functional groups. Once the above-mentioned information system is established, reduce the size of the available resources in the project organizations to a minimum, and add them to the functional group when needed. The apparent "loss of control" should be compensated for by the added visibility provided by the information systems package and by total management commitment to follow the rules, the logic, and the set of priorities, as established above.

5 CONCLUSIONS

Managing a diversified high-tech innovative company is particularly complex and difficult. Unlike with low-tech companies or mass manufacturing of strictly mature high-tech products, the work process in the innovative high-tech multiproject company is inherently stochastic. This follows from uncertainties associated with the duration of the development cycle of each work package, inducing randomness of the start and finish times of subsequent WPs. Therefore, attempts to manage the above process by deterministic tools is bound to fail.

The uncertain arrival and departure times of the WPs imply a queuing structure of the workload in the various functional groups. Concepts from queuing theory and stochastic processes were shown to be extremely useful for in-depth understanding of the delays and frequent cost overruns of projects executed in parallel in a multiproduct organization.

To quantify the above-mentioned phenomenon, the term *queuing penalty* was introduced. Analyzing its nature, it was shown that there is no practical way to completely avoid this penalty. However, a number of methods to minimize this penalty were examined, and their applicability for different situations was suggested.

The necessary condition for rational management of the queuing process is to have available real-time information. Such data should include status of all WPs, including those waiting in line as well as those being worked on in the functional groups.

REFERENCES

RD Archibald. Managing High Technology Programs and Projects: A Complete, Practical and Proven Approach to Managing Large-Scale Projects. New York: John Wiley & Sons, 1992.

AB Badiru. Project Management in Manufacturing and High-Technology Operations. New York: John Wiley & Sons, 1996.

O Berman, R Larson, and E Pinker. Scheduling workforce in a high volume factory. Management Science 43:158–172, 1997.

B Bunday. An Introduction to Queuing Theory. New York: John Wiley & Sons, 1996.

D Cleland. Field Guide to Project Management. New York: Van Nostrand Reinhold, 1996.

D Frame. New Project Management. New York: Jossey-Bass, Inc., 1994.

D Gross. Fundamentals of Queuing Theory. 2nd ed. New York: John Wiley & Sons, 1985.

H Kerzner. Project Management. New York: Van Nostrand Reinhold, 1994.

W Kevin. Manufacturing lead times, systems utilization rates and lead-time-related demand. Eur J Operational Res 89:259–268, 1996.

D Lock. Project Management. Brookfield: Ashgate, 1996.

JR Meredith, SJ Mantel Jr. Project Management: A Managerial Approach. 3rd ed. New York: John Wiley & Sons, 1994.

J Miltenburg, D Sparling. Managing and reducing total cycle time: Models and analysis. Int J Production Economics 46–47, 89–108, 1996.

G Newell. Applications of Queuing Theory. 2nd ed. London: Chapman & Hall, 1982.

H Papadopoulos, C Heavey, J Browne. Queuing Theory in Manufacturing Systems, Analysis and Design. London: Chapman & Hall, 1993.

A Shtub, J Bard, S Globerson. Project Management: Engineering, Technology and Implementation. Prentice Hall International, Inc., 1994.

12

A Multiproject Management Framework for New Product Development

Adriano De Maio, Roberto Verganti, and Mariano Corso

1 INTRODUCTION

Brilliant product innovations are at the very root of most of the greatest fortunes in the history of the industry. Nevertheless, management literature (Burgelman and Maidique, 1988; Stalk and Rout, 1990) reports many cases of mistakes committed in the development of new products, leading outstanding firms to lose their competitive edge. Moreover, there have been many imitators who, through their manufacturing superiority or through the control of some important complementary assets, have deprived innovators of any significant advantage from the innovation (Teece, 1986).

New product development (NPD), therefore, has long been regarded as a powerful but risky weapon for companies following an aggressive differentiation-driven strategy (Porter, 1980). Consequently, in the past, the process of new product development had, with few exceptions, been considered and managed as something episodic and with low interaction with the normal activity of the firm.

Adapted from the *European Journal of Operational Research*, 1994.

Today, the competitive context is changing: the growing rate of diverse and unpredictable changes in technology and environment, the increasingly demanding market, and the more and more international competition require frequent and effective management of product and process innovation. As product life becomes shorter and innovation development time increases, firms pursuing a pure followership strategy are doomed to fail (Ansoff, 1979). New product and process development ceases to be an issue of daily management to be dealt with.

Hence, there is renewed interest in management techniques and philosophies regarding innovation. Total quality control (TQC) and project management (PM) are most significant of these (De Maio and Maggiore, 1992). As is shown in Figure 1, both these techniques aim at the ability to manage

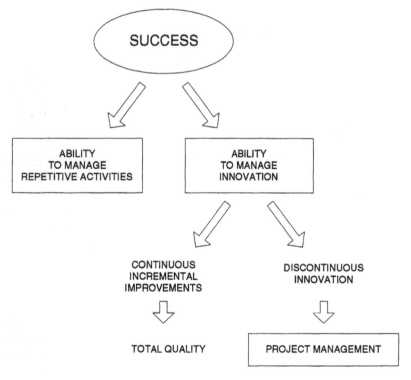

FIGURE 1 Impact of management techniques on innovation seen as a critical success factor.

innovation but, whereas TQC deals with continuous incremental improvements, PM relates to discontinuous innovation.

This chapter focuses on the application of project management, but it is worth stressing that PM and TQC are profoundly related. In a recent book, Blackburn (1991) underlines how firms excelling in incremental innovation management, through the application of TQC, are usually outstanding also in discontinuous innovation management through PM applications. This phenomenon, far from being coincidental, is a strong confirmation of the organizational and cultural nature of today's competitive challenge, which is based mainly on human resources.

Excluding the cases in which only marginal production enhancement and slight modifications are carried on, NPDs represent very important examples of discontinuous innovation (Hayes et al, 1988). Thus, one could reasonably think that a PM approach may effectively be used to manage product innovation. Even if this is true for the basic PM principles, several problems arise during the implementation of specific methods and techniques. Product innovation processes, in fact, have peculiarities that require new, tailor-made tools and interpretative models to be developed. An interesting example is the issue dealt with in this chapter; that is, multiproject management (MPM) of NPD projects.

The following section analyzes the process of product development with a new view on how a PM approach can improve product innovation performance. The problem of a multiproject management is then introduced as a critical issue in the implementation of PM systems in NPD. Further on in the chapter an interpretative model especially tailored for high-tech manufacturing firms is introduced and shown in detail, with some of its possible uses demonstrated. Finally we return to a discussion of the model's field of application, stressing its aims and main limitations.

2 PROJECT MANAGEMENT APPLICATION IN PRODUCT INNOVATION PROCESSES: THE PROBLEM OF MULTIPROJECT MANAGEMENT

Many authors have already pointed out that the new product development processes have features of complexity and interfunctionality that make a PM approach very suitable (Gilbreath, 1988; Hayes, Wheelwright and Clark, 1988). A correct application of PM can, in fact, have a positive impact on product development performance. To explain this phenomenon, the process of new product development can be seen as a sequence of stages, each one

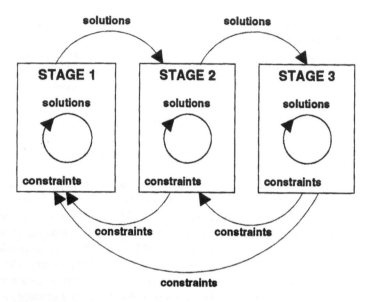

FIGURE 2   Problem-solving cycles in new product development.

characterized by a problem-solving circle (Clark and Fujimonto, 1991) [Figure 2].

Every loop between stages may lower quality and will certainly reduce productivity and increase time scales. A PM approach can be used profitably to avoid loops by "anticipating constraints" in the following ways:

1. Organizing multifunctional teams and integrating them into the firm's structure.
2. Focusing on the overall architectural design of the process. This, on the other hand, helps to take into account characteristics and needs of downstream stages.
3. Improving integration and coordination between different stages of the product. This is particularly important for facilitating the intense and continuous flow of information in overlapping activities.

Project management, therefore, can play an important role in product development. However, close attention must be paid to the fact that we are applying PM techniques in a context that is culturally and technically different from PM in engineering companies, the environment in which these techniques were originally developed.

Pioneering experiences in manufacturing industries highlight the fact that the dominant management culture tends to create a situation in which only the most superficial aspects of PM are actually applied (De Maio, 1991). Emphasis is placed almost exclusively on tools, whereas little attention is given to a number of very fundamental issues in PM organizational and managerial philosophy, such as the definition of goals and scope of work, or the focus on general project design, too often confused with technical design. In this way, PM, instead of simplifying the control system by focusing monitoring efforts on the critical success factor, leads to a strong focus on procedures and a subsequent increase in bureaucracy.

The real need, on the contrary, is to understand the contribution provided by PM basic principles in terms of competence integration, planning logic, emphasis on anticipation of constraints, and the control of critical areas. New tools and methods are then required, which, although based on PM principles, are especially tailored to suit NPD peculiarities.

One of the characteristics of product innovation processes that differs substantially from traditional engineering projects is that goals, requirements, and characteristics often change during the project lifetime. A constant, dynamic control of the validity and mutual compatibility of different project plans is, therefore, needed. One of the most critical issues becomes multiproject management: the system of actions aimed at dynamically ensuring compatibility among different simultaneous projects with a portfolio approach.

It may be of some surprise that, in spite of its criticality, this is one of the issues that has been studied least in the implementation of project management systems. The reason is that multiproject management systems were originally developed in engineering companies where, even if there are often several simultaneous projects to be managed using shared resources (Tsubakitani and Deckro, 1990), this problem does not seem to acquire particular criticality. In fact, because project implementation is the core activity and actual mission of engineering companies, integration among projects is a noncritical issue from a cultural point of view. Besides that, the main reason for MPM criticality in product development relates to the nature and degree of interdependencies existing between projects.

In fact, the choice of whether a system of processes is to be managed independently or concurrently depends on the strength of the links existing between them. Links between projects, in particular, may be classified as follows:

1. Resource interdependencies
2. Input/output interdependencies

Resource interdependencies derive from the sharing of scarce resources among different projects. As far as product innovation processes are concerned, it can be observed that resource interdependencies are currently growing in importance. On the one hand, because product lifecycle is shortening, companies are being compelled to simultaneously develop an increasing number of new products. On the other hand, the continuous technological evolution requires resource specialization to be increased so that flexibility in resource allocation cannot be exploited. The combined effect of these trends implies rapid resource saturation that turns into stronger resource interdependencies.

The current criticality of multiproject management in NPD, however, may be further underlined by considering peculiarities of input/output interdependencies. These can be due to:

- *Commonality:* When two different products require the development of some common parts.
- *System integration:* When a product is developed not only to be sold in its own market, but also to be included in a more complex system. An example could be that of computer-aided instruments that can be used either as stand-alone tools or as part of an integrated computer information management (CIM) system.
- *Technological prerequisites:* When technologies developed for one product are also to be used in subsequent projects. An example concerns customized or cost-reduced products based on previously developed platforms or core products (Clark and Wheelwright, 1992; Wheelright and Sasser, 1989; Clark and Fujimonto, 1991). More in general, we refer to all those techniques known as *carryover,* which aims at reducing the dimension of NPD projects using previously developed parts (off-the-shelf parts or shelf innovation);
- *Market interactions:* When a product could open market opportunities for subsequent projects.

Traditional multiproject techniques usually neglected the input/output interdependencies, because they related to environments where the presence of an external customer forces explicit contractual ties to be established (Lawrence and Morton, 1993). Hence we have projects, having generally autonomous and clearly defined objectives, interacting only in case of conflicts regarding resource requirements.

In product innovation projects, on the contrary, input/output interdependencies acquire fundamental importance as they induce deep strategic, and not only operative, links between projects that must be managed by a special

MPM system. To support this new managerial level, specially tailored tools and interpretative models must be developed.

3 A NEW MODEL: AIMS AND BASIC CONCEPTS

The purpose of this chapter is to put forward a model that will explain a firm's behavior in simultaneously managing different product development processes in each step from project selection to ongoing control. A comprehensive model of MPM, in fact, cannot be based on specific techniques; on the contrary, interpretative models aimed at supporting the decision-making process seemed to be more useful (Schmidt and Freeland, 1992). The model proposed, therefore, is a general explanatory tool. It is especially suitable for high-tech industries as it focuses on dynamic aspects. Moreover, it can be used as a general framework to integrate prescriptive methodologies that address more specific problems, such as sequencing and scheduling.

Going into deeper detail, the proposed model aims at helping decision-makers in five steps of the multiproject management process:

1. Individual product evaluation, classification and initial screening
2. Multiproject classification and selection
3. Actions for improvement and portfolio reclassification
4. Priority assignment
5. Ongoing control of project portfolio

In these five fundamental steps of multiproject management, projects must be compared to one another on the basis of three factors: relevance, risk, and critical resources.

- *Relevance* is the expected profitability of the project. It depends on the strategic importance of the product, the expected income, and cost.
- *Risk* represents the uncertainty involved in a particular project. For instance, in product innovation, risk often depends on the project size, the degree of technological innovation, the stability and knowledge of market needs, and the competitive situation (Moenaert and Souder, 1990; McFarland, 1981).
- *Critical resources* are those resources whose availability and quality strongly condition either project feasibility or performances. In new product development, the most critical resources are generally measured in terms of engineering hours.

These three variables are the minimum set of criteria that must be explicitly considered to avoid losing too much explanatory power. Far from being static, they change frequently according to the evolution of the internal and external environment like, for instance, modifications in exogenous factors (e.g., market, competitors, and technology), strategic changes inside the company (strategies, policies, birth or death of other projects), or changes within the project itself (caused, for example, by unforeseen risks or unexpected problems).

Let us assume that projects, both new proposals and ongoing projects, have been evaluated in terms of relevance, risk, and critical resources required. We will use the following notation:

j Project index, $j \in G$, where G is the universe of projects considered.

J^* Selected portfolio, $J^* \in G$.

X_{max} Maximum risk accepted.

X_j Expected risk of project j ($X_j \leq X_{max}$).

Y_{min} Minimum relevance accepted.

Y_j Expected relevance of the project j ($Y_j \geq Y_{min}$).

Z_j Critical resources required by project j.

Z_{tot} Total amount of critical resources available in the planning period.

U_j Utility of project j, is the attractiveness perceived for project j; it is the function of risk, relevance, and resources required.

U_{j^*tot} Total utility perceived for portfolio J^*.

From a theoretical point of view, the selected portfolio J^* could be derived from the following optimization problem:

$$\text{Max}_{J^*} \; U_{J^*tot}(X_j, Y_j, J^*)$$

s.t.

$$\sum_{j \in J} Z_j \leq Z_{tot} \quad \text{on all critical resources,}$$

$X_j \leq X_{max}$ for all $j \in J^*$, on maximum risk accepted,

$Y_j \geq Y_{min}$ for all $j \in J^*$, on minimum relevance accepted.

Unfortunately, as suggested in the previous section, such an optimization approach, although useful in cases such as those studied by financial portfolio theories, is unrealistic and useless in product development. Variables and relations, in fact, are extremely hard to estimate, as they vary according to how projects are scheduled and resources assigned. Moreover, total utility is not merely the sum of individual projects' utilities, as complex strategic interactions (which cannot be easily estimated through correlation coefficient) often arise between various projects' expected results. This approach is, therefore, not usually viable in a real situation.

We propose instead the heuristic approach depicted in Figure 3. Individual projects are classified initially, without considering resource constraints; then resource constraint is considered and an initial hypothesis of project portfolio is selected. Subsequently a multiproject portfolio evaluation is carried out to take into account complex interactions that arise between projects at portfolio level, changing both relevance or risk of the overall portfolio. Until the expected result is perceived as satisfactory, actions for improvement are taken that may act either on the firm as a whole or on individual projects; projects are then classified again and a new portfolio is selected. When a satisfactory situation is reached, the plan is consolidated and transmitted to downstream phases for further, more detailed project planning. During project

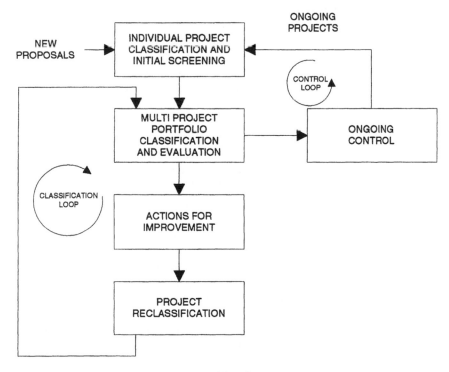

FIGURE 3 Heuristic approach to multiproject management.

execution, projects are monitored and, when some relevant changes occur, reclassified for a new cycle of multiproject management.

In the following sections, we will illustrate in detail each step of the process. Using the notations introduced above, we will propose analytical relations whose aims are purely conceptual and explanatory. A graphical approach, however, will be introduced that could be more useful as a practical guideline and as an interpretative mapping tool all along the process.

4 SUPPORTING THE MULTIPROJECT MANAGEMENT PROCESS

4.1 Individual Project Evaluation, Classification, and Initial Screening

The starting point of the proposed model is the evaluation of single projects in terms of relevance, risk, and critical resource requirement. The assessment of these three variables is not simply aimed at selecting the most promising projects. In a PM perspective, the main purpose is to identify the most suitable approach and, as a result of the anticipation of critical issues, to set the monitoring and control system of the project. Depending on their relevance, risk, and resource requirement, projects will be characterized by different organizations (e.g., functional matrix or task force; Larson and Gobeli, 1987), different attention from top management, different schedules, and different priorities in the access to shared resources.

The key concept here is "classification": decision-makers show a natural tendency to categorize every managerial problem in terms of their previous experiences. Projects, therefore, are managed following the approach used in successful experiences and avoiding those that led to failure. This hypothesis is that, even if we are dealing with discontinuous innovation and unique processes, there is a certain stability in the general environment. It is highly probable that a managerial approach that proved worthwhile in previous projects will be suitable for new projects classified as similar.

Methods of evaluating relevance and risk are outside the scope of this chapter, but classifying the different approaches could be useful in clarifying the problem. Methods proposed in the literature can be divided into three main groups.

The first group includes all techniques that can be defined *financial*, or capital budgeting (Clark, et al. 1998). The aim of these techniques is to appraise the economic effectiveness of a project, evaluating incremental discounted cash flow (DCF techniques) deriving from the investment. The main merit of these methods is the use of a widely known and accepted language, originating from the accounting tradition deeply rooted in all economic organizations. The main limitations relate to the tendency to express every cost and benefit resulting from the projects with medium-term monetary flows (Hayes, et al. 1988). These models are substantially deterministic, as they take account of the different degree of uncertainty only by requiring higher profitability when project uncertainty is high.

The second group comes from *operations research* studies. These methods aim at expressing variables, relations between variables, constraints, and utility functions analytically. Risk minimization, therefore, can be viewed as an additional goal to achieve greater utility. These methods allow for complete and conceptually solid models, with multiple control levels (Speranza and Vercellis, 1993), multiple objectives, and constraints (Mohanty and Siddiq, 1989). Nevertheless, they often result in models that are difficult to apply and that often don't suit the organizational behavior (Schmidt and Freeland, 1992).

More recently, many authors have understood the criticality deriving from the application needs in high-uncertainty environments often characterized by the presence of multiple decision-makers with different individual goals and cognitive models. Multi-Criteria Decision Making (MCDM) and Multi-Attribute Utility Theory (MAUT) researchers, in particular, have recently been shifting their interest from solving well-structured problems under often realistic assumptions to developing Multiple Criteria Decision Support Systems (MCDSSs). The latter support the decision-makers in capturing and making explicit their own preferences, interacting with them in several steps of the decision-making process (Dyer et al., 1992).

The third and final group includes methods that can be defined *strategic*, aimed at evaluating the impact of the project on the position of the firm in the competitive context. These methods can be numerical (e.g., scoring methods) or nonnumerical (e.g., check lists) and may have very different degrees of complexity (Souder, 1998), but they are all characterized by the substantial rejection of claims to optimality and objectivity and a great focus on the so-called intangibles: benefits (or costs) resulting from an investment that cannot be expressed in terms of cash flow. Risk analysis can be carried out by identifying every potential source of undesired events and by evaluating each of these events in terms of probability and impact. The weaknesses of these methods are mainly the subjectivity of analysis and the difficulties in the ex-post control.

As some authors have already suggested (Azzone and Betel, 1991; Meredith and Mantel, 1989), there is no optimum method. Techniques must be evaluated and chosen according to the specific application; moreover, these

methods should not be considered mutually exclusive, but rather as complementary techniques.

In our case, the features of high uncertainty that characterize multiproject management of new product development in high-tech industries suggest
MCDSSs and strategic methods as the most fitting solutions. At the same time,
the high impact on firms' overall strategies and financial position suggests
that further support by financial evaluations could be beneficial. Analytical
relations, on the other hand, can be used to conceptually identify relevant
variables and their mutual relations.

Leaving the choice of the specific evaluation method out of consideration, the aim of this chapter is to put forward a model that will integrate
individual project evaluation in the overall MPM process.

An effective representation to support the process could be the following: projects can be represented as circles on a two-dimensional risk-relevance
(R-R) matrix (Figure 4), with the position identified by the coordinates X_j,
Y_j, and an area proportional to the expected absorption of critical resources
(calculated without taking into account resource constraints).

Although not innovative in itself, this simple representation allows a
clear explanation of each step of the multiproject management process.

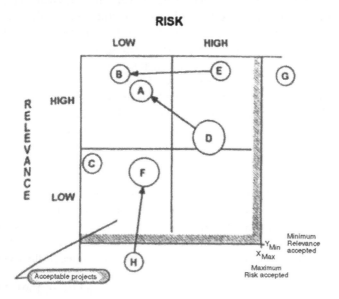

FIGURE 4 Project classification and initial screening.

The classification process is represented by the positioning of the n projects in the R-R matrix (see Fig. 4). The most important input/output interdependencies between projects are represented by arrows joining the linked projects.

Overlooking resource constraint implies that, in the first instance, projects are classified under the assumption that all linked projects will be selected. In this phase, however, an initial screening is already carried out. Projects that have higher risk or lower relevance than those (X_{max} and Y_{min}) established as "acceptable" are rejected (G and H). This implies, that, in the situation shown in Figure 4, a further reclassification of Project F is requested to take into account the exclusion of the linked project H.

4.2 Portfolio Evaluation and Selection

The next step is to take into account resources interdependencies, introducing the resource constraint: we have to select a feasible project portfolio by trying to achieve the greatest possible utility according to resources available. The different degrees of risk aversion can be represented by the slope of the straight b-b line in Figure 5: projects placed on the same b-b line are perceived by the firms as having the same attractiveness. Shifting from the top left corner

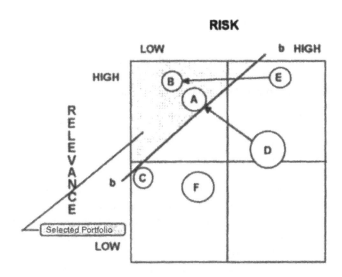

FIGURE 5 Project portfolio selection.

to the bottom right one, the line b-b meets all the projects in order of decreasing utility, from most attractive to least attractive.

The selected portfolio J^* is composed of projects placed in the area above the straight line b-b. This line can be seen as a feasibility constraint. It takes into account planned resource availability and the ability to manage risk.

A further multiproject reclassification is then required to consider inter-dependencies between the selected projects (see A and B in Fig. 5) and the rejected projects linked to them.

From an analytical point of view, this can be translated as follows: with a rough approximation we can postulate, in a relevant range, a constant degree of risk aversion and a linear utility curve. Thus, we can define:

$$\lambda(X) = \partial Y/\partial X = \Delta Y/\Delta X = \lambda$$

degree of risk aversion (constant),

λ is measured by the amount of incremental relevance required for a unit of incremental risk. Project utility, therefore, is

$$U_j(X, Y) = Y_j - \lambda X_j.$$

In first instance, we could say that the total utility is given by the sum of single projects' utilities:

$$U_{J^*tot} = \sum_{j \in J} (Y_j - \lambda X_j).$$

However, as we have already stressed, projects are not independent. Each different portfolio selection could change either the risk or relevance of each project. Thus, for every J^* we have to evaluate:

$$U_{J^*tot}(X_j, Y_j, J^*) = \Sigma (Y_j(J^*) - \lambda X_j(J^*)).$$

It becomes clear that this analytical approach is not so effective as the graphical approach, in that it does not support the identification of interactions between projects.

The purpose of the model is not only the assessment of the attractiveness of alternative portfolios, but also the identification of actions aimed at improving firms' expected performance. The next step is a careful examination of possible improvements. Actions for improvement could act either on the firm as a whole or on individual projects.

Given the expected risk and relevance of each project (X_j, Y_j for all j), the firm can attain better expected performances by carrying out the following three actions *on the firm as a whole*:

1. Actions aimed at increasing critical resource availability: Increasing the total amount of critical resource available ($Z_{tot}j7 > Z_{tot}$), a greater set ($J^{*'} \supset J^*$) of projects can be performed, thereby attaining better overall expected results ($U_{J^*tot'} > U_{J^*tot}$):

$$\sum_{j \in J^{*'}} Z_j \le Z'_{tot} \text{ with } Z'_{tot} > Z_{tot}$$

and so $J^{*'} \supset J^*$. (Fig. 6a, b, c, d)

This is represented in Figure 6a, where the line b-b shifts down and project "C" enters the selected portfolio. Possible examples of these actions are the recruitment of new resources, the conversion of existing less critical resources, the stipulation of subcontracting agreements, and so on. These actions may often be impossible or have too high a cost in the short term, as critical resources are not readily available on the market.

2. Actions aimed at improving resource productivity: Once again we attain a larger portfolio ($J^{*'} \supset J^*$) and better expected results ($U_{J^*tot'} > U_{J^*tot}$), but, this time, this is achieved through a reduction in critical resources required for each project (Z_j for all j):

$$\sum_{j \in J^{*'}} Z'_j Z_{tot} \text{ with } Z'_j < Z_{tot}$$

for all j and so $J^* \supset J^*$.

In Figure 6b, this action is represented by the reduction in surface area of the individual circles.

3. Actions aimed at enhancing firms' ability to manage and reduce risk and at improving overall project feasibility. These actions are represented in Figure 6c by a reduction of the gradient of b-b ($\lambda' < \lambda$): The firm, having enhanced ability to manage risk, is now able to select Project E instead of Project C ($J^{*'} \ne J^*$), thereby attaining better expected results ($U_{J^*tot'} > U_{J^*tot}$). Possible examples are higher investment in the firm's control system with a subsequent reduction in overall response time, or some form of diversification or insurance.

Given the amount of resources required by each project (Z_j for all j), the total quantity of critical resources available (Z_{tot}) and the degree of risk aversion (λ), the firm can improve its performances (U_{J^*tot}) through *actions on individual projects*. These actions can be classified as follows:

- Actions aimed at improving relevance at the price of an increase in risk (A-A' and C-C' in Fig. 6d): Possible examples are the enlargement of the scope of work or the reduction in planned time to market.

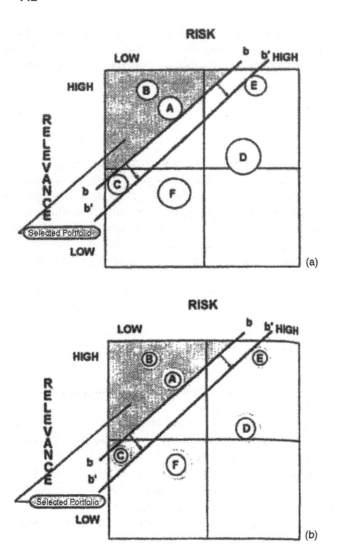

FIGURE 6 (a) Actions on the firm as a whole: Increasing critical resource availability. (b) Actions on the firm as a whole: Improving resource productivity.

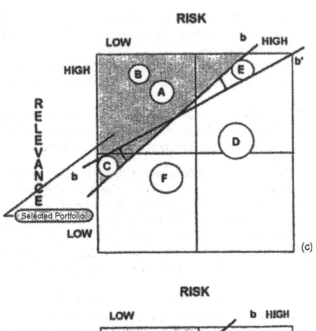

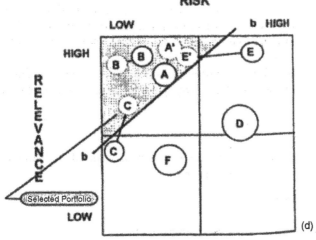

FIGURE 6   (c) Actions on the firm as a whole: Enhancing the ability of the firm to manage risk (improving overall feasibility. (d) Actions on individual projects.

- Actions aimed at reducing risk at the price of a reduction of relevance (B-B' and E-E' in Fig. 6d.): These actions can be further divided into two different classes:
- *Feedforward actions*, which are performed before project start-up to reduce sensitivity to the critical area or probability of undesired events
- *Feedback actions*, which are foreseen and planned before the project start-up, to be carried out only in the state of an emergency. Firms' response time and the impact of undesired events are reduced.

Suppose, we want to reduce the danger of people living in an earthquake zone. With a typical feedforward action, we can achieve this purpose by means of quakeproof buildings. A different, perhaps complementary, approach could be that of providing emergency measures and plans to reduce response time and time needed to rescue victims. The latter is a feedback action that reduces the impact of a negative event. In Table 1, referring to product development processes, some examples are given of critical areas and corresponding actions.

Both in feedback and feedforward actions, the reduction of risk generally has a price, which results in a reduction of the projects' overall expected relevance. These actions may be represented by arrows like those labeled B-B' and E-E' in Figure 6d.

The model allows a simple evaluation of these actions. Actions aimed at reducing risk are advantageous only if the gradient of the arrows is lower than that of b-b:

$$(Y_j - Y_j')/(X_j - X_j') < \lambda;$$

Actions aimed at increasing relevance are advantageous only if the gradient of the arrows is higher than that of b-b:

$$(Y_j' - Y_j)/(X_j' - X_j) > \lambda.$$

4.3 Priority Assignment and Ongoing Control of the Selected Portfolio

The correct selection of a project portfolio and subsequent detailed planning should guarantee resource availability. However, the unexpected changes in the duration and resource absorption of activities often force schedules to be modified. Frequent conflicts between projects arise. If not resolved in a systematic perspective, these conflicts could lead to a drastic reduction in performance. In spite of this widely recognized criticality, a clear and formal priority

TABLE 1   Critical Areas and Corresponding Actions

Critical areas	Feedforward actions	Feedback actions
Low technical specifications reliability	• Deeper client involvement in product conception	• Stricter contractual oblication (engineering to order products)
High degree of technological innovation	• Higher investment in feasibility studies • High-tech joint ventures • Long-term agreements with high-tech suppliers	• Standby agreements with high-tech subcontractors
High degree of inter-functionality	• Closer attention to overall architectural design • Physical co-location of researchers • Higher investment in communication facilities	• Closer attention to interface management • Formal definition of duties and procedures
Critical resources shared with other projects	• Overestimation of resource requirements • Formal definition and closer control of critical resources	• Formal priority assignment

policy is too often lacking: selected projects are all considered as high-priority. In such a situation, precedence in the access to critical resources is established by individual functional managers. This is done on the basis of degree of pressure perceived and from a viewpoint that is, to say the least, partial. Strong political and psychological pressures are among the causes of this costly situation: it might not be pleasant or politically advisable to tell people they are working on a low-priority project.

Priority assignment is a very complex and critical process that must be consistent with resource availability and development policy (Adler et al., 1989).

The model allows a simple representation of the process to be made. With rough approximation, we can say that high-priority projects are those

with high relevance and high degree of risk. In fact, in new product development projects, relevance is strongly related to time performance, and estimates
regarding market, environment, and technological evolution become much
more uncertain the more time scales increase. Risk is, in most cases, related
to urgency. Projects that, although relevant, are low risk, are generally less
urgent and so are lower priority than projects with the same relevance, but
higher risk.

On the basis of these considerations, we can express an initial approximation, the degree of priority PR j of project j by the following relation:

$$PRj(X,Y) = Yj + aXj$$

where $a > 0$ represents the degree of urgency related to risk. It is measured
by the amount of incremental relevance required to assign to a certain project
the same level of priority as another project whose risk is one unit higher.

In other words, using the representation shown in Figure 7, two projects
placed on the same parallel of the d-d line are perceived as having the same
level of priority.

A simple but effective approach is to identify two priority classes (De-
Maio et al., 1992):

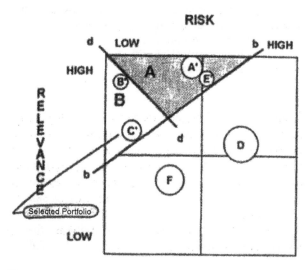

FIGURE 7 Priority assignment.

1. Class A: Projects for which no delay is acceptable. To achieve the key objective of minimization of time to market, priority in the access to critical resources is given.
2. Class B: Low-priority projects for which delays are considered more acceptable. In planning the projects, the primary effort is to assure good use of critical resources.

Projects belonging to class A are high priority and must be "protected" to avoid any delay. Projects must be selected and classified, every effort being made to limit interdependence, and the probability of conflict, between high-priority projects. From a practical standpoint, this protection involves the planning and control process in different stages:

*   In team building, more full-time highly experienced members must be assigned to high-priority projects.
*   In the allocation of critical resources, we have to ensure that no more than a certain percentage of such resources are assigned, in any given period, to high-priority projects. This assures a certain margin of resources allocated to B projects that are available for emergency actions in A projects.
*   In the architecture of monitoring and control systems, high-priority projects must receive more attention from top management and so a more frequent and detailed reporting must be provided.
*   In project monitoring, strict control over activities that, although not critical for the project itself, are physically interrelated with A projects (e.g., common parts or components).

Up to now we have seen how the model can be used as a planning tool. This model, however, can also be used during the implementation of the project, as a control tool. By monitoring relevance and risk, firms can check the state of the project and, in case of need, take adequate countermeasures to reestablish a well-balanced portfolio (Fig. 8).

The optimistic evolution of the project, if everything goes as foreseen, would be that represented by the arrows $E' - E''$ and $C - C''$ in Figure 8. During project execution, in fact, risk, which is related to uncertainty in the expected performance, is due to decrease (see Fig. 9) as estimates become more reliable. At the same time, relevance, which is evaluated on the basis of incremental income, is expected to increase as costs become "sunk" and the time incomes will be received approaches. Projects should migrate toward the top left corner of the matrix. However, external changes may substantially

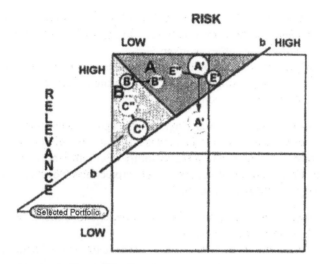

FIGURE 8   Ongoing control of project portfolio.

modify the relevance or the risk of the project, changing its priority (such as Fig. 8, the project labeled B′ − B″), or driving it out of the selected portfolio area of the R-R matrix. The latter is the case of "early project termination." For instance, suppose a firm is developing a new product and a competitor releases a similar product. This event can drastically affect the firm's advan-

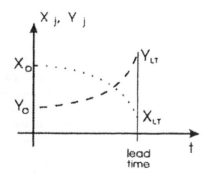

FIGURE 9   Expected risk and relevance evolution during project execution.

tage in carrying on the project. The situation, in this case, could be that shown in Figure 8, in which interest in project A ceases.

5 CONCLUSION

The application of PM techniques in NPD presents many interesting opportunities. At the same time, it raises the need to reconsider the validity of traditional methods and tools and, in some cases, to develop new ones more suitable to the processes to be managed.

Multiproject management of portfolio, in particular, is one of the points at which traditional methods and techniques appear to be less adequate. This problem is mainly related to the complexity of interproject links. Within this context, the modelization of the input/output interdependencies between projects and their integration within an explanatory framework that also considers resource interdependencies is intended as a first step toward the development of more comprehensive support systems. However, also from this prospective, the model doesn't yet appear complete: the input/output interdependencies, for example, are not confined within the planning horizon. If we can consider the coherence of competence development policies and the so-called self-innovation, they also involve past and future projects.

The widening of the explanatory framework to include these phenomena also represents the natural future evolution of the work.

In conclusion, it is worth stressing again the nature, as well as the intrinsic limits of, this chapter.

We have presented our model by means of both graphic and analytical relations; these latter have a merely explanatory function. Because firms have to appraise risk and relevance through highly subjective methods, an optimization or even analytical approach is not suitable. We have proposed instead a graphical approach that could be used effectively as a mapping tool and guideline throughout the process. This model represents the problem clearly and simply, constituting a valuable didactic and interpretative tool. We believe that this is the main merit of the model.

On the other hand the model is so general that a certain number of critical limitations arise when we can try to use it as a prescriptive methodology. The application of an earlier version of the model in the telecommunications industry, although giving us important inputs already included in this work, casts light upon several implementation problems that are still unresolved.

These limits are implicit in the difficulty of estimating project relevance and risk. The model assumes that all critical resource absorption can be expressed with a single index; this assumption is correct only when there is a single, very critical resource that limits the number of projects that the firm can undertake at any one time. Finally, it is important to observe that this model supports project selection and priority assignment at a strategic level only. Further detailed analysis could obviously highlight impediments, calling for a recycling of the process.

At the moment, we are testing the framework in the electromedical instruments industry while a modified version is being applied to information systems projects. Early evidence confirms the value of the model mainly as an interpretative and didactic tool. These and further applications in specific contexts would cast light on its potential as a framework for prescriptive methodologies.

REFERENCES

PS Adler, HE Riggs, SC Wheelwright. Project development know how: Trading tactics for strategies. Sloan Management Review, Fall, 1989.

IH Ansoff. Strategic Management. London: Macmillan, 1979.

G Azzone, U Bertele. Techniques for measuring economic effectiveness of automation and manufacturing systems. In: Control and Dynamics—Advances in Theory and Application, vol. 48: Manufacturing and Automation Systems: Techniques and Technologies. New York: Academic Press, 1991.

JD Blackburn. Tune Based Competition—The Next Battle Ground in American Manufacturing. Homewood, IL: Business One Irwin, 1991.

RA Burgelman, MA Maidique. Strategic Management of Technology and Innovation. Homewood, IL: Irwin, 1988.

JJ Clark, TH Hindelang, RE Pritchard. Capital Budgeting—Planning and Control of Capital Expenditures. Englewood Cliffs, NJ: Prentice-Hall, 1988.

KB Clark, T Fujimoto. Product Development Performance—Strategy, Organization, and Management in the World Auto Industry. Boston: HBS Press, 1991.

KB Clark, SC Wheelwright. Creating product plans to focus product development. Harvard Business Review, March-April, 1992.

A De Maio. Nuovi paradigmi organizzativi per l'nnovazione di prodotto. In: U Bertele and S Mariotti, eds. Impresa e Competizione Dinamica. Milan: ETAS, 1991.

A De Maio, E Maggiore. Organizzare per Innovare—Rapporti Evoluti Clienti—Fomiton. Milan: ETAS, 1992.

A De Maio, R Verganti, M Corso. Introduction of a project management system in a telecommunications firm. Working paper, 1992.

J Dyer. A time sharing computer program for the solution of the multiple criteria problem. Management Science 19:1379–1383, 1973.

JS Dyer, PC Fishburn, RE Steuer, J Wallenius, S Zionts. Multiple criteria decision making, multiattribute utility theory: The next ten years. Management Science 43(12), 1992.

HD Gilbreath. Working with pulses, not streams: Using projects to capture opportunity. In: DI Cleland and WR King eds., Project Management Handbook. Amsterdam: Van Nostrand Reinhold, 1988.

RH Hayes, SC Wheelwright, KB Clark. Dynamic Manufacturing—Creating the Learning Organization. New York: Free Press, 1988.

L Kurtlus, EW Davis. Multi-project scheduling: Categorization of heuristic rules performance. Management Science 28:161–172, 1982.

EW Larson, DH Gobeli. Matrix management: Contradictions and insights. California Management Review 29:4, 1987.

SR Lawrence, EM Morton. Resource constrained multi-project scheduling with tardy cost: Comparing myopic, bottleneck and resource pricing heuristic. European Journal of Operational Research 64:168–187, 1993.

FW McFarland. Portfolio approach to information systems. Harvard Business Review Sept–Oct, 142–150, 1981.

JR Meredith, SJ Mantel. Project evaluation and selection. In: JR Meredith and SJ Mantel, eds. Project Management: A Managerial Approach. New York: Wiley, 1989.

RP Mohanty, MK Siddiq. Multiple projects—Multiple resources scheduling: A multi-objective analysis. Engineering and Production Economics, Oct, 1989.

R Moenaert, W Souder. An information transfer model for integrating marketing and R&D personnel in new product development projects. The Journal of Product Innovation Management June, 1990.

ME Porter. Competitive Strategy—Techniques for Analyzing Industries and Competitors. New York: Free Press, 1980.

RL Schmidt, JR Freeland. Recent progress in modelling R&D project selection processes. IEEE Transactions on Engineering Management 39:189–200, 1992.

A Shenhar. Project management style and technological uncertainty: From low to high-tech. Project Management Journal Dec, 1991.

W Souder. Project evaluation and selection. In: DI Cleland and WR King, eds. Project Management Handbook. Amsterdam: Van Nostrand Reinhold, 1998.

MG Speranza, C Vercellis. Hierarchical models for multi-project planning and scheduling. European Journal of Operational Research 64:312–325, 1993.

GJ Stalk, TM Rout. Competing Against Time. New York: Free Press, 1990.

DJ Teece. Profiting from technological innovation: Implication for integration, collaboration, licencing and public policy. Research Policy 15:285–305, 1986.

S Tsubakitani, RF Deckro. A heuristic for multi-project scheduling with limited resources in the housing industry. European Journal of Operational Research 49: 80–91, 1990.

SC Wheelwright, WE Sasser. The new product development map. Harvard Business Review May-June, 112–123, 1989.

13

Extensions to Multiple Projects

**Robert K. Wysocki, Robert Beck, Jr.,
and David B. Crane**

1 PROGRAM MANAGEMENT VERSUS MULTIPROJECT MANAGEMENT

It must be clear at the outset that we are not dealing with program management. That is a separate topic altogether. In fact, program management is a special case of multiproject management, in that it has a single goal or purpose (put a man on the moon), whereas multiproject management treats the case of independent multiple goals (develop a client-server-based distribution system, install a new CIM package, and update the marketing information system).

2 SHARED RESOURCES: COMBINATIONS OF PEOPLE, EQUIPMENT, SPACE

Figure 1 depicts the situation we will learn about in this chapter. The assumption is that there is some contention between projects that are vying for the same set of resources. Their only linkage is through those resources, which could be people, equipment, space, or any combination of the three. In any case, they are limited resources that can be used only in one place at one time.

Adapted from *Effective Project Management*, 2000.

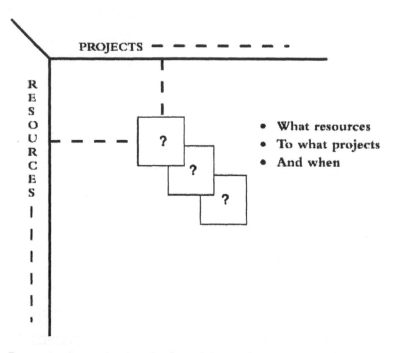

FIGURE 1 A matrix visualization of the multiproject scenario.

That is, resource scheduling is the issue. A good example is the management of the systems and programming group in the management information systems (MIS) department. One way of envisioning the project management problem is as a matrix whose rows represent available resources and whose columns are the projects that require use of one or more resources. The manager's job is to make decisions on the use of those resources so that the project requirements for cost, time, and quality are met.

The extension to multiple projects adds a number of issues that are not present in single-project management situations. For example, if the programming resource pool does not have enough hours available to meet all project requirements by the required deadlines, then one of four alternatives is available to management: utilize slack time across projects to resolve the scheduling conflict, delay one or more projects, increase available hours in the programmer pool, or reduce the requirements of one or more projects. Combinations of the four may also be feasible. For example, some delay combined with additional hours in the resource pool may be less costly than any one of the strategies used by itself. In any case, all four strategies have far-reaching implications.

Enough has been written on project management to fill the Bible and the Congressional Record several times over. Despite this wealth of information, precious little is devoted to the problems of managing multiple projects. Few would disagree that the real world is not one-dimensional (one project). Rather, we are faced with a number of projects competing for scarce resources, narrowing windows of opportunity, and the changing demands of internal and external customers. Projects are continually added, changed, and removed in response to business activity and changing market conditions. One thing is certain: the backlog of needed projects requires resources that exceed management's ability to provide. Of necessity, project priority changes are constant. Projects once scheduled now require schedule changes as any one of a number of parameters change. Out of this seeming chaos, project managers and resource managers are expected to create order.

This chapter discusses a number of considerations arising in multiple project management situations. It is not the purpose here to present solutions to all issues raised (although some are recommended). Rather, we attempt to raise levels of awareness among those who must contend with these difficult situations.

3   ORGANIZATIONAL CONSIDERATIONS

The matrix structure, or some hybrid of it, is the preferred organizational form for planning and controlling multiple projects. The traditional functional structure does not provide the necessary project management oversight required by today's businesses and is somewhat contrary to the trend toward rightsizing, worker empowerment, and business process management. Organizations are trying to shorten time to market, and the functional structure tends to work counter to that. The pure project structure greatly simplifies resource scheduling, but it is easily seen as a very inefficient resource utilization. Resources committed to one project may be underutilized, and no formal mechanism exists to share excess capacity with other projects. The resulting cost inefficiencies are obvious. One could give examples of large projects in which the project structure has worked well, but in general, these will be the exception rather than the rule.

The matrix structure has advantages and disadvantages, which we have already discussed. We simply point out that, on balance, the matrix form is generally preferred in those organizations in which projects are an important component of departmental activity and where change and adaptability are expected.

There are two hybrids of the matrix structure to consider. The first occurs in those organizations in which the project managers and resource managers report to the same manager. This variation of the matrix structure is interesting because some of the political and decision-making situations that arise in the pure matrix structure do not exist here. The fact that one operational-level manager has span of control that encompasses the projects and the resources scheduled to work on the projects means that scheduling revisions and project priority decisions are vested in the same individual. Obviously much of the politics are avoided in this case.

The other hybrid arises when user managers function as project managers. As we move to client/server architectures and applications development at the user level, the project manager is more likely to come from the ranks of the user community. This brings a lot of political baggage and fairly intense negotiation situations, but it does have a number of advantages. Probably the most significant is a much lower risk of project failure than in the other hybrid we discussed. User managers will want the project to succeed. After all, one's reputation is on the line, as is the success of the functional area. A related advantage is user buy-in. Commitment as a project manager and buy-in user go hand in hand. The major disadvantages occur in those organizations in which the user manager accepts the role of project manager in name only. This is usually signaled by the user manager deferring to the team members and not really taking a leadership role. This often happens in cases in which senior management has not made a visible sign of endorsement and commitment to the project.

Of more recent vintage is the self-directed work team (SDWT). Peter Drucker, in an article in the Harvard Business Review ("The Coming of the New Organization," Jan/Feb: 45–53, 1988), writes of the emergence of a new organizational structure. It is based on information rather than the command and control structures that have dominated the business landscape since the turn of the century. Drucker argues for a leaner organization, one in which several layers of management are no longer needed because of the easy access to information for everyone on an as-needed basis. The article is required reading for any manager trying to redesign the organization to support the systems that are oriented to business processes rather than business functions. As the organization looks to improve customer service and empower the workforce, the notion of the SWDT coupled with Drucker's Task Force begins to make good sense.

A typical organizational structure that supports these ideas was discussed in earlier in this book. The functional areas are support to the self-directed project teams (SDPT). They provide very technical consulting and training, as requested. All SDPTs are self-contained in terms of the technology and business knowledge required to complete their work. It is important to note that SDPT members must be multidisciplined. In the ideal, all team members can perform any task required of the team. This is a significant departure from the current notion of specialization characteristics of all other organizational structures. The migration toward SDPTs does not appear to be an option. As organizations consider a customer-services orientation and worker empowerment philosophy, they will come to realize that the SDPT, or some hybrid of it, is the only organizational design that makes sense.

4 STAFFING CONSIDERATIONS

The notion of a *learning organization* as described by Peter Senge in his book The Fifth Discipline (New York: Doubleday/Currency, 1990), is compatible with good project management in the organization that uses a matrix or SDPT structure. Staff development has always been an issue, and with the migration away from centralized mainframe to client/server architectures, training and staff development are on the list of critical success factors. Of paramount importance is how to address the growing skills gap. The skills gap problem is further exacerbated by the focus on business processes rather than business functions. Information systems professionals soon realize that their skill set is lacking, both in technology and business process knowledge.

In a matrix organization, the managers of staff resources are responsible for developing in their staff the skill set that is required by the organization through the projects that it authorizes. The project is a good vehicle for staff development. Researchers have concluded that the job itself is the most influential motivator of information technology professionals. Challenge, opportunity for advancement, and recognition head the list of job design parameters. One might examine the skills required to complete each project task, the inventory of staff and their skills, and then assign the individual whose skill set almost matches requirements. The needed skills will be developed in conjunction with the project task—just-in-time training.

Of course, the project manager may not be all that willing to accept that model. His or her priority is to get the project done on time, within budget, and according to specification. The project manager is not particularly interested in the need for staff development unless it contributes directly to the ability to successfully complete projects.

5 PROJECT-RELATED CONSIDERATIONS

There are two situations to consider. The first and most common is one in which the resource pool is shared across multiple projects. In this case, the projects are linked through one or more common resources. For example, they may both require the services of a telecommunications expert. When the scheduled use of the common resource on one project conflicts with the scheduled use of that same resource on one or more other projects, the dependency becomes obvious, and the resource manager must solve the resource availability problem.

The second case involves a dependency between the schedules of two or more projects. The scheduled start date of an activity in one project may depend on the actual finish date of an activity in another project. There may, in fact, be multiple such dependencies. These dependencies are particularly significant when the completion date of the predecessor activity in one project affects the start date of a successor activity in another project, and the successor activity is on the critical path. In such cases, an early finish date on the sending activity is music to the ears of the receiving activity manager. Further issues deal with who owns the slack on the predecessor activity. For any successor activities that are on the critical path, the manager of the successor activity and the manager of the associated project will make strong argument for claiming ownership of the slack.

It becomes obvious that, even for the simplest cases (say, two projects) the problem of resource scheduling may be intractable. The problem is further exacerbated in cases in which resources may be required on critical path activities of two projects whose schedules overlap. Let us step back from these multiple project scheduling problems and examine them in an orderly way.

Figure 2 graphically displays the multiple project resource situation. The area of the triangle represents the collective specifications of currently scheduled projects. The sides of the triangle represent the budget, time, and resources available in the information systems (IS) department to complete the currently scheduled projects. If a new project is requested, or changes to an existing one are made, the area enclosed by the three sides must be able to accommodate the request, or one of four things must happen:

- The request can be accommodated without affecting the completion date of the changed project or the completion dates of any other scheduled projects.
- The request can be accommodated, but the scheduled completion of the changed project will be extended.

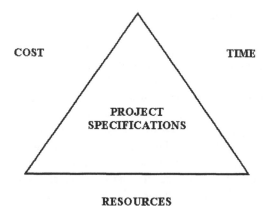

FIGURE 2   Multiple project situation.

- The request can be accommodated, but the scheduled completion of the changed project and at least one other project will be extended.
- The request cannot be accommodated with existing time, budget, and resources.

In all but the first case, negotiations will be required between the project manager, the requesting unit, resource managers, and other project managers. This is not strange turf for any of these managers. It happens in all multiple project environments. More basic to the situation is the determination of exactly which of these four situations characterizes the issue at hand. The analysis is obviously complex for a variety of reasons:

- Problem not well defined.
- No orderly way of examining alternatives.
- Solution requires sophisticated computer support.
- Alternatives will violate budget, time, resources, and/or specs on one or more projects.
- Alternatives will have to be ranked.

Some analytic support is provided by the typical project management software tools. Unfortunately, little is offered in the way of methodology. Managers are left to search the solution space in the absence of a search strategy. As an aside, D.B. Crane & Associates, a project management consulting organization in Southboro, Massachusetts, is conducting a project to assemble detailed function and features data on existing software tools for project management. The results will soon be published in a database available on diskette.

Unfortunately, there is no multiple project analog of critical path method (CPM). Furthermore, it is unlikely that any manual process could be found to solve the scheduling or scheduling update problem. There is, however, an expert system solution. We are aware of one software tool from Erudite Corporation that purports to offer a solution. The package is called Sagacity and is described in a recent book by Richard E. Westney (Computerized Management of Multiple Small Projects, New York: Marcel Dekker, 1992). Sagacity uses an expert systems approach called *assignment modeling*. Sagacity interacts with the decision-maker to propose resource scheduling alternatives for multiple project scheduling problems. The system requires the decision-maker to specify a series of prioritization rules based on user-supplied criteria. The rules are generally duration-driven or effort-driven. Duration-driven rules calculate the total work-hours of effort using inputs on the duration and resources required. Effort-driven rules calculate activity duration from inputs on the total work effort required and then calculate the resources required and activity duration. Sagacity uses the user-determined prioritization rules to sequentially schedule projects based on their relative priority. The system can be used to establish initial project schedules, as well as to update existing project schedules.

5.1   Slack Management

We will spend some time later in the chapter examining the tactical issues discussion. For now it is sufficient to know that the first strategy for the project manager or the manager of project managers is to examine the available slack. In the case of a single project, the available slack is embedded within the project, but in the case of multiple projects, the slack is distributed across several projects. The project manager will have to look for opportunities to reschedule start and end dates for activities to make the slack available to other projects. Alternatively, the project manager might use slack time to train others in the skills needed to resolve the conflict. As in the case of single projects, the project manager will want to exhaust all possibilities before going to upper management with a request for additional resources, extended deadlines, or reduced project requirements.

5.2   Project Delay

Imposing project delays may affect customer relations, cause severe financial penalties for missed deadlines, affect other projects that depend on timely completion of the subject projects, and increase the risk of meeting customer

TABLE 1 Multiproject Management Strategic Issues

- What data and information are needed by senior management for strategic decision-making?
- How do I communicate clearly to stakeholders?
- How do I decide which projects to delay, given insufficient resources to meet cost, time, and specification constraints?
- How do I determine the training and hiring mix for developing and inventorying staff skills?
- What are the strategic planning issues over the project management lifecycle?

requirements. In deciding whether this strategy makes sense, management will have to weigh the penalties for a delay in one project or some combination of projects. Before reaching a decision of this scope, the project managers will have to have exhausted other possibilities for using slack time for noncritical path activities to resolve conflicts.

5.3 Strategic and Tactical Issues

The strategic issues listed in Table 1 cannot be resolved by the project managers. They are issues that must be dealt with at a higher level. In some cases, the manager of the project managers may be able to suggest alternative strategies. In the final analysis, the client will take part in the decision. This will occur for certain if the projects are for internal clients. When the projects are for external clients, their involvement may not be perfunctory. That is, the performance contract will often include penalty clauses for late completion or out-of-specification deliverables. The strategic decision will follow from a weighing of tangible (e.g., financial) and intangible (e.g., customer relations) factors.

TABLE 2 Multiproject Management Tactical Issues

- How do I identify interproject dependencies and their impact on project completion?
- How do I schedule my resources across projects?
- How do I add new projects to an existing schedule of projects?
- How do I determine the percentage of resources to allocate to projects and the percentage to contingencies?
- When do I use automated tools for planning and/or control?

5.4 Multiproject Management Tactical Issues

The tactical issues shown in Table 2 will generally be settled at the midmanager level (manager of project managers, resource managers, project managers).

We have only introduced the topic of multiple project management. Unfortunately, there is little in the theory and application of project management to help the project manager with multiple project situations. Some of the project management software packages offer some help in resource scheduling but only as a *what-if* functionality.

14

Program Management—Turning Many Projects into Few Priorities with Theory of Constraints

Francis S. Patrick

1 INTRODUCTION

The way to get something done—quoting the well-known Nike ad—is to "just do it." Focus on the task and get it done. For those who work in organizations that rely on programs of projects—multiproject environments where resources are shared across a number of projects—there are usually a lot of things that need to get done. An environment of many projects typically generates many priorities for project resources and managers alike and can make that focus difficult to achieve.

2 DIVISION OF ATTENTION MULTIPLIES TASK AND PROJECT LEAD TIME

In an effort to take advantage of valuable new opportunities, multiproject organizations (more often than not) tend to launch projects as soon as they are understood—concurrently with existing projects, simultaneously with other

Adapted from the *Proceedings of the Project Management Institute 1999 Seminars and Symposium.*

new efforts, and unfortunately, too often without sufficient regard for the capacity of the organization. A common result is that the responsibility for sorting out an array of conflicting priorities often falls to project resources and their managers. One concern coming from this situation is that the resultant locally set priorities may not be in synch with each other or, more importantly, with the global priorities of the larger organization. A common result of trying to deal with this tug-of-war of multiple priorities is the practice of multitasking, that is, assigning resources to more than one significant task during a particular window of time, to try to move all the projects along.

In addition, many project teams rely on early starts of projects and their paths of tasks to try to achieve timely project completion. These early starts, also driven partially by the desire to see "progress" on all open projects, often translate to additional pressure on resources to multitask between both tasks and projects. There is pressure to get started on a new task in the inbox, even though we're still working on another task. As a result, these practices of early starts and multitasking have been recognized as common practice in many organizations and even institutionalized in project management software tools, which typically default to "ASAP" scheduling, and which offer "features" to apply fractional resources to tasks and to split tasks.

The question is, however, whether these early starts actually accomplish their desired effect. When multitasking is the result, the seemingly common-sense belief that "the sooner you start, the sooner you finish" becomes questionable. True progress in a project happens, as in a relay race, only at the handoffs between resources, when the work completed by one resource allows another resource to start its work. To the extent that one project's tasks are interrupted by work being performed on other projects' tasks, the first project is delayed. The common practice of multitasking results in multiplying the time it takes to complete tasks, delaying true progress in projects (see Figure 1).

If a resource divides her attention between different tasks before handing off task deliverables, all the projects involved will take longer than necessary, because all of that resource's successors from each project will have to wait longer than necessary because of time spent on other project work. If many resources in the organization become accustomed to working in this manner, then most projects will take significantly longer than necessary, in both their promise and their execution. The projects will also be affected by the variability of not only their own tasks, but also of those associated with the other projects that are interleaved within them.

The pressures of these competing priorities result in the splitting of attention and energy, loss of focus, and an inability to complete tasks and projects

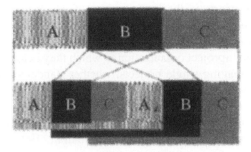

FIGURE 1 From the point of view of the project, multitasking multiplies the time required to complete a task. **A** and **B** are delayed with no gain for **C**.

in a timely manner, or even within the time in which they were planned, at least not without heroic efforts. This is not a desirable outcome for projects that want to keep their promises or for organizations that need to reliably deliver projects in shorter and shorter intervals.

One of the key challenges of multiproject or program management, therefore, revolves around the avoidance of pressures on resources to multitask and the ability to assess and direct the most beneficial use of resources when there is apparent contention for their attention. To the extent that these can be addressed, a multiproject program will minimize the pain that is encountered in the interaction of projects fighting for shared resources.

3 AVOIDING PRESSURES TO MULTITASK

The pressure to multitask comes from the combination of having more than one task in one's in-box and a lack of clear priority for the best use of one's attention. If there was a way of setting commonsense priorities for the maximum benefit of the organization, it would make sense to all that we set aside some tasks to wait for the completion of the most critical. And if there was a way of reducing the queue of tasks waiting for a resource, there would be less need for assessing and resetting priorities. If we could systematically provide clear priorities and minimize the queue, then the devastating impact of multitasking on projects and, more importantly, on organizational performance would be minimized.

Applying the management philosophy known as the theory of constraints (TOC) to the realm of project management provides a whole system view of the challenge. The TOC suggests that components of the system being managed subordinate their efforts to the larger system of which they are a part. The management of tasks and the resources that perform them must subordinate to the needs of projects, and the management of projects must subordinate to the needs of the multiproject organization to which they belong. The TOC-based solution for managing single projects, whether standalone or as part of a portfolio of projects, is known as *critical chain scheduling and buffer management*. It provides part of the answer for the priority aspect of the question ''what should I work on?'' which, if not addressed appropriately, drives multitasking behaviors in multiproject environments (Goldratt, 1997; Newbold, 1998; Patrick, 1999).

A critical chain schedule removes the pressure of artificial task due dates from the concerns of project resources. It does this by recognizing that a schedule is only a model of our expectations and by aggregating and concentrating the safety that is typically embedded in individual tasks where it does the most good: in a system of *buffers* positioned to protect the promise of the project (Fig. 2).

In the real world, we expect time variation in the execution of tasks—Murphy's Law has not yet been repealed (Patrick, 1999). Buffers are used to absorb that variation without distraction to the resource performing the task at hand, while at the same time protecting the truly critical promises of the project. The result is the elimination of meaningless intermediate task due dates and the detrimental pressures, behaviors, and practices associated with

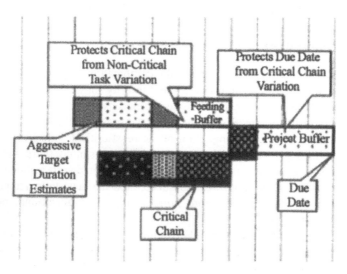

FIGURE 2 A critical chain schedule.

them. These include Parkinson's Law ("Work expands to fill the time allowed") and the "student syndrome" (delaying the start of a task when one has more than enough time to accomplish it).

Buffers also effectively absorb deviations from the baseline critical chain model, made up of target task durations from which significant safety has been removed. As long as there is sufficient buffer remaining, the project promise can, to some degree, be protected from distractions and disruptions, such as from the need to use a planned resource on another more jeopardized project or more critical task. If there is a sufficient unconsumed buffer related to a task waiting for attention, a resource can hold off on picking it up and multitasking and, instead, can maintain focus on the current task at hand until it's complete. The deliverable of the current task can be handed off before moving to the queued task, which minimizes the setdown, setup, and half-finished work that extends project lead times when multitasking is the usual response.

The buffers and the status of their consumption and replenishment during the reality of project execution also provide a clear, forward-looking indication of what chain of activities is in the greatest jeopardy of delaying the promise of a project. When a project buffer is sufficiently consumed to indicate heightened risk of the project promise, then it is clear that the priority for resources' attention should be adjusted to address the tasks associated with that project. Buffers can, therefore, provide clear direction for the most beneficial use of a resource's focused attention.

Even with these safeguards at the individual project and task level, the pressures to jump from a task on one project to another—to multitask across projects—can still be overwhelming and distracting if resources are faced with an overflowing inbox of tasks clamoring for attention.

This is due to the fact that if projects are pushed into an organization without regard for the system's capacity and capability, work-in-process (in the form of started but unfinished projects) quickly clogs the system. The buildup of work-in-process creates queues of work that dilute and diffuse the time and attention of resources and management alike and often expand project lead times beyond the comfort zone. There is still pressure to multitask. It is therefore necessary to look beyond the individual projects, or even pairs of them, to the larger system encompassed by the organization responsible for accomplishing many projects.

4 SYNCH OR SINK

In addition to providing controls and measures for individual project status or determining priorities between projects, TOC, when applied to multiproject systems, also provides guidance on assessing the capacity of such systems and related mechanisms for the synchronized launch of projects.

When faced with assessing system capacity, many organizations typically go into a major data-collection and number-crunching exercise in an attempt to balance the availability of all resource types with the demand on the system. To support the scheduling and monitoring of projects, however, the required process is far simpler than that usual approach. Theory of constraints tends to focus on maximizing flow of work through a system rather than balancing capacity. This higher-level view of system capacity, rather than resource capacity, leads to the conclusion that it is enough to keep as little as one resource effectively utilized to manage and maximize the throughput of the system. Indeed, to do so, it is required that other resources have sufficient protective capacity to protect that throughput (Goldratt, 1992).

Therefore, determining a starting point for synchronizing the flow of work through the system can simply involve identifying an aspect of the multiproject system that can approximate its throughput potential. One possible candidate for this *synchronizer* might be a resource that is commonly used across projects and more heavily used relative to most other resources (Jacob 1998; Newbold 1998).

The role of the synchronizer is to set the pace at which projects are launched into the system. They provide a stagger that is intended to allow overlap of project schedules, yet minimize peak loading on all resources and the pressure to multitask that is the usual result of these peak loads. Once a synchronizer has been identified, a synchronization schedule for the multiproject program can be put together; one that, combined with individual critical chain project schedules, will provide the basis for responsive, realistic, and reliable project promises. To develop this schedule, projects are first assigned a strategic precedence. The priority against which projects will be serviced by the synchronizer is determined. When desired project commitments result in conflicts for synchronizer attention, the higher-precedence project's synchronizer tasks are moved earlier in time, along with the remainder of its schedule, minimizing the impact of lower-precedence execution variability on higher-precedence projects.

In addition to the ordering and staggering of projects provided by the synchronizer, the synchronization schedule must also take into account that not all projects are consistent in the use of the synchronizer. This may result in occasional windows of time when the stagger is insufficient to protect other resources from both peak loading and pressures to multitask. To prevent this situation, additional stagger is added between the projects in the form of a capacity buffer. Based on the expected variability of synchronizer work within the earlier project, the capacity buffer also provides a level of cross-project

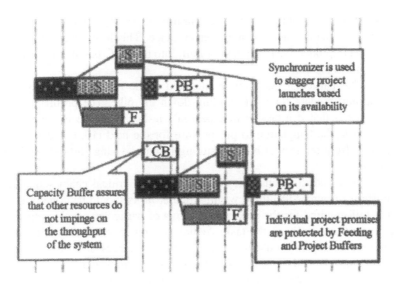

Synchronizer is used to stagger project launches based on its availability

Capacity Buffer assures that other resources do not impinge on the throughput of the system

Individual project promises are protected by Feeding and Project Buffers

FIGURE 3 Staggering projects via a resource-based synchronizer.

protection and time for recovery and other nonproject uses for synchronizer resources.

The synchronization schedule therefore consists of the precedence-ordered synchronizer tasks, capacity buffers whenever a synchronizer moves from one project to another, and natural gaps that result from the actual demand placed on the synchronizer. These gaps are important aspects of the schedule, as they allow new projects' synchronizer tasks to be interleaved among already committed projects, enabling the organization to take on new opportunities without affecting existing project promises.

The resultant rhythm of project launches (Fig. 3), its pace set by the capacity and capability of a commonly used and heavily loaded synchronizer resource, is well within the ability of less-loaded resources to maintain. More importantly, combined with the individual critical chain schedules' systems of buffers, this synchronization schedule of projects allows resources and their projects to recover from delays and disruptions in a timely, rational, and non-heroic manner. Without synchronized project launches, the risk of sinking into a swamp of muddy priorities is too great for comfort.

5 ASSIGN NO TASK BEFORE ITS TIME

In addition to a healthy respect and accommodation for inevitable variability in execution and an emphasis on flow of throughput over balanced capacity, most applications of the theory of constraints also recognize that human behavior plays a major role in system performance. This leads to another fail-safe against nonproductive multitasking built into the TOC-based approach to program management.

The particular behavior in question is the normal propensity to look ahead and prepare for work coming down the pike. The problem with this behavior is that if a task is in a person's in-box while he is tending to another task, the temptation to pre-prepare for the next task could lead to distraction from the task at hand, resulting in multitasking and delay of project progress.

To avoid this behavior, when developing critical chain schedules for projects, resources identified with particular tasks should be done in terms of the skill required for the task, not in terms of particular people who actually perform those skills on the task. Actual assignment of personnel to tasks by resource managers should be held back until predecessor tasks are complete and the task is ready to start. With the synchronization schedule and its resultant protective capacity now available in most resource pools, resources will wait for tasks more frequently than vice versa. This designed situation will now provide flexibility for assignment to appropriate, available people and yield maximum flow of undistracted work through the system.

6 SUMMARY—MANY PROJECTS, A FEW CLEAR PRIORITIES

In *A Guide to the Project Management Body of Knowledge* (Project Management Institute, 1996), a program is defined as ''a group of projects managed in a coordinated way to obtain benefits not available from managing them individually.'' Most organizations that depend on the accomplishment of projects as a source of products, profits, or process improvements do so with shared resources that must be ''managed in a coordinated way.'' In such a system, proficiency at managing single projects individually without proactively dealing with the interactions between them is not sufficient to assure the attainment of the goals of the organization. The system that really needs to be managed in most cases is greater than the sum of the single projects. It is a larger, complex system of projects, priorities, policies, and practices that guides the behaviors of managers and resources and requires consistent and coherent coordination for maximum effectiveness.

By applying the TOC prescription for multiproject/program management, an organization honors its priorities by scheduling its programs through the strategically defined precedence of the synchronization schedule.

Project managers avoid unnecessary changes in priority by relying on buffers to absorb most of the normal, expected variability in the execution of tasks and projects.

Resource managers find clear direction and priority for assignment of tasks in the status of the buffers, which indicate the best use for available resources to support the promises made by the organization.

Resources have a single priority—the current task to which they are assigned. Without the distraction of pressures to multitask or to meet false priorities of task due dates, they can concentrate on the task at hand and "just do it," do just it, and do it justice to assure a quality handoff, successful projects, and maximum throughput for the organization.

REFERENCES

EM Goldratt. The Goal. 2nd Revised Edition. Great Barrington, MA: North River Press, 1992.

EM Goldratt. Critical Chain. Great Barrington, MA: North River Press, 1997.

D Jacob. Introduction to Project Management the TOC Way—A Workshop. New Haven, CT: The A.Y. Goldratt Institute, 1998.

R Newbold. Project Management in the Fast Lane. Boca Raton, FL: St. Lucie Press, 1998.

FS Patrick. Getting out from between Parkinson's rock and Murphy's hard place. PM Network 13 (April): 57–62, 1999.

Project Management Institute. A Guide to the Project Management Body of Knowledge (PMBOK® Guide), 1996.

15

Operational Measurements for Product Development Organizations

Tony Rizzo

1 INTRODUCTION

The details of the critical chain method could easily fill a book. In fact, the reader is directed to Eliyahu M. Goldratt's own book, *Critical Chain* (The North River Press, 1997). So, rather than exploring every minor detail of the critical chain method, let's focus on the overall approach.

The following steps summarize this simple yet elegant strategy:

- Plan your project well, striving to build as much concurrency into the project plan as possible.
- Assign resources to all tasks, and have those resources estimate task duration not at a low-risk, protected value, but at a more aggressive, average value. No protection time may be allocated to any one task.
- Resolve resource contention and identify the longest chain of tasks, taking into account not only precedence dependencies but also resource dependencies. This longest chain is the project's critical chain.

Adapted from the *PM Network Organization*, 1999.

- Protect the project's commitment date with a properly sized buffer; that is, concentrate protection time at the end of the critical chain rather than spreading it throughout the project.
- Protect the critical chain itself. This is achieved by inserting buffers wherever a critical chain task is expected to receive input from a feeding task. The critical chain also is protected by reserving key resources at an appropriate early time in the project.
- Ensure that all working resources perform their tasks in a highly focused manner.

The application of these steps to a project plan results in a plan that resembles Figure 1. In the exhibit, the colors indicate resources. The numbers indicate the estimates of average duration of the respective tasks. The tasks with dark borders make up the critical chain of the project.

As the figure illustrates, the project buffer is the primary source of protection for the project's due date. No protection time is associated with any individual task. The feeding buffers protect the starts of the only two critical chain tasks that require input from noncritical chain tasks, Red 15 and Blue 15. The critical chain is protected further by the advance booking of key resources; the corresponding tasks are indicated by the starbursts.

The sense of urgency with which team members need to work their respective tasks is communicated best with a relay race analogy. If the project were a relay race, the race would be won by causing the critical chain to be completed as soon as possible. Thus, the critical chain method requires that all the tasks be worked at a full level of effort, but this must also be a *sustainable* level of effort.

Now that we've discussed the basics of the critical chain method, it's time to move on to Goldratt's multiproject management method. As we'll see,

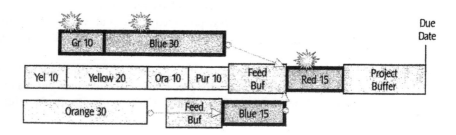

FIGURE 1   Feeding buffers protect the critical chain from variability in the feeding chains. The project buffer protects the customer.

the multiproject management method is to product development productivity and speed as Goldratt's drum-buffer-rope method is to manufacturing productivity and speed.

2 MULTIPROJECT MANAGEMENT METHOD

The critical chain method gives us a highly effective system model for an individual project. However, most product development organizations are described best not as single-project systems but as multiproject systems. They have fixed sets of resources, and they are tasked with performing unending streams of projects with those resources. For all its usefulness, the single-project critical chain method does not address the needs of multiproject organizations.

The single-project critical chain method deals effectively with resource contention within an individual project, but it does little to address resource contention across projects. Unfortunately, nearly all the projects of a multiproject organization share many resources. Predictably, attempts to manage a collection of individual projects in such a shared-resource environment create competition for resources among the projects. One outcome is a demolition derby of projects at those shared resources.

Another outcome is the creation of a severe conflict for the organization's resource managers. Imagine that you're such a resource manager. Existing projects already fully use your people when a new project is launched by the executive of your organization. You are now held accountable for showing progress on the new project as well as the earlier projects.

If you're like most people, you feel pressure to delay the start of the new project so that your people can complete work on the earlier projects, but this requires that you tell your executive that the start of the new project is being delayed purposely. In essence, it requires that you say "No!" to your executive. Stop and think for just a moment. How many managers do you know who have enhanced their careers by saying "No!" to an executive? When you consider that the bank still owns a big piece of your home and that your teenager is filling out college applications, this heroic solution just doesn't seem very attractive. You have to begin showing progress on the new project, ASAP, but where can you find the resources? How can you solve this ubiquitous, severe conflict without jeopardizing your child's college education?

There is only one safe solution to the conflict: multitasking. You time-share your people across projects. Consequently, your people are faced with spending a fraction of their time on one project and a fraction of their time on another project; a third party probably gets their overtime.

Multitasking is a compromise solution, but it's a lose-lose solution. The earlier projects lose because their progress is slowed. The new project loses because its progress isn't nearly as great as it might be. You and your people lose, too, because your common sense is severely violated by this necessary survival tactic. Ultimately, the organization loses even more because all its projects are delayed and all the earnings from those projects are delayed *and* diminished.

Goldratt's multiproject management method resolves this widespread conflict, and it does so with a compromise solution, but one that is a win for everyone concerned, particularly for the organization and the bottom line.

The multiproject management method (not to be confused with the Theory of Constraints' five focusing steps) consists of five common-sense steps: (1) Prioritize the organization's projects. (2) Plan each project per the critical chain method. (3) Stagger the projects so as to ensure that everyone in the organization has more than enough time to do all the work of the projects. (4) Measure and report the buffers. (5) Manage the buffers.

Let's focus on the outcome of the third step.

2.1 Staggering the Projects

Staggering the projects is not done without thought. Figure 2 illustrates the outcome of staggering the projects' start times. All the tasks in the figure are shown grayed, except those of the blue resource. In Goldratt's terminology, this resource would be selected as the drum resource.

The drum resource is the one whose schedule is used to stagger the projects. By staggering the projects with the use of the schedule of a single resource, we automatically eliminate (or at least reduce significantly) resource contention for all other resources across all projects. This simple yet powerful observation is the basis for Goldratt's multiproject management method.

Ideally, the drum would be a heavily loaded resource for many of the organization's projects. In practice, it is often difficult to identify exactly the one resource loaded more heavily than all the others. Further, resource loading may change somewhat from project to project. Even if resource loading remained constant across projects, however, we would still have to expect many instances of resource contention during the course of any project simply because task duration is an unpredictable, statistical quantity. This is where the buffers come in. This is also where Goldratt's genius really shines.

Observe in Figure 2 that every task in a project precedes either a feeding buffer or the project buffer. Accordingly, if any task requires more time than previously estimated, the corresponding buffer is replenished. By continually

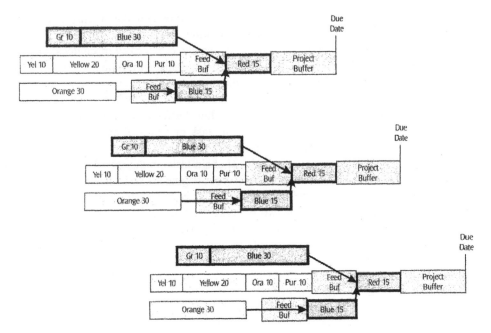

FIGURE 2 For multiproject organizations, speed requires the elimination of damaging multitasking. This is achieved by staggering the projects via the drum resource schedule and using the buffers as risk indicators.

tracking both the size of a buffer and the total days of work that precede the buffer we can assess the level of risk that the buffer might be consumed entirely.

In a very real sense, the buffers are risk gauges. If we happen to be tracking a feeding buffer, we get a measurement of the risk that the corresponding critical chain task might be delayed; note that every feeding buffer feeds a critical chain task. If we happen to be tracking a project buffer, we get a measurement of the risk that a project's due date might be missed. In practice, we track all the buffers of all the projects with the use of a software specifically designed for this purpose. This is all good, but there's more to it.

2.2 Providing Operational Measurements

The buffers, in fact, are exactly the operational measurements we need for our product development organizations. Like a tachometer or an oil pressure gauge, an operational measurement tells us the (nearly) instantaneous state of the system. The buffers tell us the instantaneous level of risk to the organization's projects. For this reason, everybody in the organization can use them as the basis for day-to-day operational decisions.

Imagine that you're a resource manager. Your key mechanical engineer is needed by three projects, apparently simultaneously. You know this because you have work for her from all three projects. How can you prioritize your engineer's work for this week? The answer is in the buffers. Each of the three tasks is associated with either a feeding buffer or a project buffer. Consequently, each task is either a feeding task or a critical chain task. Priority is always given to the critical chain task.

What if there are two critical chain tasks in the set? Again, the answer is in the buffers. If two or more of your engineer's tasks happen to be critical chain tasks, the task whose project buffer is in greater jeopardy gets priority. The same holds true for two or more feeding tasks: the task whose feeding buffer is in greater jeopardy gets priority. With the buffers as operational measurements, you are always able to prioritize your people's work correctly,

When a product development organization undertakes a successful implementation of a multiproject management method and uses the buffers as operational measurements, everyone in the organization gains information with which to make day-to-day decisions that are always in the best interest of the bottom line. With the operational (risk) measurements provided by the buffers, all conflicts for resources are immediately eliminated, because all project managers and all resource managers, indeed, all working resources, have access to the same, valid information about the instantaneous state of the organizational system; they are all driven to the same, correct decision.

The organization's decision-maker gains tremendous insight into the operations of his or her organization. The organization's weekly buffer report becomes top management's instrument panel; the buffers are the gauges on that instrument panel. Where once a review of a moderately sized organization's projects took days, with the global buffer report a more effective review takes less than one hour. An organization's management team, whose implementation is now mature and fabulously successful, reviews more than 30 projects every week during a brief conference call with the organization's managers and resources in four distant locations.

2.3 Providing a Clear View of the Organization

The buffers do even more for a management team. Rather than offer an occasional look in the rearview mirror as current project management tools do, the buffers provide a management team with a clear view through the organization's windshield. Problems that normally would take the managers and the decision-maker by surprise are detected very early in a project. The organization gains the ability to avoid many problems that would otherwise delay many projects. But there is another, even more significant benefit.

As a result of this organization-wide project management system and its accompanying system of operational measurements, every working resource in the organization is able to focus consistently on the right thing at the right time. In a very real sense, the efforts of everyone in the organization become synchronized and directed most effectively in the direction of the product development organization's goal: speed! Specifically, by constantly making decisions that safeguard the buffers, everyone automatically makes decisions that cause *all* the projects to finish as early as possible. With this management system, a product development organization whose people are currently forced to multitask can cut its cycle time in half while simultaneously propelling its on-time performance to near perfection. Real-world implementations of the multiproject management method are the basis for this statement.

Goldratt's multiproject management method is a practical, extremely effective, enterprise-wide project management system with which an organization can transform itself from an industry follower to an industry leader. If your organization is already an industry leader, with this system it can become *the* industry.

3 A STRATEGIC WEAPON

Eli (Dr. E. M. Goldratt) was on a roll, but finally, he saw my hand in the air, he pointed to me. I was but one among the hundreds in the audience.

"Eli, has any company ever driven a competitor out of business with TOC?" I asked.

My question caught him by surprise; his face was proof of that. But I needed to know. If the Theory of Constraints is really such a powerful paradigm, then somebody, somewhere, must have used it to kill the competition. He took more than a comfortable pause before he answered my question.

"Yes! It has happened," he admitted.

The predicted effect that I was looking for existed. I could see that my question troubled Eli. So I didn't pursue the topic. He quickly moved on to another person's question.

That was in 1995. I was new to TOC at the time; my thirst for common sense had just begun to be quenched. I heard that TOC was powerful, and I had concluded that, like all things powerful, TOC, too, could be dangerous. But I had no experience with it at the time.

Now, I do have experience. My hunch was right; TOC is extremely dangerous . . . in the hands of your competitors. With it, your competitors can render your entire product line obsolete in a few short years.

Currently, the rate and regularity with which nearly all companies bring new products to market are haphazard, random. Project launches often are driven by the annual budget cycle. Once top management approves the research and development budget, all pending projects are launched. The projects begin tripping over each other immediately, and they continue to trip and delay each other at every step. Inevitably, some projects are delayed until they wither and die. The ones that survive bring products to market in spurts, unpredictably, ineffectively, late.

With TOC, this irregular release of products is replaced by the rat-a-tat of a rapid-fire weapon, which quickly drives the competition from the battlefield that is the market. The key is synchronization. The releases of projects are placed, synchronized. As a result, the projects don't interfere with each other, and cycle time is reduced significantly. The project's completions and, consequently, the products' releases to the market are also synchronized and accelerated. Any business that encounters such an opponent finds itself striving to match its competitor's last product, only to watch in stunned desperation as the competitor obsoletes its own product even faster.

What does your business do if it encounters such a competitor? It dies. It dies because it cannot make the change to TOC fast enough. It can take anywhere from 6 months to 1 year to make the change effectively. Even if a business succeeds in making the change, it runs headlong into the next constraint: marketing. As soon as the business achieves speed in the development of its new products, it realizes that its ability to define innovative new products can't keep pace with its newfound ability to execute products rapidly, regularly. The rat-a-tat begins and ends abruptly as the rapid-fire product development weapon's magazine is emptied with surprising speed. In the meantime, the rat-a-tat of the competition becomes deafening, overwhelming, fatal.

What should you do if one of your employer's competitors brings the new TOC weapon to your new-product-development battlefield? Whatever you do, don't update your resume in the hope of getting a job with that competitor. It is true that your capable competitor will find itself flush with cash as it conquers your customer base. It is equally true that it will want to expand to new markets; it will have the cash with which to do just that. That competitor will not need many new employees. The TOC strategic weapon gives your opponent's workforce at least twice its previous firepower, twice the capacity to develop new products, with essentially the same development costs. So, what should you do? Sit tight, particularly if you work for a large organization. It's likely that your top management will offer an early retirement package soon.

16

New Problems, New Solutions: Making Portfolio Management More Effective

**Robert G. Cooper, Scott J. Edgett,
and Elko J. Kleinschmidt**

1 INTRODUCTION

Most companies' development portfolios suffer from too many projects for the limited resources available, ineffective project prioritization, Go/Kill decisions made in the absence of solid information, and too many minor projects in the portfolio. The result is poor performance: low-impact projects, too long to get to market, and higher-than-acceptable failure rates. Solutions are proposed based on the experiences of firms in the study. The first is to implement a systematic gating or stage-gate new product process, complete with tough Go/Kill decision points. Next, build in resource capacity analysis—a quantitative assessment of resource supply versus demand in your new product pipeline. A third solution is to develop a product innovation and technology strategy for your business to help guide the selection of the best projects. Finally, integrate portfolio management into your gating process with one of the two approaches used by leading companies in the study.

There are two ways for a business to succeed at new products: doing projects right, and doing the right projects. Most new product prescriptions

Adapted from *Research • Technology Management*, 2000.

focus on the first route; that is, on effective project management, using cross-functional teams or building in the voice of the customer. Portfolio management, the topic of this chapter, focuses on the second route; namely, on doing the right projects.

Despite all the publicity about portfolio management and the many portfolio methods proposed, managers have identified major problems and have raised serious concerns about the effectiveness of portfolio techniques. This chapter reports the results of continuing research into portfolio management practices [1,2]. It highlights some of the problems and offers some tentative solutions—solutions that have been witnessed in typical firms as they try to address the issue of picking the right projects (see Section 8 "Research into Portfolio Management").

2 AN ELUSIVE GOAL

Portfolio management is fundamental to successful new product development. Portfolio management is about resource allocation—how your business spends its capital and people resources, and which development projects it invests in. Portfolio management is also about project selection—ensuring that you have a steady stream of big new product winners! And portfolio management is about strategy—it is one method by which you operationalize your business's strategy.

Recent years have witnessed a heightened interest in portfolio management, not only in the technical community but in the cheif executive officer's office as well. According to our recent survey of Industrial Research Institute member companies, portfolio management has gained prominence for a number of reasons [3]:

- Financial—to maximize return on research and development (R&D) and technology spending
- To maintain the business's competitive position
- To properly allocate scarce resources
- To forge the link between project selection and business strategy
- To achieve a stronger focus
- To yield the right balance of projects and investments
- To communicate project priorities both vertically and horizontally within the organization
- To provide greater objectivity in project selection

The problem is that effective portfolio management has proven to be an elusive goal for many businesses. Management rated the effectiveness of

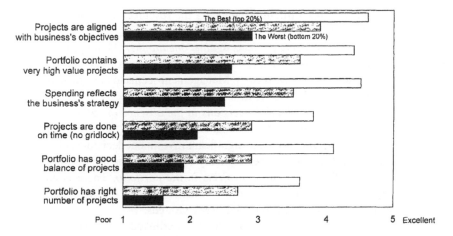

FIGURE 1 Businesses' portfolio performance results are on average fairly good across six key metrics, but there are weaknesses in terms of too many projects, pipeline gridlock, and the right balance of projects. Also, there are major differences between the Best and Worst performers.

their project selection and portfolio management methods, and the results are provocative [2] (Fig. 1):

- Portfolio methods in use were given high marks for ensuring strategic alignment—that R&D spending and projects undertaken are consistent with the business's strategy.
- Portfolio methods also fared well in terms of selecting high-value projects.
- Portfolio methods were rated much weaker in terms of having the right number of projects (there are far too many projects in most business's portfolios), promoting timely completion of projects (there is gridlock in the pipeline), and having the right balance of projects (too many minor, incremental projects).

Note the major significant differences in Figure 1 between the best and worst performers: clearly a number of companies are struggling with their portfolios, whereas a minority seem to have it right!

Why are managements so disappointed with their first attempts at portfolio management? More in-depth research has probed these issues and has identified four main challenges or problem areas in portfolio management:

1. *Resource balancing.* Resource demands usually exceed supply, as

management has difficulty balancing the resource needs of projects with resource availability.

2. *Prioritizing projects against one another.* Many projects look good, especially in their early days, and thus too many projects "pass the hurdles" and are added to the active list. Management seems to have difficulty discriminating between the Go, Kill, and Hold projects.

3. *Making Go/Kill decisions in the absence of solid information.* The up-front homework is often substandard in projects, the result being that management is required to make significant investment decisions, often using very unreliable data. No wonder so many of its decisions are questionable!

4. *Too many minor projects in the portfolio.* There is an absence of major revenue generators and the kinds of projects that will yield significant technical, market, and financial breakthroughs.

These four problems are clearly interlinked. For example, the inability to discriminate between projects invariably leads to a resource balancing problem. Insufficient resources on key projects in turn result in project teams short-cutting key activities. Cutting corners on projects results in poor information and difficulty in making sound Go/Kill decisions.

Inadequate resources and poor information invariably lead to a tendency to do short-term, quick, and simple projects. And so the portfolio problems continue, feeding one another in an endless downward spiral (Fig. 2).

We now consider each of these challenges in detail:

2.1 Too Many Projects, Not Enough Resources

Pipeline gridlock plagues many business portfolios. There are simply too many projects and not enough resources to do them well. This is a universal complaint within product development groups. The demand for more new products than ever coupled with corporate restructuring has helped to create this resource crunch.

One frustrated new-product project leader at her company's technology conference exclaimed: "I don't deliberately set out to do a bad job. Yet, when you look at the job that the project leaders around here do, it's almost as though our goal is mediocrity. But that's not true . . . we're good project leaders, but we're being *set up for failure.* There simply isn't enough time and there are not enough people or the right people to do the job we'd like to do!"

She went on to explain to senior management how insufficient resources and budget cuts along with too many projects were seriously compromising

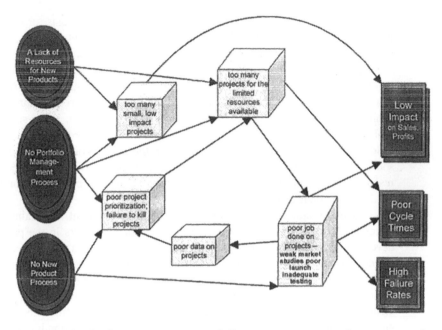

FIGURE 2 Lack of resources, no portfolio management, and no new product process **(left)** are the root cause of many problems, which feed on one another, resulting in a downward spiral of negative effects and results.

the way key projects were being executed. She was right! The point is, for positive results, the resource commitment must be aligned with the business's new product objectives, strategy and processes [4].

Lack of resources is part of the problem. The other part is the failure to allocate resources effectively. Here, portfolio tools and methods are partly at fault, along with a lack of will on the part of senior management to cut back the number of active projects, to say "no" to some worthwhile initiatives.

The fact is that most project selection and portfolio management methods do a poor job of resource balancing. Projects are evaluated, Go decisions are made, but resource implications are often not factored in. For example, one of the most popular methods for evaluating projects and making Go/Kill decisions is the use of financial models, such as net present value (NPV) [2, 5]. More advanced versions introduce probabilities and uncertainties into the financial calculation. Management is presented with the NPV of the projects, along with probability distribution curves. These same models, although so elegant in their handling of financial estimates (revenues, costs, profits) are notably lacking in their handling of the resource constraint problem, as resource availability is rarely part of the financial calculation.

The majority of project selection techniques are weak when it comes to making Go/Kill decisions or choosing the portfolio in light of constrained resources. There is really no way to check that the required resources are available when using most of these selection tools. Indeed, these selection tools consider individual projects one at a time and on their own merits, with little regard for the impact of one project on the next. Worse yet, people resources are assigned to projects, but only later is it discovered that the same resources are committed to multiple projects and that some people are committed 150% of their time.

In one major beverage company, there were constant complaints that major bottlenecks were encountered in new product projects in the package development department. Only after a demand analysis was undertaken on a project-by-project basis was it discovered how heavily committed certain players were. Each project team member was assigned to projects (number of person-days each month). When the packaging department's time commitments were totaled across all active projects, it turned out that this three-person group had been committed to about 100 person-days each month—a 160% commitment. No wonder there were logjams in the process!

The results of too many projects in the pipeline are serious. Here are some of the negative effects we have observed:

- Time to market starts to suffer as projects end up in a queue waiting for people and resources to become available. A senior technology manager in one Xerox division, concerned about project timelines, undertook a quick survey. He picked a day at random and sent an e-mail to every project leader in his division: "How much work got done on your project today?" The shocking news: more than three quarters of the projects had no work done on them at all! Subsequent follow-up revealed that a minority had legitimate reasons for inaction, such as waiting for equipment to be delivered or for tests to be completed. The great majority were simply in a queue, waiting for people to get around to doing something on them. His best guess was that he could have halved time to market for most projects simply by having fewer active projects under way and thereby avoiding queues.

- People are spread very thinly across projects. With so many "balls in the air," people start to cut corners and execute in haste. Key activities may be left out in the interest of being expedient and saving time, and quality of execution starts to suffer. The result is higher failure rates and an inability to achieve the full potential of would-be winners.

One major chemical company undertook an audit of its new product practices and performance across its many businesses. One common conclusion, regardless of business unit, revealed a lack of good market knowledge and customer input in the typical new product project. A task force was set up to study why. Its conclusions: marketing people were so thinly spread across so many new product projects that they barely had time to oversee the launch of new products, let alone even think about doing market studies and solid market research.

• Quality of information on projects is also deficient. When the project team lacks the time to do a decent market study or a solid technical assessment, management is often forced to make continued investment decisions in the absence of solid information. Consequently, projects are approved that should be killed, and the portfolio suffers.

• Finally, with people spread so thinly across projects and trying to cope with their "real jobs" too, stress levels go up and morale suffers. As a result, the team concept starts to break down [6].

2.2 Project Selection Methods Fail To Discriminate

Most project selection tools—scoring models and financial tools, for example—weigh the project against some hurdle or "minimum acceptable value." In the case of NPV, for example, the NPV is calculated using a risk-adjusted cost of capital. If the NPV is positive, the acceptable hurdle rate is achieved and the project is deemed a *pass*.

The trouble is, lots of projects pass the hurdles. They are rated against objective criteria but then rarely force-ranked against one another. So there is little discrimination between projects—they are all Go's!

An international banking organization had established a well-oiled new product process, complete with rigorous Go/Kill decision points built in. These Go/Kill decisions were based in part on a scoring model and on traditional profitability criteria. Unfortunately, many projects "passed" the hurdles at the gates and so kept getting added to the active project list. As the list got longer, the resources were spread thinner and thinner! The gating method looked at projects, each on their own merits, but failed to distinguish the top-priority ones from the rest.

Forced-ranking of projects means making tough decisions. The result is a prioritized list of projects, with the best ones at the top. Projects are listed until the business runs out of resources. Below that point, projects are put on hold or killed outright. All too often these tough decisions are not made; as one executive put it, "No one likes to drown puppies in our business!"

This lack of discrimination among projects, where the best rise to the top of the list, is in part due to weaknesses in the particular selection tools used:

1. NPV was designed for one-off decisions; for example, the decision to buy a new piece of equipment. However, NPV was never meant for portfolio decisions, where multiple projects compete for the same resources. Ranking projects according to their NPVs does not yield the right portfolio either—the method ignores resource constraints. Finally, NPV calculations are always suspect in the early stages of a new product project. As one senior manager remarked, "What number do you want to hear? The project team always delivers the right number to get their project approved!"

2. Scoring models are valuable decision aids for evaluating projects. They, too, tend to rate projects against absolute criteria, rather than against each other. Admittedly, one might consider ranking projects according to their project scores. Again, the issues of resource constraints and "bang for buck" are ignored.

For example, one major financial institution developed a scoring model to rate projects. Four fairly typical criteria were used: strategic fit and importance, market attractiveness, competitive advantage, and magnitude of the profit opportunity. Projects were scored on these criteria by senior management on 0-to-10 scales and the scores were added to yield a Program Attractiveness Score. Projects falling below a certain minimum score were discarded, and the remaining ones were rank-ordered according to the score.

A review of the resulting three-page prioritized list of projects revealed an artifact of the ranking scheme. All the big-hit projects were on page 1 at the top of the list, and the small ones on page 3. A closer review of the projects showed that many of these big-hit projects also consumed large resources, whereas some of the projects on pages 2 and 3 of the list, although having lower scores, were also relatively inexpensive to do. The scoring model had missed the notion of efficient allocation of resources.

A final complaint about scoring models is that often they fail to discriminate well. They tend to yield middle-of-the road scores—60 out of 100—which makes it difficult to spot the stars from the dogs. This is especially true when a large number of scoring criteria are used: high scores on some criteria cancel out low scores on others, and the result regresses toward the mean—a project score of 50 or 60 out of 100.

3. Bubble diagrams, another popular tool for visualizing one's portfolio, have the advantage of looking at all projects together. Figure 3 illustrates how resource requirements are displayed by the size of the bubbles or shapes

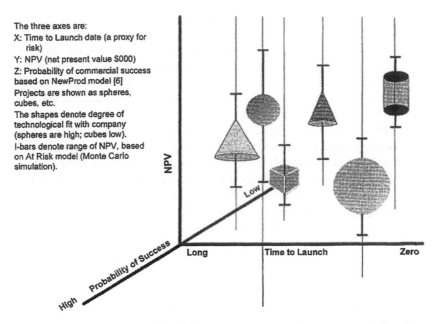

The three axes are:
X: Time to Launch date (a proxy for risk)
Y: NPV (net present value $000)
Z: Probability of commercial success based on NewProd model [6]
Projects are shown as spheres, cubes, etc.
The shapes denote degree of technological fit with company (spheres are high; cubes low).
I-bars denote range of NPV, based on At Risk model (Monte Carlo simulation).

NPV

Low

Probability of Success

High

Long   Time to Launch   Zero

FIGURE 3   The risk-reward bubble diagram, as used at Procter & Gamble, portrays projects in terms of NPV, commercial success probability, and time to launch [7].

[7]. The problem is that bubble diagrams tend to be information displays only—a discussion tool—and do not generate a list of prioritized projects.

2.3   Go/Kill Decisions Without Solid Information

This issue was mentioned in the discussion of Problem 1 above, but it is so pervasive that we expand on it here. Here's a typical case:

A major tool manufacturer has dozens of development projects under way at any one time. To help prioritize projects and make better Go/Kill decisions, management has implemented a "Go to Development" gate decision point. The project team is required to submit a business case, which includes estimates of market size, expected revenue, and profits. These data are key inputs to the prioritization decision. The trouble is, these numbers are best guesses, often based on numbers pulled out of the air. Hence, management is lulled into believing that it is making rigorous Go/Kill decisions based on objective criteria. In reality, the numbers it is using to make these decisions are *pure fiction*.

Early in the life of a project, management must make some important Go/Kill and resource commitment decisions on specific projects. The dilemma is that the up-front homework is rarely done well enough to provide the quality of information that management needs to make sound decisions. For example, a study of more than 500 projects in 300 firms revealed major weaknesses in the front end of projects: weak preliminary market assessments, barely adequate technical assessments, dismal market studies and marketing inputs, and deficient business analyses, on average [8]. These are critical homework activities, yet in study after study they are found wanting; the up-front homework simply does not get done well [9]. Even worse, these activities are strongly linked to ultimate project outcomes. The greatest difference between winning and losing products lies in the quality of execution of the project's homework activities.

Why is quality of execution of these early-stage activities so pivotal to new product success? There are two reasons:

1.   When the quality of this early-stage work is better, an excellent foundation is laid for the project. Thus, subsequent activities are more proficiently executed: better product design, better testing, better launch and production start-up, and success rates rise [8, 9]. As an example, better up-front homework usually results in sharper customer input, which, in turn, means earlier, more accurate and stable product definition. Note that unstable product specifications are one of the major causes of long cycle times, whereas sharp, early product definition that is fact-based is strongly connected to product profitability [10].

2.   When the early work is done better, market and technical information on the project is superior. Thus, management has the information it needs to select the winning projects (and to remove the dogs). The result is a much better portfolio of projects and, again, higher success rates. For example, bad market information plagues many new product projects. Lacking good data on market size, expected revenue, and pricing makes it difficult to undertake a reliable financial analysis. Indeed, one company's analysis of the accuracy of its financial analyses undertaken just before development revealed a 300% error in NPV estimates on average! Because so many firms rely on NPV numbers as the dominant decision criteria [2], such errors render the decision-making process a hit-and-miss exercise. One might be better off tossing a coin!

The overriding message here is that doing projects right will ultimately lead to better project selection decisions and higher odds of doing the right projects. "Right projects right" becomes the means to achieving a higher success rate.

2.4 Too Many Small Projects, Too Few Major Hits

The shortage of major hits or big breakthroughs in the portfolio is a problem common to many firms (Fig. 2). Anecdotal evidence from our research suggests many reasons for this:

- A preoccupation with financial results and overemphasis on shareholder value (financial evaluation techniques inevitably favor small, well-defined, fast projects over long-term, less defined ones).
- Management impatience and its desire for some quick hits. One executive called this the Nike theory of management: "Just do it!"
- A lack of discipline. "Urgent things always take precedence over important things!" exclaimed a frustrated manager, annoyed with his business's preoccupation with quick-hit projects.
- The dynamic nature of markets and the competitive situation, making it difficult to predict the long term (and hence more difficult to predict and justify long-term projects).
- The difficulty in finding major revenue generators. Markets are mature, and the opportunities for major breakthroughs just are not there, according to some people in certain industries.

Short-term projects (extensions, modifications, updates, fixes) are clearly important projects if the business wishes to remain competitive and keep its product line current. If these projects consume almost all your development resources, the issue becomes one of balance. A certain proportion of your resources must be committed to bolder projects that promise breakthroughs or to changing the basis of competition: genuine new products, platform developments, and even technology developments.

Part of the problem is the absence of a product innovation strategy that gives direction to the business's development efforts and spending priorities. With no strategy in place, tactics take over, and tactics favor the small, quick project. Another root cause is the lack of deployment decisions in the business. Many companies we interviewed did not consciously address the deployment or resource allocation decision across project types. For example, there was no attempt to set aside envelopes or "buckets" of money for different project types—major projects, long-term projects, technology developments versus shorter projects, extensions, modifications, and fixes [11]. With no conscious envelopes or buckets in place, every would-be project is thrown into the same bucket and the results are predictable: the quick, short-term, and well-defined extensions, modifications, and fixes win out in the competition for resources, often to the longer-run detriment of the business.

3 FIRST THINGS FIRST

Fix the quality of information problem! No matter how elegant or sophisticated your portfolio selection and decision tools, if the information input is poor, then so will be the decision-making. As one manager exclaimed, "If we had spent as much effort improving the quality of information as we did on the software for our new portfolio model, we would have been further ahead. The elegance of the model far exceeds the quality of the data inputs!"

How can your business strive for better quality information on its projects? Many companies have adopted a stage-and-gate approach to managing their new product projects to drive new products to market (Fig. 4) [12]. Stage-Gate™ approaches are relatively common in industry today: an estimated 60% of U.S. product developers now use a Stage-Gate method in their product development efforts [13].

Stage-Gate processes are instrumental in improving the quality of information generated in your projects:

1.   Stage-Gate methods define the key tasks, activities, and accountabilities within each stage. Thus, in the typical Stage-Gate process, there is a heavy emphasis on the up-front or front-end of the new product process and assurances that the market information activities are conducted in concert with the technical appraisals.

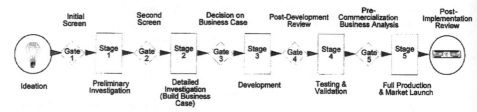

FIGURE 4 The typical Stage-Gate™ new-product process has five stages, each preceded by a gate. Stages define best-practice activities and deliverables, whereas gates rely on visible criteria for Go/Kill decisions. An estimated 60% of product developers in the United States now use a Stage-Gate process to guide development efforts [4].

2. Next, gating processes define the deliverables required for the gate decision: every gate has a menu of deliverables, a list of information items that senior management needs to make effective Go/Kill decisions at each gate. Thus, project teams are well aware of what information they must deliver; these deliverables become the team's objectives.

3. Finally, Stage-Gate methods specify the criteria against which each project is evaluated. Gatekeepers (the senior management) judge the project against a list of criteria, such as strategic fit, technical feasibility, market attractiveness, and competitive advantage. If the discussion that centers on each criterion results in shrugged shoulders and comments like, "we're not sure," this is a sure signal that the quality of information is substandard: the project is recycled to the previous stage rather than being allowed to progress.

Our benchmarking studies, which by now include more than 300 companies, reveal that businesses that boast such a new product process fare much better: higher success rates on launch (by 37.5%); meet new product sales objectives more often (88% better); and meet profit objectives more often (72.0% better) [14].

So, Step 1 is to overhaul your new product process: install a Stage-Gate process complete with defined stage activities that emphasize the upfront homework, a menu of deliverables for the key decision points or gates, and defined criteria at each gate against which the project is judged. Experience dictates that it is very difficult to implement portfolio management without an effective new product process, such as Stage-Gate, in place.

4 INTRODUCE RESOURCE CAPACITY ANALYSIS

The problem of too many projects and too few resources can be partly resolved by undertaking a resource capacity analysis. This analysis attempts to quantify your projects' demand for resources (usually people, expressed as person-days of work) versus the availability of these resources. You can do this analysis in one of two ways [15]:

1. *Do you have enough of the right resources to handle projects currently in your pipeline?* Begin with your current list of active projects. Determine the resources required to complete them according to their timelines. Then look at the availability of resources. You usually find major gaps and, hence, potential bottlenecks. Finally, identify the key resource constraints—the departments, people or capabilities that you run out of first (see section 8.2).

2. *Do you have enough resources to achieve your new product goals?* Begin with your new product goals. What percent of your business' sales will

come from new products? Now, determine the resources required to achieve this goal. Again, you will likely find a major gap between demand based on your goals and capacity available. It's time to make some tough choices about the realism of your goals or whether more resources are required (see section 8.2).

This capacity analysis is not a total solution, but it does provide information necessary to begin work on a solution. The experience in companies is that capacity analysis often:

- Detects far too many projects in the pipeline, resulting in an immediate prioritization and pruning effort. The result often is that half the projects are killed or put on hold!
- Causes senior management to rethink its goals (often new product goals, such as percentage of sales by new products, are based on wishful thinking or an unrealistic corporate dictum).
- Identifies departments or groups that are major bottlenecks in the innovation process, leading to decisions to increase or shift personnel.

Resource capacity analysis is a tactical move, but it is relatively straightforward and provides real insights into the nature and magnitude of the resource constraint problem. So when looking at resources and resource allocation, this is a good place to begin. You cannot manage what you cannot measure!

5 DEVELOP A PITS FOR YOUR BUSINESS

Developing a product innovation and technology strategy (PITS) for your businesses is one way to improve the balance of projects in the portfolio [16]. Some would argue that such a strategy is necessary to ensure a reasonable balance between short-term, quick, small projects and major breakthroughs, and that if your portfolio has too many small projects consuming too many resources, then chances are it is because you lack an innovation strategy or have failed to operationalize one. *Strategy becomes real when you start spending money.* Thus, strategy guides the split in resources across project types, between short-term and long-term projects, between high-risk and low-risk initiatives, between new products and platform development versus extensions, updates, and fixes.

Your product innovation strategy should:

- Define the goals for your new product and development effort; for example, what percent of your business' sales will come from new products? What percent of profits or growth?

- Define arenas for focus; that is, the key markets, technologies, and product types that your development effort will focus on.
- Define deployment of resources, approximate splits in resources or spending across project types (platform developments, new products, extensions, fixes and updates), across markets, and across product types.
- Define the attack plan (or strategic stance) for development; for example, being the innovator (versus fast follower) in a given arena, or focusing on superior product performance versus best cost.

At Allied Signal, for instance, senior management in each business unit first defines its business vision, goals, and strategy. Then it translates this strategy into a spending split in technical resources across three project types: platform projects, new product projects, and "other" (modifications, fixes, improvements). After the spending split is decided across project types, projects within each of the three categories are listed and ranked against one another. Different criteria are used to rank the projects within each category—strategic criteria for platform developments, multiple criteria typical of a scoring model for new products, and financial criteria for "other." In effect, three separate portfolios of projects are defined, and projects within one category or portfolio do not compete for resources against projects in another category. In this way, resource spending is forced to reflect the business's strategy.

6 INTEGRATING PORTFOLIO MANAGEMENT

By putting a Stage-Gate process in place, you are taking the first step toward effective portfolio management. First, quality of information should improve. Second, the gates should, at minimum, kill poor projects, thereby improving the overall quality of the portfolio. A gating process engages senior management in the right way. Next, introducing resource capacity analysis is also a good step: you will have a much better understanding of resource needs, resource availabilities, and potential bottlenecks.

Where Stage-Gate processes fall short is in project prioritization and resource balancing (Problems 1 and 2 above). That's the role of portfolio management methods.

Portfolio management goes beyond mere project selection, and it is more than simply making tough Go/Kill decisions at gates. Portfolio management is a dynamic decision process whereby a business's list of active new product (and R&D) projects is constantly updated and revised; new projects are evaluated, selected, and prioritized; existing projects may be accelerated, killed, or deprioritized; and resources are allocated and reallocated to the active projects [5].

A new-product process, such as Stage-Gate, is a step in the right direction, but is only a partial solution. Gating processes focus on individual projects and evaluate each project on its own merits. They deal with the fingers. By contrast, portfolio management, by considering all projects together, looks at the fist!

Our research reveals a number of companies experimenting with different approaches to portfolio management. These attempts are new—portfolio methods have been in place for an average of 3 years—thus, the approaches are tentative [17]. Virtually all the firms finding success here had already implemented a systematic new product process (above), and had designated one gate at the point where portfolio management kicks in. Typically this is Gate 2 (which precedes the detailed investigation stage in Fig. 4) or Gate 3 (which opens the door to development).

From this point on, however, there is divergence of opinion, with many different portfolio tools and techniques used. Indeed, two broad portfolio approaches were observed in practice, and each has its own merits.

We present now a summary of the various portfolio tools used. Next, we outline the two fundamental approaches to portfolio management. Note that although the two approaches share some of the same tools, and on the surface look similar, each is fundamentally different from the other in terms of how it is put into practice.

6.1 Portfolio Tools

A variety of portfolio tools, charts, and techniques are used to assist in the review of all projects. Our research uncovered three goals of portfolio management, and different tools appear best suited to each of the goals. The three goals are:

Goal 1: Value Maximization. To allocate resources so as to maximize the value of the portfolio in terms of some business objective, such as profitability. Tools used to assess ''project value'' include:

- *NPV*: The project's net present value (or some other financial metric) is determined and must exceed some minimum acceptable value. Projects can also be ranked by NPVs.
- *ECV*: This is a variant of NPV and introduces probabilities of technical and commercial success along with an incremental decision process (options pricing theory) [18].

- *Checklists*: A list of Yes/No questions is used to rate the project in checklist format. A suitable pattern of scores (often the absence of definite "No's") signals a Pass decision.
- *Scoring model*: Decision-makers rate the project on a number of questions that distinguish superior projects, typically on 1–5 or 0–10 scales. These ratings are added to yield a quantified Project Attractiveness Score, which must clear a minimum hurdle. This score is a proxy for the "value of the project to the company," but incorporates strategic, leverage, and other considerations beyond just the financial measures.

The values of projects to the business are determined, and projects are ranked according to this "value" until there are no more resources.

Goal 2: Balance. To achieve a desired balance of projects in terms of a number of parameters: long-term projects versus short-term ones; high-risk versus sure bets; and across various markets, technologies, and project types.

Visual charts display *balance* in new product project portfolios. These visual representations include portfolio maps or *bubble diagrams*, such as the risk-reward bubble diagram used at Procter & Gamble, plotting NPV, probability of success, and time-to-market (Fig. 3) [5]. Other visuals include pie charts that show the breakdown in numbers of projects or spending by project types, product lines, or markets [19].

Goal 3: Strategic Direction. To ensure that the final portfolio of projects reflects the business's strategy, that the breakdown of spending across projects, areas, markets, etc., mirrors the business's strategy, and that all projects are "on strategy."

The Strategic Buckets approach is used by some leading firms to ensure that portfolio spending mirrors their strategic priorities. Here, management preallocates funds to various "buckets": project types, markets, technologies, or product lines. These splits are based on strategic considerations (for example, Allied Signal splits development resources into three buckets: platform projects, new products, and minor projects). Projects are categorized by bucket and then rank-ordered within a bucket Thus, multiple lists or portfolios of projects are created, with each portfolio managed separately.

How are these various portfolio tools used in conjunction with a gating process? There are two fundamentally different approaches:

6.1.1 Approach 1: The Gates Dominate

Here, the philosophy is that if your gating or Stage-Gate process is working well, the portfolio will take care of itself. Therefore, make good decisions at the gates! The emphasis of this approach is on sharpening gate decision-making on individual projects.

In Approach 1, senior management or gatekeepers make Go/Kill decisions at gates on individual projects. Also at gates, the project is prioritized and resources allocated. Gates thus provide an in-depth review of projects, one project at a time, and project teams leave the gate meeting with committed resources, with a check in hand! This is a *real-time decision process*, with gates activated many times throughout the year. By contrast, the periodic Portfolio Review, held perhaps once or twice a year, serves largely as a check to ensure that real-time gate decisions are good ones.

This ''gates dominate'' approach is often used by companies that already have a Stage-Gate process in place, and one that is working well. They then add portfolio management to their gating process, almost as a complementary decision process. Our research found this approach used most often in larger companies, in science-based industries, and where projects are lengthy (such as the chemical process industry).

Here's how it works: Projects proceed through the Stage-Gate process as portrayed in Figure 4. Projects are rated and scored at gates, usually by senior management, especially at more critical gates (Gate 3 and beyond in Fig. 4).

To introduce portfolio management, gates become two-part decisions (Fig. 5). The first part or half of the gate is a Pass-versus-Kill decision, where individual projects are evaluated using the financial, checklist, and scoring model valuation tools described above.

The second half of the gate meeting involves *prioritization* of the project under discussion versus the other projects (Fig. 5). In practice, this means making a Go-versus-Hold decision, and if Go, allocating resources to the project. A rank-ordered list of projects is displayed to compare the relative attractiveness of the project under discussion to the other Active and On-Hold projects. Here, projects can be ranked on a financial criterion (for example, NPV or, better yet, the ECV) or on the Project Attractiveness Score derived from the scoring model.

Additionally, the impact of the proposed project on the total portfolio of projects is assessed. The question is: Does the new project under discussion improve the balance of projects (or detract from balance), and does the project improve the portfolio's strategic alignment? Bubble diagrams and pie charts are the tools used for visualizing balance and alignment, as outlined above.

Note how the gates dominate the decision process in this approach: Go/Kill, prioritization, and resource allocation decisions are made in real time, right at the gate meeting. But other projects are *not* discussed and reprioritized

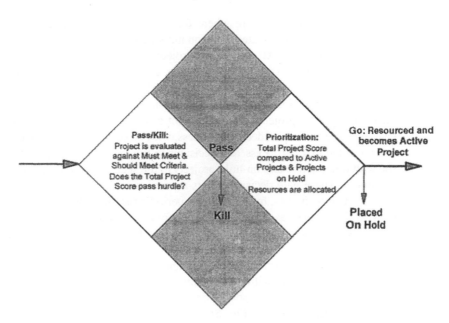

FIGURE 5 Decisions at gates are a two-part process. The first part evaluates the project against a set of Must and Should Meet criteria—a Pass versus Kill Decision. In part 2, the project is prioritized against other Active or On-Hold projects.

at the gate; only the project in question is given a relative priority level versus the rest.

What about looking at all projects together? That's the role of portfolio reviews. In this approach, the portfolio reviews serve largely as a check that the gates are working well. Senior management meets perhaps once or twice a year to review the portfolio of all projects:

- Is there the right balance of projects?
- The right mix?
- Are all projects strategically aligned (fit the business's strategy)?
- Are there the right priorities among projects?

If the gates are working, not too many decisions or major corrective actions should be required at the portfolio review. Some companies in our research indicated that they don't even look at individual projects at the portfolio review but only consider projects in aggregate!

To recap, the gates are where the day-to-day decisions are made on projects in Approach 1. Gates focus on individual projects, one at a time, and are in-depth reviews. At gates, each project is evaluated and scored before moving on to the next stage—a real-time decision process. At gates, poor projects are spotted and weeded out, and good ones are identified and prioritized accordingly. Note that resource decisions, that is, committing people and money to specific projects, are made right at these gate meetings. Thus, the gates become a two-part decision process, with projects evaluated on absolute criteria in the first part (Pass/Kill decisions in Fig. 5), followed by a comparison with other active and on-hold projects in the second part (Go-versus-Hold decisions). These gate decision points are real-time decisions.

Portfolio reviews, by contrast, are periodic meetings, held perhaps twice per year. They serve as a check on the portfolio and oversee the gate decisions being made. If the gates are working well, the Portfolio Reviews are largely a rubber stamp.

Note that the portfolio reviewers and the senior gatekeepers are most often the same people within the business. The result of the gating process working in tandem with the portfolio reviews is an effective, harmonized portfolio management process (Fig. 6).

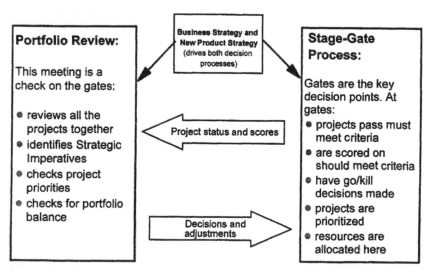

FIGURE 6   Portfolio Approach 1 relies on a gating process **(right)** to make the key decisions. The portfolio review **(left)** serves as a check. Both decision processes are driven by strategy **(top)**.

6.1.2   Approach 2: Portfolio Review Dominates

The philosophy of the second approach is that every project must compete against the others. A single decision on all projects replaces one of the gates in the gating process.

Here, the leadership team makes Go/Kill and prioritization decisions at the portfolio reviews, where *all projects* are up for auction and are considered on the table together. This review occurs two to four times a year. The gates in the Stage-Gate process serve merely as checks on projects, ensuring that projects remain financially sound and are proceeding on schedule.

The result of this "portfolio review dominates" approach is a more dynamic, constantly changing portfolio of projects. The method may suit faster-paced companies, such as software and electronics firms, but it requires a much stronger commitment by senior management to the decision process, spending the time to look at all projects together and in depth several times a year.

Approach 2 uses many of the same portfolio tools and models described above, but in a different way. The result is a more dynamic portfolio of projects. In this approach, the project enters the portfolio process typically after the first stage (at Gate 2 in Fig. 4) when data are available.

The main difference from Approach 1 is that early in the life of projects, a combined Gate 2 and Portfolio decision meeting takes place. All new Gate 2 projects, together with all projects past Gate 2, are reviewed and prioritized against one another. Every project at Gate 2 and beyond is in the auction, and all these projects are ranked against each other. Active projects, well along in their development, can be killed or reprioritized here, and resources are allocated here rather than at gates. This Portfolio/Gate 2 decision meeting takes place about four times a year.

The role of gates in Approach 2 is very different from Approach 1. Successive gates (after Gate 2) are merely checkpoints or review points. They:

- Check that the project is on time, on course and on budget
- Check quality of work done—the quality of deliverables
- Check that the business case and project are still in good shape

If No, the project could be killed at the gate, recycled to the previous stage, or flagged for the next Portfolio/Gate 2 meeting.

The major decisions, however, occur at the combined Gate 2/Portfolio decision point, which is a more extended, proactive meeting than portfolio reviews in Approach 1. Although this is a periodic process, it is almost real-time because this Portfolio/Gate 2 meeting is held every three months.

As an example, EXFO Engineering, a midsized entrepreneurial and very successful instrument manufacturer, has implemented both a Stage-Gate process and portfolio management Approach 2. Four times a year, the leadership team of this business, chaired by the CEO, evaluates the complete slate of new-product projects during their portfolio review meetings. Any project at or beyond Gate 2 is included in this prioritization exercise. Projects are rated according to the following criteria:

- Confidence in the project team and in their proposed costs, revenues, and schedules
- Revenues (times a commercial risk factor) versus expenses (development and commercialization costs, including a technical risk factor), over a two-year period.
- Match to the strategic plan (specific growth directions, with a weighting factor on each)
- Profitability index (return on investment)
- Availability of technical resources and commercial strengths

Projects are then force-ranked against one another. The result is a prioritized list, with some projects placed on hold.

The format of this vital, quarterly Gate 2/Portfolio decision point is typically this: all Gate 2 and beyond projects are "on the table." The portfolio managers (senior management) first identify the "Must Do" projects, the untouchables. These are projects that are either well along and still good projects or are strategic imperatives. Then, management votes on and identifies "Won't Do's," which are killed outright.

Next, the projects in the middle are evaluated. There are different methods here:

- Some firms use the same criteria they use at gate meetings, and in some cases, the most recent gate 0–10 scores; that is, the Project Attractiveness Score from the gate meeting is used to rank-order the projects.
- Other managements rescore the projects right at the Portfolio/Gate 2 meeting (using a shorter list of criteria than the list found in the typical scoring model).
- Forced ranking on criteria is also used. Here management ranks the projects against one another, 1 to N, on each criterion. Again, a handful of major criteria are used, such as those used by Kodak at its portfolio review [20]:
- Strategic fit
- Product leadership (product advantage)

- Probability of technical success
- Market attractiveness (growth, margins)
- Value to the company (profitability based on NPV)

We recommend the forced ranking method because it yields better discrimination than a traditional scoring model, forcing some projects to the top of the list and others to the bottom. One of the weaknesses of a scoring model, in contrast, is that projects tend to score middle-of-the-road—everything is 60 out of 100. Any of these three methods, however, yields a list of projects, rank-ordered according to objective scores. Projects are ranked until one runs out of resources. This ranked list is the first cut or *tentative portfolio.*

After this, it is necessary to check for balance and strategic alignment: the proposed portfolio is displayed using some of the bubble diagrams and pie charts described above (summarized in Fig. 7). The purpose here is to

Prioritized Scored List of Active and On-Hold Projects

Project	Rank (Priority Level)	Total Project Score	Portfolio Balance Factor	Adjusted Total Project Score
Soya-44	1	80	1.10	88
Encapsulated	2	82	1.00	82
Legume N-2	3	70	1.10	77
Spread-Ease	4	75	1.00	75
Charcoal-Base	5	80	0.90	72
Projects on Hold				
N2-Fix	1	80	1.00	80**
Slow-Release	2	70	1.10	77*
Multi-Purpose	3	75	.90	68
etc..	etc..			

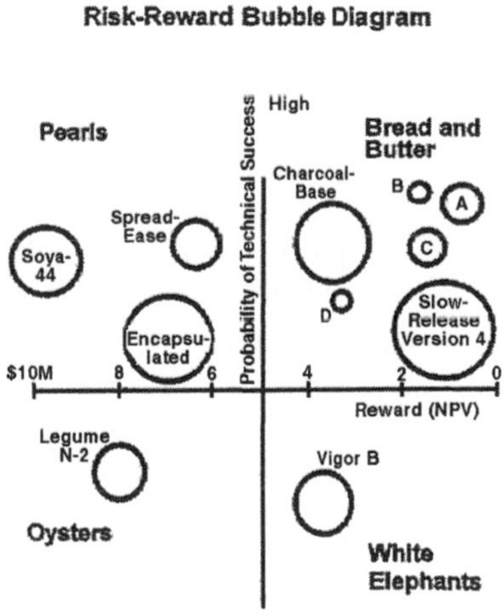
Risk-Reward Bubble Diagram
High
Pearls
Bread and Butter
Probability of Technical Success
Charcoal-Base
Spread-Ease
Soya-44
Encapsu-lated
B
A
C
D
Slow-Release Version 4
$10M
8
6
4
2
0
Reward (NPV)
Legume N-2
Vigor B
Oysters
White Elephants

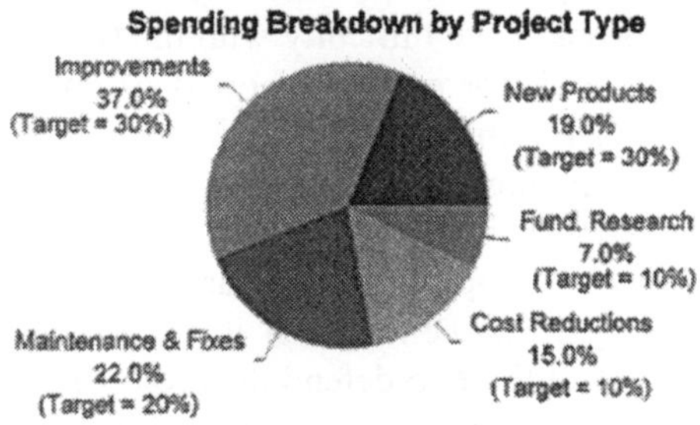
Spending Breakdown by Project Type
Improvements 37.0% (Target = 30%)
New Products 19.0% (Target = 30%)
Fund. Research 7.0% (Target = 10%)
Cost Reductions 15.0% (Target = 10%)
Maintenance & Fixes 22.0% (Target = 20%)

FIGURE 7 In portfolio Approach 2, at the end of the project ranking exercise, the resulting portfolio of projects is displayed on various charts. These charts enable management to check for portfolio balance and strategic alignment.

visualize the balance of the proposed portfolio and to check for strategic alignment. If the tentative portfolio is poorly balanced or not strategically aligned, projects are removed from the list and other projects are bumped up. The process is repeated until balance and alignment are achieved.

To recap, the Portfolio/Gate 2 decision meeting is where the key decisions are made in Approach 2. The portfolio review is really a Gate 2 and portfolio review all-in-one, held two to four times a year. It is here that the key Go/Kill decisions are made, and, consequently, is a senior management meeting. With all projects at or beyond Gate 2 on the table, the meeting:

- Spots Must Do and Won't Do projects
- Scores (forced ranking) the ones in the middle
- Checks for balance and strategic alignment (using various portfolio charts and bubble diagrams)
- Decides the portfolio: which projects, what priorities, how much resources

The gates serve mainly as a check. Projects are checked as they progress from stage to stage to ensure that they are on time, on budget, and remain good projects. Kill decisions are still made at gates to weed out poor projects. Gates rely on criteria, and the scores at these gates are often used as inputs to the portfolio meeting.

Approach 2 thus lashes together the two decision processes: the gating process and the portfolio review. Gate 2 is really the integrative decision point in the scheme and the point where the two decision processes intersect (Fig. 8).

Approach 2 has some advantages (and disadvantages) versus Approach 1. Management indicates that it is easier to prioritize projects when looking at all projects on the table together (rather than one at a time at real-time gates). Additionally, some people have difficulty with the two-part gate approach in Approach 1 and Figure 5; for example, how does one find resources for a good project when that is the only project being considered at the meeting? Finally, some managers like the notion that prioritization of all projects is redone regularly. No project is sacred!

There are also disadvantages to Approach 2 and areas in which Approach 1 is superior. Many managements believe that if projects are to be killed, then the project team should be there to defend the project (or at least to provide updated information), such as happens at an in-depth gate meeting. Another criticism is that Approach 2 requires a major time commitment from senior management; for example, senior management in the midsized firm in the instrument business cited above takes three days every quarter to conduct this Portfolio/Gate 2 decision meeting!

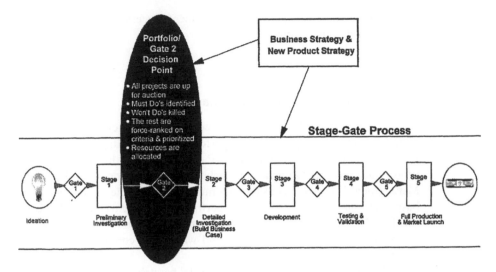

FIGURE 8 In portfolio Approach 2, portfolio management intersects with the new-product process (*black oval*). Projects are force-ranked against each other in this combined Portfolio/Gate 2 decision meeting. Prioritization is established, and resources are allocated here. Subsequent gates serve as checks.

A final advantage of Approach 1 is that gate reviews provide a much more in-depth assessment than is ever possible when all the projects are considered at a single meeting.

7 JUST DO IT!

New-product portfolio management has become a vital concern, particularly among leading firms. For example, senior executives in top-performing businesses consider new product portfolio management to be ''of critical importance'' [2]. Although a number of tools have been described that help to select projects and visualize a portfolio, the choice of tool may not be that critical; indeed, the best performers use an average of 2.4 tools each—no one tool can do it all!

Two different approaches to portfolio management—where the gates dominate and where the portfolio review dominates—have also been outlined. Both have their merits, and both are recommended. Regardless of which portfolio method or which specific tools you favor, do move ahead: choose a method and implement it! Our research [2] shows clearly that those businesses that feature a systematic portfolio management process, regardless of the specific approach, outperform the rest.

8 NOTES

8.1 Research into Portfolio Management

This chapter reports the findings of a continuing research investigation into portfolio management practices and performances, done in part with industrial research institute member companies. Part I of the study looked at 35 leading firms' portfolio management approaches and was reported in Technology Management [1]. Part II considered a much larger sample of companies (205 businesses) and was able to correlate performance results versus methods used [2]. Part III of the research, reported here, probes some of the difficulties uncovered in portfolio management and what some companies are doing to address these difficulties.

The 30 companies in Part III were deliberately chosen, based on prior knowledge of their approaches and the fact that they were actively addressing portfolio management issues. Further, they are more representative of industry-at-large (typical companies, as opposed to Part I, which focused on leading firms only). The research is case study in nature (i.e., interviews with management in the firms).

8.2 Two Ways To Analyze Resource Capacity versus Demand

1. **Demand Created by Your Active Projects**
Determine demand.

- Begin with your current list of active development projects, prioritized from best to worst (use a scoring model to prioritize projects or one of the financial approaches mentioned in the text). Develop a prioritized project list table.
- Then consider the detailed plan of action for each project (use a timeline software package, such as Microsoft Project).
- For each activity on the timeline, note the number of person-days of work (or work-months), and which group (or department) will do the work.
- Record these work-day requirements in the prioritized project list table, one column per department. In other columns, note the cumulative work-days by department.

What is your capacity?

- Next, look at the capacity available—how many work-days each department (or group) has available in total. (These work-days look at all people in that group or department and what proportion of their time they have available for new products. Be sure to consider their "other jobs" in this determination; for example, the fact that a marketing group likely has 90% of its time consumed by day-to-day assignments).
- Then mark the point in your prioritized list of projects table where you run out of resources—where demand exceeds capacity.

Results

You will likely learn three things from this exercise:

- You really do have too many projects, often by a factor of two or three.
- You can see which department or group is the constraining one.
- You also begin to question where some departments spend their time (and why such a small proportion is available to work on new products!).

2. Demand Generated by Your Business's New Product Goals
Determine demand.

- Begin with your new product goals—what sales or percentage of sales you desire from new products.
- Translate these goals into numbers of major and minor new product launches annually.
- Then, using your attrition curve, how many Stage 1, Stage 2, Stage 3, etc. projects does it take to yield one successful launch? determine the number of projects per year you need moving through each stage.
- Next, consider the work-days requirements in each stage, broken down by function or department. The numbers of projects per stage combined with the work-day requirements yield the demand, namely, the work-days and personnel requirements to achieve your business's new product goals, again by department.

What is your capacity?

- Now turn to availability. How many work-days are available per department (as per the second part of method 1 above)?

Results

- Again, you are likely to find a major gap between demand and capacity.
- At this point, you either modify your goals, making them a little more realistic, or make tough choices about adding resources or reassigning people to achieve your goals.

These two exercises [18] can be done either with work-days (people × days) or dollars as the measure of resources.

REFERENCES

1. RG Cooper, SJ Edgett, EJ Kleinschmidt. Portfolio management in new product development: Lessons from the leaders—Part I. Research • Technology Management Sept.-Oct. 16–28, 1997; also: RG Cooper, SJ Edgett, EJ Kleinschmidt. Portfolio management in new product development: Lessons from the leaders—Part II. Research • Technology Management Nov.-Dec. 43–52, 1997.
2. A study of portfolio management practices and what results were achieved (IRI member companies). See: RG Cooper, SJ Edgett, EJ Kleinschmidt. Best practices for managing R&D portfolios. Research • Technology Management July-Aug: 20–33, 1998.
3. RG Cooper. Product leadership: Creating and Launching Superior New Products. Reading, MA: Perseus Books, 1998, p. 189; and based on a study reported in RG Cooper, SJ Edgett, EJ Kleinschmidt. New product portfolio management: Practices and performance.'' Journal of Product Innovation Management 16: 333–351, 1999.
4. RG Cooper. The invisible success factors in product innovation. Journal of Product Innovation Management 16:115–133, 1999.
5. RG Cooper, SJ Edgett, EJ Kleinschmidt. Portfolio Management for New Products. Reading, MA: Perseus Books, 1998.
6. CM Crawford. The hidden costs of accelerated product development. Journal of Product Innovation Management 9:188–199, 1992.
7. See this and other examples of bubble diagrams in [5].
8. RG Cooper. New products: What separates the winners from the losers. In: MD Rosenau Jr., ed. PDMA Handbook for New Product Development. New York: John Wiley & Sons Inc, 1996.
9. RG Cooper. Winning at New Products: Accelerating the Process from Idea to Launch. Reading, MA: Perseus Books, 1993. Also, an excellent review of success/failure studies is: MM Montoya-Weiss, RJ Calantone. Determinants of new product performance: A review and meta analysis. Journal of Product Innovation Management 11:397–417, 1994.

10. RG Cooper. Developing new products on time, in time. Research • Technology Management Sept.-Oct: 49–57, 1995; and RG Cooper, EJ Kleinschmidt. Determinants of timeliness in new product development. Journal of Product Innovation Management 11:381–396, 1994.
11. This strategic buckets method is described in Portfolio Management [5].
12. Stage-Gate™ processes are described in Winning at New Products [9] and Product Leadership [3].
13. A Griffin. Drivers of NPD success: The 1997 PDMA Report. Chicago: Product Development & Management Association, 1997.
14. RG Cooper, EJ Kleinschmidt. Benchmarking firms' new product performance and practices. Engineering Management Review 23:112–120, 1995.
15. This resource capacity analysis method is taken from the article cited in [4].
16. RG Cooper. Product innovation and technology strategy. Research • Technology Management Jan.-Feb: 38–40, 2000.
17. As reported in the portfolio study cited in [2].
18. For a discussion of Options Pricing Theory, see Product Leadership [3], and: T Faulkner. Applying 'Options Thinking' to R&D Valuation. Research • Technology Management May-June: 50–57, 1996.
19. For a complete illustration of these various pie charts and bubble diagrams, see Portfolio Management [5]; also the two articles in [1].
20. E Patton. The strategic investment process: Driving corporate vision through portfolio creation. Proceedings: Product Portfolio Management: Balancing Resources with Opportunity. Boston: Management Roundtable, 1999. Describes Kodak's portfolio management approach.

17

Juggling the Interdependent Project Portfolio

Michael Singer Dobson

1 INTRODUCTION

''The move to a new computer center is the biggest single project I've ever managed, Sarah observes. To make it even more difficult, it has to be accomplished while keeping all the other projects and activities of my department running smoothly. On top of everything, if this project doesn't go well, it could turn into a first-class disaster for the company . . . not to mention my own career!

I've been on projects like this before. They start off smoothly all right, but then comes crunch time, right toward the end when everybody's pulling all-nighters and it's anybody's guess whether we'll make it out or not. That's what worries me.

On top of everything else, my entire collection of projects is really part of the overall move of the entire company! It could be worse. I could be in charge of everything. Still, I have to make sure that I coordinate my work so that if fits into the overall move schedule.''

Adapted from *The Juggler's Guide to Managing Multiple Projects*, 1999.

2 DEFINITIONS

An *interdependent project* is a project that is part of a portfolio of projects aimed at achieving a common outcome. Not only must the project goal be reached, it also must be reached in a way that fits with the other projects in the portfolio to achieve the overall goal.

No-fail budgeting is the process of allocating total portfolio resources to each project in the portfolio so that each has the minimum resources necessary to succeed. Once each project has the minimum resources, the project manager can use the remaining resources to increase total portfolio quality.

Total portfolio quality is the achievement of the overall portfolio goal, as opposed to the achievement of individual project goals within the portfolio. This concept helps you and your project managers remember that what is good for an individual project is not always what is good for the portfolio as a whole.

Crunch time is a common experience on major projects. The work all seems to go perfectly until the very end, when suddenly everyone must work around the clock to cope with unanticipated disasters.

The *control point identification chart* is a tool for identifying problems to allow for early solution.

Finish-to-finish dependency describes a situation when the finish of task B depends on the finish of task A. (It can start earlier.)

Frontloading is a strategy for doing as much of the project as you can up front. This builds in additional margin if things go wrong as you approach the deadline.

Lag time is extra time built into a project at the end to allow time to respond to emergencies. Unlike a lag activity, this time is not associated with any task. It can be used freely to respond to any emergencies.

Overlap dependency means the start of task B can begin sometime after the start of task A, but before task A finishes.

Start-to-start dependency is when the start of task B depends on the start of task A. In a normal finish-to-start dependency, the start of task B depends on the finish of task A.

Task slack belongs to a single task, allowing it to be delayed without affecting the next task.

Path slack is slack that is shared among a sequence of tasks. Free slack is the amount of time a task can be delayed before affecting the next task in the sequence.

Total slack is the amount of time a task can be delayed before affecting the deadline of the project.

3   ABOUT INTERDEPENDENT PROJECT PORTFOLIOS

Projects in an interdependent project portfolio often vary dramatically in subject matter. In Sarah's case, her projects range from managing a physical move to purchasing new hardware, developing strategic documents, and developing computer programs, all aimed at the common outcome of making the move happen.

Who has expertise in every single one of these areas? Very few, indeed. When you manage an interdependent project portfolio, you can expect to be stretched professionally into new fields. You need to be an outstanding delegator, able to find and motivate professionals with the skills and experience you do not have.

Sarah's situation also involves the reality that projects take place inside organizations. Sarah has regular management duties, meetings to attend, special assignments, and other elements of work. So does her staff.

Part of her situation, and one common to most interdependent project portfolios, is that she is responsible for ongoing work and projects while trying to let this major additional function into her schedule. As a result, and similar to Patrick's situation, the techniques in this situation are in addition to, not instead of, the techniques for managing the interdependent project portfolio, as well as the task-oriented project portfolio.

Interdependent project portfolios tend to be long term and substantial in size, scope, and complexity. Individual projects in the portfolio may be of any size, from small and easy to huge and cumbersome.

You can also be in the situation of managing an interdependent project portfolio from the inside. Sarah's situation is complex enough to be called an interdependent portfolio on its own, but her portfolio can also be considered a project in an even larger interdependent portfolio consisting of the entire company move!

Notice that this reality adds a series of issues and problems for Sarah. She cannot just pick a time for the move, based on the convenience of her own department; she must coordinate her move with the corporate move. Otherwise, the loading dock might be in use or the build-out of her space might conflict with other important priorities.

When managing a project within an interdependent portfolio, no matter how complex your issues are, you must remember that you can only succeed if your outcome dovetails with the other elements of the portfolio. Make sure you always keep your eye on the big picture.

4   INDEPENDENT PORTFOLIO MANAGEMENT VERSUS INTERDEPENDENT PORTFOLIO MANAGEMENT

As with the independent project portfolio, your interdependent project portfolio can benefit if you use the techniques of professional project management. Because independent projects are *independent*, the Gantt chart is an ideal way to display and understand them. Because interdependent projects require more attention to the idea of connectedness, you will find that in most cases the PERT chart is a more useful tool for understanding and control. Again, keep in mind the key concept

$$\text{Project} = \text{Task}$$

to allow managing multiple projects by using the techniques of single project management.

Another difference between the two types of portfolio is that failure is not allowed. If Patrick's schedule becomes unmanageable, he can let a project of lower priority slip, or cancel it completely. Sarah does not have that option, at least not in her core projects. She must use the concept of no-fail budgeting to ensure that her resources are allocated to achieve every single project in the portfolio, at least to a minimally acceptable level of quality. She can use remaining resources to increase total portfolio quality, but she needs to be aware that increasing the quality of one project in the portfolio does not automatically increase total portfolio quality.

4.1   The Irony of Interdependent Project Portfolios

Sarah's computer center portfolio has another special issue in it—one that is common to interdependent project portfolios. The issue is this: *she has never done this before.* She is an experienced data processing manager, but this particular situation has never occurred. In fact, there are many outstanding and experienced professionals in this field who have never had to move a computer center. Plus, Sarah is unlikely ever to move another computer center, and if she does, she will not move very many in an entire career.

There is an irony in interdependent project portfolios: the project manager and the team have probably never done this before. That is true even with some major projects.

The Smithsonian National Air and Space Museum, a $30 million federal project that opened in 1976 (ahead of schedule and under budget, by the way), was managed by Mike Collins, then director of the museum. Collins, best known as the Apollo 11 command module pilot, had never built a museum. Neither had his senior staff. The team did it anyway.

World War II Allied Command General Dwight D. Eisenhower had never managed an international military alliance to coordinate a continental invasion before D-Day. He did it anyway.

Imagine the pastor of a church who decides to expand into a new building. Like Sarah and her computer center, the pastor may never have done it. If the pastor has, it will not have been very often. Yet, church building projects happen all the time. They do it anyway.

When you are put in charge of an interdependent project portfolio, and if you say to yourself, "I have no idea what I am doing because I have never done this before," relax, you are in good company. Just do it anyway.

5   PLANNING AN INTERDEPENDENT PROJECT PORTFOLIO

Sarah would have preferred more notice, but the overall decision to move into a new building has already been made, the plans are in progress, and the deadline is set. She can't do much about it. Her goals in planning are as follows:

- Make sure the physical move happens on schedule without any data loss. (This includes ensuring that backups are completed and protected.)
- Make sure new equipment is installed, tested, and operational by the deadline.
- Keep critical department functions operating during the move.
- Avoid crunch time as much as humanly possible.

The process for planning the interdependent project portfolio is the same as that for the independent project portfolio.

5.1   Step 1: Define the Portfolio Goals

Make sure that you have a clear understanding of the portfolio goal and that you have prepared the objective in triple-constraint terms. You then need to determine the triple-constraints for each of the projects in your portfolio. It is not necessarily the case that they will be the same.

In Sarah's case, the goal is to have a successful move without losing data or production time. The triple constraints are as follows.

- *Time*   Move-in has been scheduled for the week of September 20. All activities needed for the move-in must be ready by then. (Certain activities may take place after the move-in week, such as unpacking.)

- *Performance*   Critical computer services are not interrupted, data are not lost, new equipment is installed and operational, and the staff is trained.
- *Budget*   There is a budget for new equipment ($1 million), and the overall move budget is $150,000.

Put the triple constraints in order. You can determine them by looking at the consequences of failure. The weak constraint is pretty obviously budget, as the damage done by going over budget is less than the damage done by missing the move-in or losing data and critical services.

Performance is probably the driver, because missing the move-in date, although costly and embarrassing, would be less serious than failing to deliver critical services or losing data. That gives us:

- Driver: performance
- Middle: time
- Weak: budget

Remember, when you determine the triple constraints, you often look at the consequences of failure. This does not mean that you intend to fail or want to fail. In fact, you want to achieve all three constraints. You need to understand the order of the constraints so you can make good decisions in the event of unforeseen difficulties.

5.2   Step 2: Prepare a Work Breakdown Structure

This portfolio consists of four interrelated projects: (1) the physical move, (2) new equipment procurement, (3) continuing operations and transition management, and (4) new center implementation (training, documenting, dry run, debugging) (see Fig. 1). Those projects become level 2 of the work breakdown structure (WBS). Each project consists of one or more tasks, which go in level 3 of the WBS. Some tasks may be large and complex enough to be considered projects of their own. You may break them down further into levels of the WBS.

Use the WBS to plan the management of your project. First, you need to assign a manager to each of the projects in the portfolio.

Tip! Let the managers help you plan. This not only lowers the amount of work you have to do, it also helps get buy-in and acceptance of the workload.

Verify triple constraints of each project. For example, the physical move project is time-driven, but continuing operations is performance-driven. New equipment may be performance-driven, but it could be budget-driven, depending on the organizational issues that affect your decisions.

Remember that individual project managers on your team manage their

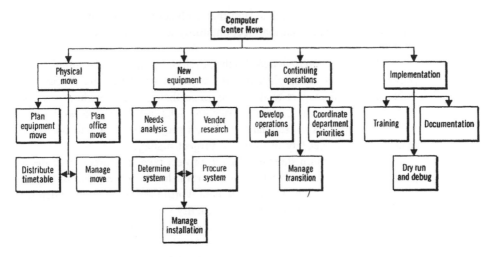

Figure 1   Work breakdown structure for moving computer center to new location.

projects according to their goals. Your job is to ensure that their work fits into your overall strategy.

5.3   Step 3: Conduct the Task Analysis Process

When you analyze tasks at the level of an interdependent project portfolio, you need to think of that as an entire process, rather than just filling out forms. An enormous amount of strategic and tactical thinking takes place, and this is one of your chief opportunities to get the members of your senior project team properly oriented and prepare them to get results.

Determine available resources. One of the frequent situations in managing an interdependent project portfolio is that the portfolio comes on top of a normal load of projects and work. You and your team need to determine what time you can realistically commit to the portfolio projects. This often means making decisions about what functions can be delayed until after completion of the portfolio. Delay everything that can be delayed so you will have maximum time to accomplish what cannot be delayed.

Assign clear responsibilities. It is easy for important matters to slip in project situations like this. People can easily get wrapped up in day-to-day activities. As the cartoon says, "When you are up to your rear end in alligators, it is hard to remind yourself that your original objective was to drain the swamp."

To overcome this, make sure that each activity is in the hands of a specific person or team, and that accountability and authority have been clearly defined.

Determine good enough. Each individual project in the interdependent portfolio has to be accomplished, but the quality standards vary. Because individual project managers tend to maximize their projects without regard for the portfolio as a whole, one of your key jobs is to establish *minimum* and *maximum* performance standards for each project. It is best to do this as a team activity, to get buy-in from the project managers.

What maximum standards? Each project takes resources from the total pool. If a project is satisfactory at a certain level, and exceeding that level takes more resources, is the improvement worth the cost? You must determine this by contribution to total portfolio quality.

Brainstorm ways to monitor progress. Use your team resources to do some extensive brainstorming when faced with an interdependent project portfolio. Look for ways to save time, improve quality, and lower cost. Look for ways to reinvent methods of doing the individual projects.

Determine ways to monitor program. You will need a regular schedule of meetings and reports to stay on top of the process. Plan them in advance and be sure to follow good meeting practice, such as always having an agenda.

One good tactic to both monitor and motivate progress is to make a wall chart. Take one large, empty wall and display PERT and Gantt charts on it. Mark all progress issues on the charts so that they are in view of all staff.

Motivate early action. On a portfolio of any size and complexity, one key tactic is to get started early. *Crunch time* may be inevitable, but you can minimize it if people start early.

5.4   Step 4: Prepare a PERT Chart for the Portfolio

Place the tasks from the work breakdown structure (WES) and the PERT-chart sequence (Fig. 2). You inserted two milestones: Start and Project Finish. As with all milestones, they will have a time estimate of zero. They help organize your chart. One task, Move-in week, is a must-start activity; it is already scheduled and you need to work around it. Most tasks have to be done in time for the move-in; the move-in tasks are done during the move-in (they have a start-to-start dependency relationship).

Remember, the decisions you make in laying out your PERT chart are strategic decisions that affect your project. One of Sarah's most important goals is to minimize the crunch time on this project. She followed two strategies in laying out her PERT chart.

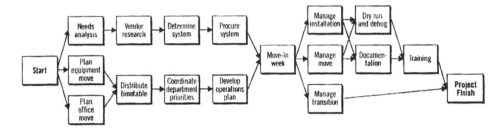

FIGURE 2 A PERT chart showing the sequence of tasks involved in the computer move.

1.   Frontloading: The more of this project you can get out of the way before the move-in date approaches, the better off you are. When managing a deadline-sensitive project with the possibility of unforeseen complications, put as much as possible up front.

2.   Build in lag: Schedule the project to allow as much free time as possible between the end of the tasks immediately preceding the move-in week and the move-in week itself. Internal lag time lowers risk and increases safety.

5.5   Step 5: Determine the Critical Path

Place time estimates on your PERT chart and determine the longest (critical) path. Identify available slack time. Slack time has several benefits.

First, slack is a way to lower risk. If you use the optional PERT time-estimating formula and calculate sigma (σ) for the paths, try to have 2σ of slack and lag available. This gives you a base 95% chance of reaching the deadline on time. If 2σ is unrealistic, take all you can get.

Second, slack sometimes gives you the opportunity to optimize resources. If you have paths with excessive slack (more than 2σ), look to see if you can reassign people and resources from tasks on that path to critical tasks. The noncritical tasks take longer, but that is okay as long as you still have slack. The critical tasks go faster, which improves your total project performance.

Our computer-center PERT chart contains some special situations that might affect your planning (Fig. 3).

Task slack versus path slack. The task, *Plan office move*, contains 1 week of task slack. That means it can finish 1 week late without delaying the start of the next task or the end of the project. (This is also called free slack). The entire task sequence from *Plan equipment move* through *Development operations plan* is scheduled to take 11 weeks.

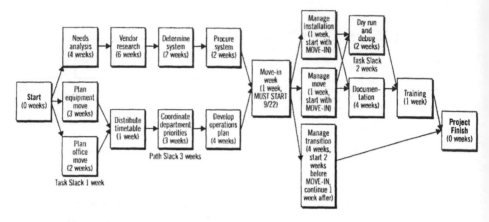

FIGURE 3 PERT chart for computer move showing task slack.

The corresponding critical-path section (*Needs analysis* through *Procure system*) takes 14 weeks. The difference, 3 weeks, is slack time.

Unlike the task slack situation, this 3-week period belongs equally to all tasks. If *Plan equipment move* is late 1 week, it delays the start of *Distribute timetable*, which delays the start of *Coordinate department priorities*, which delays the start of *Develop operations plan*, but it does not delay the start of move-in week! In other words, all the tasks in the sequence can be a total of 3 weeks late (in any combination) before affecting the start of the next task.

The 3 weeks in this case are also called total slack. *Plan equipment move* has 3 weeks of total slack, which is how late it can be without affecting the critical path. It has no free slack because any delay in the task delays the start of the next task in the path. *Develop operations plan* has the same 3 weeks of total slack but it also has 3 weeks of free slack—assuming all its predecessors finish on time!

Internal log. Move-in week is a must-start activity (fixed in time, rather than just following its predecessor task), but that does not automatically mean that the project start date is fixed. Working backward from the move-in week task, the critical path is 14 weeks to that point, which means that the project portfolio must start no later than the week of 6/16 to make the 9/22 deadline. However, this assumes that everything will go perfectly. A better strategy is to move the start day back. If you add 2 weeks of lag time to the critical path, backing the start date up to 6/2, you add that margin of safety to the portfolio (also lowering the crunch-time problem.)

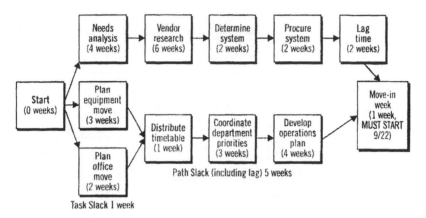

FIGURE 4   PERT chart showing lag times as an activity.

Figure 4 shows lag time as an activity. This is always a legitimate option, but it is not strictly necessary. Do it if it helps you keep better track of your project.

5.6   Step 6: Prepare a Gantt Chart for a Calendar Management

In managing an interdependent portfolio, you should put greater emphasis on the PERT chart, because it does a much better job of showing connections among the projects that make up the portfolio. As mentioned, displaying a wall-sized PERT chart can be a powerful tool to help keep people focused on the goal.

A Gantt chart, however, does provide advantages in any time-sensitive project, because it shows the activities in a calendar form (Fig. 5). There is no reason you must limit yourself to only one project view, especially if you are using project management software. Creating a Gantt chart from a PERT chart (or vice versa) is simply a matter of selecting the option from the menu and hitting "Print."

In this chart, you chose not to show the lag as a separate activity; that is why there are no critical tasks in the project until you reach the move itself. Even the tasks you previously designated as *critical* can be late up to 2 weeks before they jeopardize the start of the move.

As in the independent project portfolio, you can use the Gantt chart as a way to monitor progress in calendar terms. You should also update the PERT chart to see progress in terms of dependency relationships.

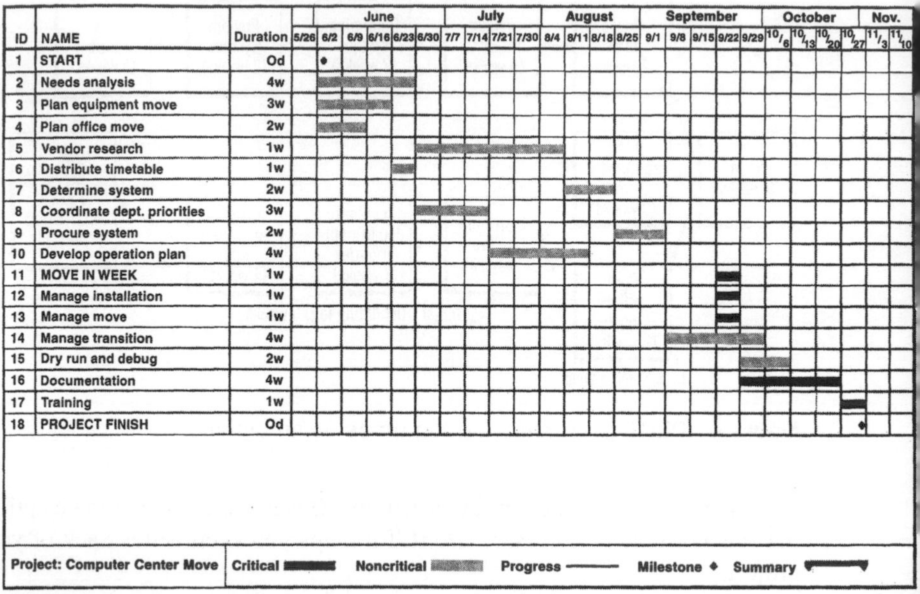

ID	NAME	Duration	June						July				August				September				October				Nov.	
			5/26	6/2	6/9	6/16	6/23	6/30	7/7	7/14	7/21	7/30	8/4	8/11	8/18	8/25	9/1	9/8	9/15	9/22	9/29	10/6	10/13	10/20	10/27	11/3	11/10
1	START	0d	◆																								
2	Needs analysis	4w																									
3	Plan equipment move	3w																									
4	Plan office move	2w																									
5	Vendor research	1w																									
6	Distribute timetable	1w																									
7	Determine system	2w																									
8	Coordinate dept. priorities	3w																									
9	Procure system	2w																									
10	Develop operation plan	4w																									
11	MOVE IN WEEK	1w																									
12	Manage installation	1w																									
13	Manage move	1w																									
14	Manage transition	4w																									
15	Dry run and debug	2w																									
16	Documentation	4w																									
17	Training	1w																									
18	PROJECT FINISH	0d																									◆

Project: Computer Center Move — Critical ▬ Noncritical ▨ Progress —— Milestone ◆ Summary ▼▬

FIGURE 5 Gantt chart for computer center move.

5.7 Step 7: Prepare a Control Point Identification Chart for Critical, High-Risk Activities

The control point identification chart is a tool to help you identify something that might go wrong—or right—that would be out of the ordinary. Use a brainstorming session for each project in your portfolio to identify potential problems and opportunities. Then, identify early warning points, and list possible solutions and strategies (Fig. 6).

Project/Task	What could go right/wrong?	How/when would I know?	What would I do?

FIGURE 6 Control point identification chart.

The planning of issues for the interdependent portfolios are similar to those of other projects; however, it is important that you adjust your perspective to the special issues that make this type of project different. By taking into account the differences in size and internal relationships, you will be well on the way to success.

6 HOW TO MANAGE MULTIPLE PROJECTS IN AN INTERDEPENDENT PORTFOLIO

"Making a good plan and thinking about strategic issues is obviously important," Sarah observes. "I still wonder about the actual management, however. What if things don't go as expected? What about outside pressures? Will my team stay motivated? In other words, how do I manage the portfolio and achieve the goal?"

Sarah's concerns include:

- How can I keep my team focused on the goal without either panicking or getting distracted?
- How can I make sure my team chooses the right balance between ongoing work and this important move?
- How can I keep crunch time from becoming a disaster?

As with our other project portfolios, the management phase is different from the planning phase. Take a look at the special issues involved in managing a successful interdependent project portfolio.

6.1 Definitions

Here are the key terms you will need to know:

An *escalating objective* is a project situation in which the agreed-upon objective grows during the process (also called *mission creep*).

A *change order* is a change in the project objective requested by the customer (internal or external).

The *Godzilla principle* states that if you catch a problem early, it is easier to solve.

The *pop-up principle* states that when you solve a problem, the solution itself usually contains a problem.

6.2 The Art of Managing the Interdependent Portfolio

The process of managing multiple projects is additive: you need to do all the elements of managing the task-oriented portfolio and the independent portfolio and then add the special features of the interdependent portfolio on top.

The interdependent project portfolio is defined as a large project with major divisions important enough to be considered projects in their own right. The first key to managing this type of portfolio is not to allow any individual project to fail without fundamentally compromising the success of the portfolio.

The Smithsonian National Air and Space Museum was both a large project and an interdependent project portfolio. Each individual exhibit gallery clearly qualified as a project; each aircraft restored was a project; the construction of the building itself was a project. The failure of any project within the portfolio would compromise and possibly destroy the success of the entire portfolio. For example, if all the exhibit galleries had been successfully completed but the building construction had been delayed, the museum would not have opened on time. Essentially, the quality of the galleries would have been irrelevant if there had been no building in which to put them.

As Ed Harris said in the movie *Apollo 13*, "Failure is not an option."

6.3   Your Role as Portfolio Manager

From a management point of view, one of your critical responsibilities is to help your individual project managers stay focused on the goal. It is all too easy to become distracted by the individual requirements of a project within the portfolio and pursue them in a way that is detrimental to the interests of the portfolio as a whole.

What is best for an individual project in the portfolio is not necessarily best for the portfolio itself. For example, in the portfolio involving the computer center move, there is an obvious conflict between *Manage transition* and *Manage installation*. The manager of the transition has a primary responsibility for ensuring that critical functions run smoothly.

6.4   No-Fail Budgeting in the Interdependent Portfolio

Another key management issue in the interdependent project portfolio is resources allocation. Given the reality that resources are always limited and opportunity is unlimited, you must allocate the available resources to the projects in your portfolio. To ensure that you meet your most important objectives, you should allocate resources in a two-pass process.

First, identify the minimum acceptable performance level for each project in the portfolio and the resources necessary to achieve that minimum level. This is called *no-fail budgeting*. Allocate the minimum resources. If you have no more resources, the minimum is now the best you can do.

Second, allocate any remaining resources to achieve maximum portfolio achievement. Do not allocate resources evenly across your projects, because some of your projects do not improve portfolio quality once they have achieved the minimum. For example, in construction, no one paints the inside of the drywall, because it does not add to the quality of the building as a whole.

6.5 Coping with the Escalating Objective

Certain management problems can affect any manager in any situation at any time; however, one particular nightmare for the project portfolio manager is the circumstance of *escalating project objectives*. This occurs when the initial project objective, although properly approved, starts creeping upward as the project progresses. Time compresses, budgets shrink, and performance criteria increase.

Changes in projects lead to *change orders*. Whether change orders are formal or informal, they tend to be common to project management experience. You must learn how to cope with the change.

Try the following techniques, especially at the beginning of your project:

- Do the entire triple-constraints process. This may be the source of some problems if you have not fully negotiated and explored the triple constraints. Too many project portfolio managers neglect identifying the underlying project reason and the management, organizational, and customer issues that influence it.
- Identify the players. As part of the triple-constraints process, remember that a project has a central objective and, often, secondary objectives that are the related interests of all those who form the project constituency. You must discover who your project constituency is, interview him, learn his goals and perceptions, and integrate as many of those goals as possible without compromising the central objective. Do not forget personal as well as external motivations.
- Put it in writing, and shop it around. A good goal is a written goal. Make sure people know the goal in advance and in writing, and have an early opportunity to challenge that goal. It can be difficult to negotiate a workable compromise, but it is much easier than coping with a late-project major change order that virtually guarantees disaster. People can change a written goal; however, it is harder than changing an unwritten goal. As a famous Hollywood mogul said, ''An oral contract is worth the paper it's printed on.''
- Show others your plans, schedules, and budgets. You cannot assume that others in management will understand the consequences of a proposed project change as well as you do. Document the

consequences of a change clearly and objectively. When a change is requested, print out a current plan and budget. Next, integrate the change into the existing schedule and print out the revised plan and budget. Third, brainstorm the most proactive ways of achieving the new goal. Revise the schedule and budget to accommodate the change. Print that out. Now, go to management or the customer. Show them the three versions: (1) no change, (2) integrate the change and proceed, and (3) best ideas to integrate the change while achieving the time, budget, and performance goals. Ask for suggestions. You may still have to make the change, but you may better negotiate the corresponding changes in time, budget, and performance.

- Build change into the process. In many projects, the nature of the work makes change orders inevitable. It may not be possible to identify all the real needs until work has progressed to a certain point. In this case, you need to schedule change into the process. Set milestones in your project schedule for customer view and expectation development, tasks for integration of requirements changes, and redevelopment to accommodate changes. Build this into your initial schedule and budget. If it is inevitable, plan for it.

6.6 Problem-Solving Strategies

The first—and still the best—problem-solving strategy is to avoid the problem. Effective planning, including the control point identification chart, reduces both the number and severity of the project problems.

Here are a few additional pointers to help you in solving problems.

The Godzilla principle. In Japanese monster movies, there is frequently a scene where the monster du jour (Godzilla, Mothra, Gamora, and so on) is a cute baby monster. People say, "Oh, what a cute little monster!" Obviously, no urgency exists. They ignore the monster.

They wait until the monster is full-grown and busily stomping downtown Tokyo, then they shout, "What are we going to do!" The answer is, of course, nothing. When Godzilla is rampaging through downtown Tokyo, there is very little you can do about it. The best option is past.

On your projects, spend time on baby-monster patrol. Every time you find a little problem with the power to later grow into a big one, stomp on it at once.

There are three times when problem solving is possible: (1) when you first think of it, (2) when you first detect it, and (3) when it actually happens.

The rule of problem solving is, the closer you get to the problem, the fewer the options available to solve it.

If you are planning a summer picnic and rain is a possibility, you can schedule a rain date. You have solved the problem at the moment you thought of it.

Perhaps you missed that opportunity, but you heard a weather report forecasting rain a few days before the picnic. It is too late to recall the invitations and set up a rain date, so you rent a tent, increasing the cost. At least people will be dry. You have solved the problem when you first detected it.

Perhaps you do not watch the news, and you missed the weather report. You wake up the morning of the picnic and it is raining cats and dogs. Now you are madly scrambling for umbrellas, changing activities, and trying to keep the picnic from becoming a complete muddy ruin. You have solved the problem when it happens.

You cannot anticipate everything or solve every problem, but you can improve your problem-solving effectiveness by using this strategy.

Pop-up principle. Every time you solve a problem, something pops up.

Schedule a rain date for the picnic? New problems pop up, such as extra time, effort, and costs to book the site for a rain date, such as loss of perishable food and some loss of available guests on the second date.

Rent a tent? New problems occur: additional costs and activity cancellation.

Pop-ups do not invalidate a problem-solving strategy; they present one more challenge to overcome. When you come up with a solution to a problem, ask yourself "What are the pop-ups?" What negative consequences can arise from this solution? Sometimes, the negative consequences are minor, even insignificant. In that case, you can ignore the pop-up. Sometimes, the cure is worse than the disease. If the solution is worse than living with the problem, do not choose that particular solution. Sometimes, the negative consequences of the pop-up can be minimized. Look for ways to adjust the solution. Of course, this can create another pop-up!

Use the triple constraints. Every problem affects one or more of the triple constraints; that is what makes it a problem. A problem may be one of the following four types:

1. Time problem: tasks take longer than expected.
2. Budget problem: tasks cost more than expected.
3. Performance problem: tasks are not delivering the expected result.
4. Resource problem: resources are not available to do the work. This causes problems in one or more of the constraints.

Because the triple constraints are always in priority order, the seriousness of a problem depends on which constraint is affected. If a problem affects the driver, it is very serious and must be solved. If a problem affects the weak constraint, it may not be worth the effort required to solve it.

For the picnic, imagine you are thinking about renting a tent. If budget is the driver, the tent may cost too much. It is not an acceptable solution. If budget is the weak constraint, then extra cost may be irrelevant. Use the order of the constraints to determine the seriousness of problems, and use the flexibility in the weak constraints as a tool to help you solve them.

7 A FINAL WORD ABOUT MANAGING MULTIPLE PROJECTS

Futurist Alvin Toffler predicted that the concept of bureaucracy would give way to a new organizational strategy, the *ad-hocracy*. He might have been talking about project managers of single and multiple projects.

As a project manager, you traditionally have more responsibility than authority. In fact, you are often in a situation when you need the willing and voluntary cooperation of people over whom you have no authority to achieve your goals. You do this through persuasion, negotiation, planning, communication, and professionalism. You do this by developing your skills and knowledge. You do this by using the tools of project management and fitting them to the circumstances of your organization and your work.

When you do, you will find yourself fitting the traditional definition of a project manager: people responsible for doing something that has never been done before, for people who don't know what they want, who must first predict the unknown, make a plan to cope with the unforeseen, and execute the plan with too-limited resources that they do not control, and who are held completely responsible for the results, even if miracles are required.

You can do it. Good luck.

18

Program Management: A Key for Integrated Health Care Delivery Systems

Ken Jones and Jolene Weiskittel

> *I was myself last night, but I fell asleep on the mountain, and they've changed my gun, and every thing's changed, and I'm changed, and I can't tell what's my name, or who I am!*
> — "Rip Van Winkle," by Washington Irving

1   INTRODUCTION

Change is rocking the health care industry. Much like Rip Van Winkle's experience, it seems sudden, confusing, and sometimes frightening. The market forces for change are demanding high-quality care at reduced cost. In virtually every major metropolitan market, hospitals are consolidating while new competitors enter markets. Competition, market share, quality, and cost reduction are the focus of health care delivery systems today. The driver of this change is managed care.

This chapter presents the experience of The Health Alliance of Cincinnati and Ernst & Young LLP in establishing a program management office to manage a large portfolio of information technology projects. It describes the business

Adapted from the *Proceedings of the Project Management Institute 1997 Seminars and Symposium.*

drivers behind The Health Alliance, the need for significant new information technology investments, and it explores how program management has been implemented and its impact on the organization. Finally, lessons learned during the first year in operating the program management office are summarized.

2   THE DRIVERS OF CHANGE

In January 1995, The Health Alliance of Greater Cincinnati, a network of hospitals in the greater Cincinnati/northern Kentucky region, was formed. The Alliance began with Christ and University Hospitals, and later incorporated St. Luke Hospitals (mid 1995) and Jewish Hospitals (January 1996). The Alliance was created to position the member hospitals and physician organizations to compete under managed care as it evolves in the United States. Under managed care, insurance companies set the rates doctors, pharmacies, and hospitals can charge for services. This is a significant change in the economics of health care delivery and is forcing institutions to get much bigger to leverage economies of scale and drive down costs.

The formation of The Health Alliance was a first step in developing an integrated health care delivery network (IHDN) in Greater Cincinnati. As managed care takes over as the dominant method of health care financing in the United States, the IHDN will become the dominant form of health care delivery. Integrated health care delivery networks like The Health Alliance will compete aggressively for market share, and because of this market competition, will offer the promise of:

- Increased quality of services rendered
- Reduced costs
- Improved access to services
- Stronger physician support and training
- Improved operational efficiency
- Delivery of service by the system far beyond what any hospital could do individually

The key strategy for achieving these outcomes is to shift quickly and significantly to investments in information technology. Information systems are the critical component in enabling new organizational structures and care delivery processes. The objectives of these investments are to:

- Provide integrated care delivery systems
- Move patient information seamlessly among Alliance members
- Maintain a high level of patient confidentiality
- Consolidate financial management systems

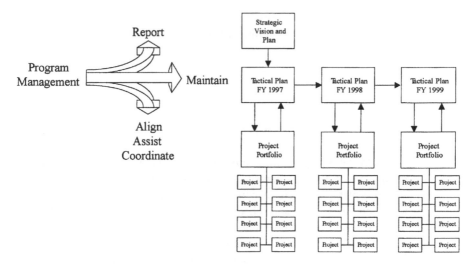

FIGURE 1   Project portfolio management.

- Consolidate system operations
- Implement enterprisewide networks
- Establish electronic data interchange with key suppliers and payers

Common systems and easy information exchange for care management and financial processes are central to the ability of The Health Alliance to reduce costs while maintaining high quality and patient satisfaction.

As if the imperative for market change were not sufficient, The Health Alliance, like most organizations, faced significant Year 2000 issues. These issues mandate a large number of system replacements or significant new investment in antiquated systems. Most of the Year 2000 corrective actions must be in place by the summer of 1999 to assure minimal interruption of services. The world that Rip Van Winkel faced when he woke up on the mountain is truly the world of health care today (Fig. 1).

3 POSITIONING FOR CHANGE

To meet the challenges of managed care, executive management concluded that significant new information systems investment was required. New systems were needed to support:

- Patient care systems (registration, utilization analysis, documentation, results/order entry, etc.)
- Alliance-wide ambulatory care

- Managed care systems
- Financial accounting, HR/payroll, materials management, and fixed assets
- Patient accounting
- Pharmacy management
- Infrastructure
- Decision support
- Enterprise master patient index

Once the scope of the change was understood, a 3-year information technology (IT) tactical implementation plan was developed and aligned with the strategic plan. For each year in the tactical plan, a portfolio of projects was identified, prioritized, and scheduled. As it became apparent that a large number of projects would be needed over the 3-year period, the issue of overall coordination and alignment became critical to achieving a successful outcome. One analysis of the situation indicated that under the status quo for managing projects, The Health Alliance could experience cost increases of 12% to 15% above planned capital outlays annually because of poor project performance and lower business benefits. To mitigate these risks, The Health Alliance embraced program management as a key component of its implementation strategy and created a Program Management Office (PMO) in the summer of 1996.

The PMO was chartered as a project with responsibilities to:

- Ensure project consistency through the establishment of planning, reporting, and knowledge-capture standards
- Monitor compliance with established program standards and recommend corrective actions as needed
- Coordinate the program's projects with other related initiatives in the areas of knowledge sharing, issues resolution, and work plan synchronization
- Provide overall control and coordination of program progress, quality, and performance

Promote efficiencies by providing shared administrative services

- Procedurally, the PMO is responsible for providing the following services to the project teams and executive management:
- Portfolio risk and performance analysis with recommendations
- Financial tracking and reporting
- Integrated planning and support

- Knowledge coordination
- Project management process training
- Risk and quality management
- Technology enablers for project control and project accounting

As it has evolved at The Health Alliance, program management reports how the overall program is performing to the strategic plan, maintains the alignment of the tactical plan to the strategic plan, and aligns, assists, and coordinates the actions of the project team to function within a portfolio of projects.

Overall, the PMO acts both as the role of coach and "cop." The PMO is the group of individuals whose goal is to make projects as successful as possible. This is accomplished by eliminating redundant tasks, providing a common technical infrastructure for project management, and assisting in all phases of plan development, performance, and conclusion. However, the PMO is also charged with enforcing the standards of the program. In this capacity, the PMO reports project performance that falls outside of expected norms and is proactive in working with project managers to clarify and correct deviations.

4 COORDINATING MULTIPLE PROJECT THREADS

With time to market and Year 2000 as critical drivers, projects have been sequenced in parallel threads of execution as much as possible. Parallel execution reduces elapsed project execution time, but it also increases the risk of poor project performance through reduced knowledge reuse, poor coordination, poor communication, inefficient deployment of resources, and duplication of effort. To keep the multiple parallel threads tied together as a coordinated group moving toward common objectives, the PMO acts as the agent to assure overall synchronization.

Program synchronization occurs on a periodic basis designed to detect problems early and provide a constant flow of information for executive decisioning. Each week, all projects report a balanced scorecard of project performance data, including project scope (financial, temporal, and deliverable) and project management process performance (issue management, change management, work plan management). The individual project reports are combined into a program dashboard report that uses colored indicators (red, yellow, green) to report project performance to executive management (Fig. 2).

Monthly, the PMO reports overall project portfolio performance to an IT Governance Board that reviews the program's financial performance and progress toward tactical goals. Issues that cannot be resolved at the project or program level are elevated to the Governance Board.

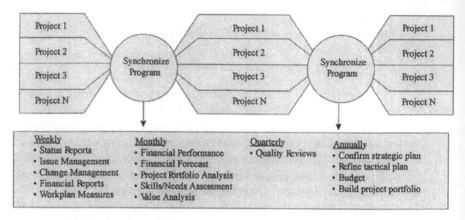

FIGURE 2   Synchronizing threads of project execution.

Quarterly, projects conduct process quality reviews. Each project receives a quality rating that measures 18 different aspects of the project's performance, as well as the effectiveness of project sponsorship. The quality review provides an opportunity for the project manager to gain perspectives from independent third parties. The review also gives the program manager the opportunity to identify systemic problems that may impact other projects.

A rolling 3-year tactical plan is updated annually. The process requires realignment of the tactical plan to the strategic business plan, tactical adjustments based on actual project performance and project reprioritization, and finally, identification of a new set of project objectives in the third year of the plan.

5   KEY TECHNOLOGY ENABLERS

Coordinating the financial and project information from a number of different teams at dispersed physical locations required tools to support project accounting and project management. Two key technology enablers were deployed by the PMO: (1) the Project Accounting System (PAS) and (2) the Program Workbench.

The PAS is a Microsoft Access-based application to track project financial data to the resource and deliverable level. The key unit of tracking is the project deliverable as defined and maintained in a deliverable breakdown structure (DBS). Using a DBS code and resource information, the program office is able to monitor compliance of vendors to contracts (timing and dollars), manage budget to actual performance, track commitments to projects separate from expenses incurred by projects, and report, on a near real-time basis, the financial performance of the project portfolio.

The Program Workbench is an application developed by Ernst & Young to support large project/program team environments. At the core of the Program Workbench is a set of Lotus Domino databases with Internet browsers (Netscape, Microsoft Internet Explorer, etc.) and the Lotus Notes client supported on the desktop. Program Workbench is designed to provide an integrated workgroup environment that supports virtually all aspects of project management control, reporting, and knowledge-sharing processes. The key components of Program Workbench are shown below.

5.1 Projects and People Management

This part of the application provides access to information concerning all initiatives, projects, and personnel working on projects at The Health Alliance. The initiative and project documents contain specific information such as goals, objectives, value propositions, and organization. The personnel forms allow users to enter, update, and manage information about themselves and their teams.

5.2 Project Control

On a day-to-day basis, this is the most widely used portion of the application. Project control includes:

- Weekly status reporting (individual and project)
- Issue management
- Change management
- Work plan actuals reporting
- Consolidated resource forecasting

All forms to support these key project management processes are created, stored, and communicated electronically. The tool interacts with Microsoft Project for work plan development and scheduling.

5.3 Deliverables

The deliverables management repository provides centralized storage and sharing of project outputs. The repository allows sponsors, the project team, and project teams not directly involved with a project to view and use deliverables. The two primary functions of the database are to:

- Share and store knowledge for project teams
- Allow all Health Alliance personnel access to the completed deliverables

5.4 Standards

The standards define the "rules of the road" for all projects. A readily available body of program standards helps new team members become familiar with the program and builds a common understanding of program and project management processes. Some examples are:

- Frequency of status reports
- Quality assurance measures and processes
- Issue management guidelines
- Issue escalation procedures

6 IMPACT OF PROGRAM MANAGEMENT

Looking back on our experience since July 1996, program management has made a number of impacts on the organization.

1. The PMO was able to quickly implement a project accounting system that provides project financial performance data on a weekly basis. The project accounting information leads the general ledger by as much as 120 days and supports a level of detail tracking and analysis that is not currently available in The Health Alliance financial management systems. Timely and detailed project financial information is critical to effective decision making.

2. Use of automated tools for project control (status reporting, issues management, change management, deliverable management, work plan management) went from almost 0 to 65 active users. The key success factors in gaining system acceptance and utilization were:

- Commitment by project managers and executive sponsors to use the tools
- Support for HTML (Netscape) clients
- Application training
- Project management awareness and skill-building training

3. Program management became recognized as having a positive impact on IT project performance and is beginning to have an impact at the executive leadership level outside of IT. Success in program management for IT is generating interest in the same kind of approach in other change efforts.

4. Executive decisions (as they are affected by IT projects) are now more likely to be based on data rather than individual perceptions. Prior to having detailed project data, project decisions were based largely on subjective criteria. Now, managers look at project management performance, project

financial performance, resource deployments, and the project queue when making decisions.

    5. A portfolio approach has provided an understanding of where individual project performance stands in relation to the larger view. Many projects are important, but some are more important. Project priorities can shift, depending on technical, organizational, or environmental factors. The portfolio approach allows management to "see the forest" and exert more effective management control.

    6. As the program matures, new sets of issues start to arise. Now that a number of projects have been completed, the task of organizing the project outputs into knowledge objectives becomes more critical. The teams are comfortable using a workgroup environment and are capable of sharing knowledge effectively. The tools must continue to evolve to support a more sophisticated knowledge management and sharing process.

7 LESSONS LEARNED

As we continue to improve our program management processes, we have identified a number of "lessons learned." By incorporating these lessons learned into our ongoing processes, we hope to improve the program's overall performance and mitigate risk. Some of the key lessons learned are:

    1. The Health Alliance was formed from four separate organizations. In many cases, The Health Alliance was a single organization in name only and not able to move at the pace dictated by the tactical plans. Infrastructure building projects are generally less threatening and less visible politically and are, therefore, "safer" in the initial execution of the tactical plan. More visible projects that touch core business processes should have added contingency for time and more emphasis and investment in organizational change management.

    2. Technology for project accounting and project control is critical to enabling executive decision-making and project management processes. The overhead to support this technology tends to be ongoing throughout the life of the program. You must commit resources (human, financial, and technology) to the program technology.

    3. Plan on significant and ongoing investment in project management training and skill building. Training needs to be appropriate to the level of the individual. Use just-in-time and reinforcement training to help teams improve specific areas of performance (status reporting, issue management, scheduling, etc.).

    4. Resistance to change was greater than anticipated, which resulted in incorrect assumptions on pace of change. People's ability to participate in

and support change is a larger constraint on project and program performance than is the availability of financial resources.

5.   Program management and project management is not only educating IT but also educating the business unit sponsor and the end user. A greater degree of project discipline is required from IT; business users need to learn how to become partners in the process. As partners, they share responsibility for the outcome, not just final acceptance or rejection of the end product.

6.   Use an implementation team to focus on bringing up the Program Management Office. If possible, the PMO should be started before other projects are launched to establish the common process and technology environment. A focused implementation team can work out the logistics of the program office, perform initial training, and establish the initial set of program standards quickly. Projects that launch before the PMO is ready are harder to pull back under the program umbrella.

7.   Run the PMO as a project. It should have a project charter, work plan, and required deliverables. As a project, the PMO is subject to all the standards established for any other project in the program.

8   CONCLUSION

Rip Van Winkle eventually adjusted to his new environment. He embraced the strange new world that he encountered and actually found that world preferable to the one he had left behind. The IT organization at The Health Alliance is significantly different today than what it was a year ago. Project management processes are better understood, a number of projects have been successfully planned and completed, and components of the future state information systems are starting to be deployed and benefit the organization.

In health care today, far-reaching change is upon us. The Health Alliance is aggressively moving to embrace this change. Program management provides the structure, coordination, and information needed to rapidly implement and achieve a functioning, competitive, and growing integrated health care delivery system that can fully realize the goals of decreased cost and exceptional quality.

19

Managing Multiple Projects in Large Information Systems Organizations

Steve Yager

1 INTRODUCTION

It is useful to review briefly the history of project management in the information systems (IS) field before proceeding with a discussion of the issues involved with multiproject management. Contrary to what seems to be the commonly held belief, project management is not a new undertaking for the IS industry. In truth, IS was one of the first to attempt to implement the project management discipline and project management software in the late 1960s and early 1970s. The concept of identifying "projects" and tracking the status of project tasks and the effort expended on them has been in place in most IS organizations since then. Compared with the sophisticated application of project management techniques in other industries, such as utilities, petrochemicals, and aerospace, however, IS has not been in the vanguard. Information systems project management, for the most, has been considered a budgeting exercise in the planning phase, and a time keeping effort in the tracking stage. Information systems did not embrace the critical path concept as quickly as did their counterparts in other industries. One fundamental reason for this

Adapted from the *Proceedings of the Project Management Institute 1997 Seminars and Symposium.*

was that the early project management software systems were particularly oriented to managing large, complex, single projects. Information systems very often did not even participate in the selection of project management software for other departments, even though this software was going to operate on IS-maintained computers, predominately mainframes. The evolution of project management software to today's client/server systems has finally produced tools that can be readily applied to large IS organizations with hundreds of projects running simultaneously.

2 INFORMATION SYSTEMS MULTIPROJECT ENVIRONMENT

There are some fundamental differences between the so-called traditional project management applications and today's IS application. These are:

1. IS applications are fundamentally multiproject.
2. Both project and non-project (maintenance) work must be planned and tracked.
3. The major emphasis is on resource utilization, rather than task and project completion.
4. Many IS projects are abandoned before completion.
5. There are many repetitive types of projects.
6. Project work is budgeted, usually on an annual basis.

The fact that the very nature of a large IS organization is that it handles many projects simultaneously is why there is so much potential for payoff in implementing project management techniques properly. On major complex projects, such as in the aerospace industry, external factors most often affect project timetables. Managers do not have as much opportunity to control project priorities. In the IS field, managers can actually use the project management data they receive to make adjustments to priorities and assignments to accomplish their business objectives. But the most critical concept to grasp in managing multiple projects for IS is that rather than assigning resources to tasks, IS managers assign tasks to resources. This is the reverse of the traditional project management technique in which more emphasis is placed on the project/task than the resource/task. Information systems multiproject management is actually "resource utilization" management. This difference perhaps accounts for the lack of ready adoption of the critical path method and earlier implementation of project management software based on CPM.

Information systems managers have to answer three critical questions in the multiproject environment:

1. Are resources assigned to the highest-priority work?
2. Are my resources used fully?
3. Are my resources completing their assignments on time and within budget?

The emphasis is on "resources" because, unlike their counterparts in other industries, IS managers don't have the luxury of being able to add 20 programmers or analysts for two months to complete a critical project. The main goal of the IS manager in a multiproject environment is to adjust his resource assignments to accomplish the most critical tasks, in a situation in which estimates are not always accurate, external factors do come into play (such as project cancellations), and there is a sizable amount of "non-project" work to accomplish. Proper implementation of project management techniques and software can greatly improve the manager's and organization's efficiency in such an environment.

3 IMPLEMENTING PROJECT MANAGEMENT

One of the first steps to take is an assessment of the project management maturity of the IS group. Much has been written about the fact that more than 80% of software development organizations are classified at the lowest (Level 1) on the Software Engineering Institute's Capability Maturity Model. It is my opinion that the real goals of assessing an organization's project management maturity should be:

- So that the organization knows what its current capabilities are before attempting to implement a formalized multiproject management approach.
- As a measuring guideline to check on future progress. Are we really making progress in managing our project?

It is recommended that this assessment be formal and that it be done before implementing a project management software system. This is critical because project management software does not cure process-related problems. The implementation of formal project management techniques is part of managing a fundamental change in the business processes of an organization. Investment in high-technology hardware, software, and systems alone is inadequate. Meaningful changes occur only when people are committed to and capable of performing new roles in a new business environment.

The formal assessment should consist of three parts:

1. Structured interviews
2. Individual self-assessment

3. A workshop with the team leading the project management implementation and operational staff to obtain consensus.

What this assessment does is measure the organization's project management competence at a given point in time. Some of the key competence issues to be measured and questions to be asked might be:

3.1 Skill Levels

- Is there a formalized skill assessment process?
- Is there a program to develop new skills?
- Is there a clear understanding of the types of skills required for particular tasks?

3.2 Resource Assignment Competence

- Do managers have awareness of available capacity once project plans are approved?
- At what point are specific resource/task assignments made?
- What is the review/approval process for resource assignment?

Figure 1 is a simple diagram showing the results of such an assessment.

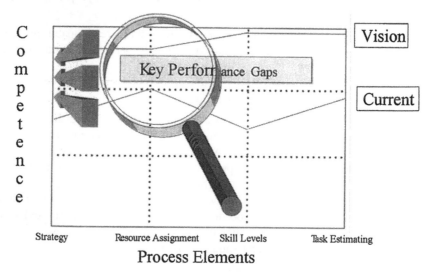

FIGURE 1 Resource assignment competence.

One of the key items on which consensus should be reached is the "vision" or "where would we like to be?" Properly done, the project management competence assessment will show many areas for potential improvement. Just as all projects can't be handled at once, improving an organization's project management maturity in all key areas takes time. So it is important that the entire organization has a plan that is understood by all concerning what will be the key focus areas for the future. It is recommended that this assessment process be repeated at regular intervals so that management has a clear picture of where the organization stands relative to the "vision." Another clear benefit of the assessment process is that it will show progress being made as a formal project management process is implemented.

4 THE PROCESS CONTROL GROUP

One question which can be raised is who should lead the project management maturity assessment. It is my recommendation that this effort be run by a Process Control Group. The inherent multiproject, repetitive types of projects, project/nonproject environment of a large IS organization makes the establishment of a Process Control Group almost essential to successfully implementing project management. This responsibility can be combined with others in a project or program support office if desired, but the critical factor is to recognize that project management implementation is about managing changes in business "processes."

In addition to conducting an initial and regular assessment of project management maturity, this group charter should include:

1. Standardizing the procedures for scheduling, statusing, and reporting both project and nonproject work
2. Piloting new processes before general implementation.

5 MULTIPROJECT AND PROGRAM-BASED

As has been noted earlier, IS organizations are inherently multiproject. In today's business process re-engineering climate, they are also inherently "program-based." Figure 2 illustrates this.

A *program* is a collection of related projects that facilitate the realization of corporate strategic business objectives. *Program management* is that set of management activities and processes that facilitates the translation, conversion, prioritization, balancing, and integration of new strategic initiatives within the context of the current organization and planned time and cost

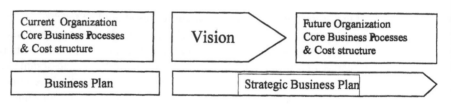

FIGURE 2   IS organizations are inherently multiproject and program based.

constraints, thereby minimizing risk and maximizing benefit to the organization. Large IS organizations support the program management activities of the corporation with their multiple project operations.

6   THE TECHNOLOGY

A successful project management implementation in a large IS department will require installation and operation of project/resource management software. What are some of the key requirements of such software for this particular environment?

1. Usability
2. Standardized, open database
3. Multiproject and multiuser capability
4. Security functions
5. Resource management orientation
6. Template capability
7. Simplified statusing mechanism

Usability is probably the most critical factor to a successful implementation of project management software. Every single member of the IS group will be a user of the system. The system should be adaptable to the organization's way of doing business, not the reverse. One of the principal reasons that IS did not embrace earlier project management software was that it was cumbersome to use and not oriented to the inherent multiproject, resource-focused needs of IS managers. An important point to emphasize is that members of the IS organization perform many different roles; the same user interface doesn't have to be used by all. In fact, a project management system that offers a role-based or customizable user interface has many advantages regarding acceptance by the user community. Usability can best be judged, not by how flashy the graphical user interface (GUI) is, but how oriented the interface is to the particular user's responsibility. Not every user will be producing bar chart graphics from the system, so not every user should be exposed to a fundamental bar chart interface. The second requirement is the use of a standard, open database as the project management repository. Because most IS organization's have chosen a commercially available database management system for other corporate applications, there is no reason not to use the same database for project management information. One of the latest trends resulting from the business process re-engineering impact on corporate culture is a move to ''managing by projects'' as a core business philosophy. This concept treats project management information as a strategic corporate resource, just like financial and human resource data. The general availability of enterprise-wide project management systems based on standard, open database architectures provides a convenient mechanism to corporations moving to the ''management by projects'' philosophy.

The ability to handle multiple projects and multiple users is also key to IS. There should be no practical limits on the number of projects that the project management system can handle. It should be recognized that there will be performance differences when running queries or reports against hundreds of projects, which should be extremely fast, versus a complex resource analysis of the same number of projects. It should also be understood that few team members need to perform such analysis, whereas many may need to run reports. Another factor that should be evaluated before choosing a system is the flexibility of the identification system for projects, tasks, resources, and codes. This is a key area in which the project management system can adapt to the IS ways of doing business rather than vice versa. An IS organization needs an enterprise-wide project management system, which means a true capability of handling multiple users. A purely desktop-based system could never be implemented for this reason. Users need accurate and timely project/resource data and can't wait for another user to free up a locked project on his desktop. It is in the area of handling multiple users that today's project management software systems offer different approaches. Some restrict project access to a single user at a time, just as the pure desktop approach does. Others allow unlimited access with the consequent potential for lack of change control, and some offer a flexible middle ground, with access control for certain functions and open reporting access.

This brings us to the next key requirement; namely, security. As noted above, there are many project management roles in the IS environment. Consequently, there should be functionality that allows an administrator to control who has access to what data and the type of access they have. In the project management field, this situation is more complex than simply read/write privileges at a file or record level. Consider a resource working on a project and the project manager both need write access to update certain status data on tasks. The project manager, however, by the simple act of changing the relationship between two tasks with the resultant downstream effect on all other in-progress and planned tasks on the project, affects much more data. What is needed for this environment is a combination of data-level security and functional security, which can be specified by individual user. The data-level security controls what projects and resources a user has access to (including whether the user even knows of the project's existence), whereas the functional security controls what functions (analysis, mass updating, task progressing, etc.) the user can perform on the particular project/resource. The administrative effort that is required to implement such a security mechanism should not be underestimated, but this effort will result in smooth operation of the project management system.

There are many repetitive types of projects in IS work, so it makes sense to use a template approach to project planning and to implement project management software that supports the template concept. Ideally, once the major project templates have been established, a project manager should be able to construct his detail project plans in short order. The template functionality should have a mass updating/editing capability to enable this. Consideration should also be given to assigning the initial creation of the project templates to the Process Control Group mentioned earlier.

Resource orientation is probably the next most important requirement (after usability) when implementing a project management system in IS. The fundamental philosophy for IS managers is to maximize utilization of their limited resources. So the project management software must approach the problem in this way also. Tasks are assigned to resources and, therefore, data entry should be structured in this fashion. As a manager, I need to know:

- Who hasn't reported project effort (timesheets)?
- Where and when is my available capacity?
- What is the effect of a transfer of one of my resources?
- Can I substitute resources with similar skills?

It should be possible to obtain this information in a timely way and, ideally, without running reports. Most IS managers would prefer to see answers in an on-line query rather than a report. Most would also prefer exception-based reporting, being notified perhaps by a programmable "agent" when a deviation to plan or budget occurs within some limits they can establish and control. Another important "resource oriented" consideration is the resource analysis results presented by the project management software. The IS multiple project environment is one of constant change, and managers should recognize that the resource analysis results obtained from today's project management software give guidance to a manager for planning his resource assignments. None gives a 100% perfectly optimized answer. Adjustments can be and should be made by the responsible manager. One of the best approaches to this problem is the "rolling wave concept." Because the most critical projects and tasks are those that are either under way or in the near term, detailed resource assignment planning for those should be the focus. As work progresses, the analysis time frame can be moved along.

The final key requirement that should be considered when implementing project management software is a simplified method of statusing resource effort and task progress. Because the analysis produced by any project management system depends on the timeliness and accuracy of the progress data, it must be easy for the users to enter this data. They must see the system as an aid to them, not a burden! The preferred status mechanism is moving to automated time tracking systems that tie to the project management database. This is a natural occurrence as most IS organizations already have some form of timesheet system implemented for chargeback purposes. As part of the implementation process, consideration should be given to either enhancing the current timesheet system to allow task status data to be entered or implementing a new time tracking system. The commercially available systems do offer many advantages, including automatic filling in of project and task data based on planned work, multiple approval levels, chargeback interfaces, and web-enabled timesheets.

One common problem raised by those attempting to implement multiproject management in an IS organization is that there may not be any detailed project plans that can be used as templates. In other words, no formal project management history exists. In this case, consideration should be given to implementing a data collection effort, first by using any new or enhanced timesheet system. After several months of operation in this manner, sufficient data will be available to begin pilot project planning system operation.

7 CONCLUSION

Large-scale IS organizations present one of the best opportunities for implementing project management techniques that can show real results. Because every staff member is a project management system user, the project environment has so many projects, and changes occur so frequently, the implementation requires careful planning. Serious consideration should be given to the aforementioned Process Control Group concept and, most importantly, the pilot project roll-out approach. It is unrealistic to think that an enterprise-wide implementation will be accomplished in two months.

20

Human Resource Allocation in a Multiproject Research and Development Environment

Martien H. A. Hendricks, Bas Voeten, and Leon H. Kroep

1 INTRODUCTION

Ultra short time-to-market and low costs of projects require effective and efficient project-oriented organizations. As progress in projects is not always what is foreseen and new projects need to be started up all of a sudden during the year because of fast changing results, for example, competitors, an adequate human resource allocation process is essential. Allocating people to projects in multiproject environments is difficult and often faces problems. Important in this process is the coupling of day-to-day planning for each individual to the long-term business plan.

Our study on how to optimize an existing resource allocation process in a large research and development (R&D) organization pointed out that five elements are vital in the set-up of an adequate resource allocation process. A central element is the so-called medium-term-resource-allocation. The main output of the medium-term resource allocation is a "rough-cut capacity planning" that shows what projects will be active for the coming months, including a rough allocation of the resources for each project.

Adapted from the *International Journal of Project Management*, 1999.

2 MULTIPROJECT ENVIRONMENT

In research and development organizations, human knowledge is the most important and scarce resource. Allocating the right human resources to a project is vital. The more projects that are involved and the more specific knowledge that is needed in every project, the more important, but also the more difficult, is the allocation process. In many R&D organizations, the matrix structure is commonly used (Fig. 1). According to the literature, as well as in practice, the methods used for resource allocation in such matrix structure are various.

Most organizations are looking for an material requirements planning (MRP)-like system based upon Bills of Materials in which projects are treated in the same way as goods that can be ordered with a certain delivery time. Therefore, everyone begins by looking at integrating their present planning system for single-project situations that occur on a day-to-day basis. They want to consolidate the data of all current and future projects with one push on a button while, on the other hand, the horizon is extended from short term to medium term. Because of the great uncertainty in the planning of projects in an R&D environment, the detailed task planning is only useful when updated frequently. When not up to date, planning is useless. Therefore *all* activities need to be entered into the system on a *detailed* level; otherwise the outcome is too unreliable. Also, new projects that may be activated in the portfolio of projects have to be entered in such a detailed way.

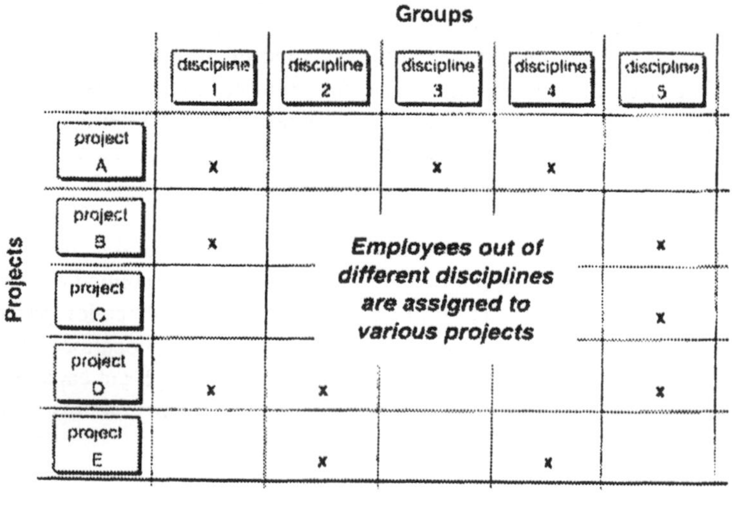

FIGURE 1   Multiproject situation in a matrix organization.

2.1 Resource Allocation Methods

During the last years, several authors wrote on the subject of resource allocation for projects. These articles focused mainly on a method for the short-term resource allocation: a model for day-to-day planning and priorities is given. The articles present a theoretical review, and implementation issues are not mentioned. Pillai and Tiwari (1995) mention a resource allocation for a longer period than short-term level, but the short-term resource allocation is missing. In 1994, a ''rough-cut project and portfolio planning'' was published by Platje et al. In this method, the planning and control cycles for single projects and the portfolio of projects is made (Fig. 2).

2.2 Rough-Cut Project and Portfolio Planning

In 1994, we implemented the concept of the rough-cut project and portfolio planning in a young R&D organization that had grown very fast, with 200 professionals in various disciplines working in 80 different projects. The allocation process was designed in such a way that every quarter an inventory was made on a proposed project portfolio by using simple resource claim and resource offer spreadsheets in the matrix organization (Figs. 3 and 4). This provided a quick and global overview of the requested project portfolio. Each claim and each offer was made clear by a percentage of workers needed for the next quarter. The claims by the project leaders needed to be discussed with the group leaders. By doing this, the rough-cut project and

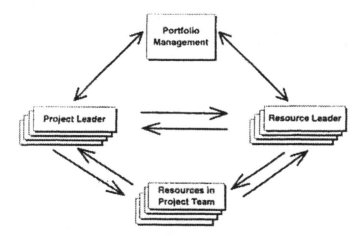

FIGURE 2 Portfolio planning process in multiproject organization.

Claims of the Project Leaders
Medium-Term Resource Allocation for 1st Quarter of 1997
100 = 100% of the specified person needed during the whole quarter

	project 1	project 2	project 3	project 4	project 5	project 6	project 7	project 8	TOTAL CLAIM	available	difference
Total	500	260	270	310	165	415	270	480	2670	2400	-270
project scatter factor	2.4	2.7	3.3	3.5	6.1	2.4	2.6	1.5			
Development	400	220	215	285	125	245	230	340	2060	1800	-260
Mechanical	140	60	80	115	20	40	80	130	665	450	-215
Hendriks, M.	30		30					50	110	100	-10
Wolff	60	60		65	10		80	80	355	100	-255
Clauser				25		40			65	100	35
Pollart	50		50		10				110	50	-60
Manuael			25						25	100	75
Electrical	85	30	80	40	35	95	20	70	455	400	-55
Broadhead	20			10	10		20		60	100	40
Castellana	65		40	20	10	80		60	275	100	-175
Goldstein		10	40	10	10				70	100	30
Loutfy		20		5	15		10		50	100	50
Fault analysis	125	100	40	120	50	40	110	80	665	600	-65
Michelsen	55		30						85	100	15
Noonan					20		70		90	100	10
Plaumann		40		30	40		80		190	100	-90
Ransley	20		10	50		10			90	100	10
Wilkes		50	40			20			110	100	-10
Voeten	50	10			10	10	10	10	100	100	0
Engineering	100	40	55	25	40	170	40	140	610	600	-10
System	50	30	15	10	20	70	20	60	275	350	75
Kroep	20		15	10			10		55	50	-5
Wismer	30	30				20			80	100	20
Larson					20	50		60	130	100	-30
Verhagen						10			10	100	90
Software	50	10	40	15	20	100	20	80	335	250	-85
Pietersen	40		20		10	50	20	80	220	100	-120
Slepers	10	10		15	10	10			55	100	45
vacancy software			20			40			60	50	-10

FIGURE 3   An example of the collected resource claims.

portfolio planning was a tool to have the project leaders contact the group leaders in a structured way. Also, management was forced to decide on what projects were placed in the portfolio and decide on the allocation of the resources. Without such a quarterly rough-cut capacity planning, the decisions on the portfolio were made too late and owing to the pressure of all days,

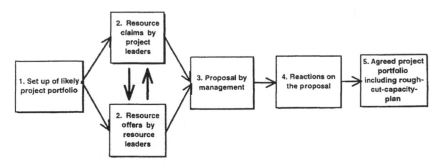

FIGURE 4   Flow chart of medium-term resource allocation.

often no time was left for a rough resource discussion between project leaders and group leaders.

3   FIVE ELEMENTS

In 1996, we conducted a study on how this rough-cut capacity planning method could be further improved. A great number of small projects were not explicitly looked at, so big projects got almost all the resources. Furthermore, the link to the day-to-day resource allocation, answering whether resource X needed to work on project A today and on project B tomorrow afternoon, was very weak.

In our study, we found that five elements are vital for human resource allocation in multi project situations. These five elements are:

1.   Long-term resource allocation
2.   Medium-term resource allocation
3.   Short-term resource allocation
4.   Links
5.   Feedback

The relationship between these five elements us shown in Figure 5. By using these elements in a correct way, this allocation method gives an organization a flexible day-to-day planning based on and in line with the business plan.

3.1   Long-Term Resource Allocation

Seeing that a certain discipline within an R&D organization is understaffed and determining the moment that such a discipline is staffed appropriately takes several months at least. Therefore, a long-term plan of the needed resources is required. A long-term plan is based on the business plan that speci-

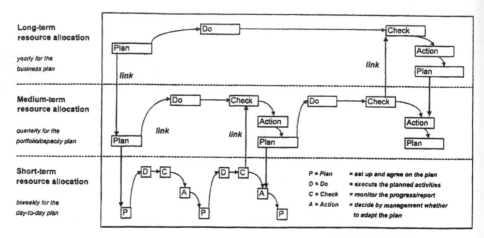

FIGURE 5 Links between the various resource allocation processes.

fies what the needs are for each discipline, at least for the coming year, and is translated into yearly budgets for the departments and groups. Distribution of the resource budgets must give a rough indication of the needed efforts of a discipline. A discipline in which efforts will decrease during the coming years must get more resources and, therefore, an increasing budget.

3.2 Medium-Term Resource Allocation

A periodic review of the project portfolio is needed. Using day-to-day planning for this purpose seems to be undesirable as it often is very unstable. In contrast, the project portfolio must be more or less stable. Planning the portfolio once a year can be effective, but when we look at development organizations in practice, the time between reviews is too long. Changes in the portfolio within a year are inevitable. Therefore, a new level of resource allocation must be set up to determine the project portfolio. The main input for this medium-term resource allocation is the long-term resource allocation. The output must be in line with the short-term resource allocation (Table 1).

The main characteristics of the medium-term resource allocation are:

- The contents of the *project portfolio*. The medium-term resource allocation can be a good tool to provide a link between the budget and day-to-day planning when the right projects are chosen. Therefore, the first result of the medium term must be the contents of the portfolio.

TABLE 1 Three Resource Allocation Processes with Their Specific Goals

Resource allocation process	Purpose	Output	Frequency	Horizon
Long term	Needed capabilities for accomplishing the business plan	• Department plan, budget per capability	Yearly	5 years
Medium term	Rough cut capacity planning for the project portfolio	• Portfolio check, which projects must be executed • Decision rules for group leaders • Analyses of the effects of the milestones of the projects (changes in targets) • Agreed rough allocation as input for the short-term resource allocation		
Short term	Operational day-to-day assignment of people	• Assignment of tasks to persons, within the medium-term resource allocation assignment	Biweekly	±6 weeks

- Although the budgets and project portfolio generate a realistic portfolio, there is always a possibility of resource overload. To give the project leaders and group leaders a hand in solving these problems, the medium-term resource allocation has to give *decision rules*. The main goal of these rules is to make clear which task has to be executed first in case of resource conflicts.
- When the portfolio is determined and the main decision rules are made, *rough-cut capacity planning* must be set up in which the resources over the projects are assigned roughly. This is important input for the short-term resource allocation.
- The rough-cut capacity planning has to be an *agreement* between the project leaders and resource leaders. Mainly, the claims for resources by the project leaders together exceed the number of resources. The project leaders know the resource planning and, therefore, they can estimate the project delay. The project delay can be communicated with all people involved and eventually a new plan can be made.

3.3 Short-Term Resource Allocation

Using the rough-cut capacity planning and the decision rules as main input, the short-term resource allocation must be the main input for the day-to-day planning of the individual resources for the coming weeks. Now almost all deviations can be treated by group leaders in close harmony with the project leaders. Interference by management can, in this way, be very limited.

3.4 Links

The long-, medium-, and short-term allocation process have their own goals, but together they must be linked to provide the organization with the results for doing business. These links must give the information needed to make the right decisions.

3.5 Feedback

The links give input to make the right decisions. This input can be made better by evaluating the input versus the real effort, when the evaluation must be used for the long- and medium-term resource allocation. The allocation process can be made better by the feedback.

TABLE 2 Growth Possibiliies of the Five Vital Elements
for the Resource Allocation Method

Element		Growth Possibility
Long-term resource allocation	Not done	Assignment of budgets related to business plan
Medium-term resource allocation	Not done	Set up a project portfolio related to business plan Assignment of tasks to persons/disciplines and decision rules
Short-term resource allocation	Ad hoc	Resource leaders assign persons according to medium-term allocation
Links	Not available	Synchronization of the allocation processes, execution of the allocations on the right level, data exchange between the allocation processes
Feedback	Not available	Feedback of the tasks, the projects, and the portfolio in all three allocation processes

3.6 Growth model

The five elements used in this method can be implemented in almost every organization. How, and to what level, the five elements can be implemented is situation-dependent. In Table 2, a model of how to grow to a mature level of resource allocation is presented.

4 R&D ENVIRONMENT

Allocation of workers in a multiproject environment is an issue for lots of organizations, such as software houses, R&D organizations, and construction and engineering companies. This chapter especially fits in with R&D organizations where multiple projects are running concurrently. Specific for R&D is that:

- Project results and project timing are *very uncertain* because of the unique characteristics of each project based on a high degree of innovation.

- Human resources are the main and scarcest resource in R&D projects. *Knowledge* is scarce. Therefore, almost everybody provides his or her small, specific contribution to every project.
- The progress of each project strongly depends on the state-of-the-art building blocks that need to be ''invented'' by scientists and engineers. Human ingenuity is very much dependent on the *motivation and involvement* of each individual engineer.

These three characteristics make the process of resource allocation difficult. The allocation method needs to be flexible because of a fast-changing project portfolio.

4.1 Project Scatter Factor

In an R&D environment the allocation of specialists to one project may be difficult because of the specific knowledge most of the people have. The number of people needed to staff a 1-year task is what we called the project scatter factor (Fig. 6). A higher project scatter factor means more people are needed for one task; therefore, the project team will be bigger and the devotion and efficiency of the work done within each project by the experts decreases. In Figure 7, the effect of the project scatter factor is shown. Devotion of the staff and the efficiency are also shown. As stated in Berenschot, the project scatter factor has great influence on the project progress.

A project of 4 man-years is done by 20 part-timers

Project-scatter-factor =

$$\frac{\text{\# of employees}}{\text{\# of menyears}} = \frac{20}{4} = 5$$

FIGURE 6   Project scatter factor.

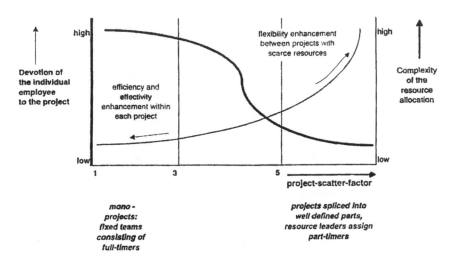

FIGURE 7   Effects of the project scatter factor.

An acceleration in the product development process is only possible in a *good* project organization with *empowered* project leaders and by allocating people *full-time* (or almost full time) and working as a *team* under control of the project leader. (Bureau Berenschot by order of the Dutch Ministry of Economic Affairs, Report on Technology Reconnoitre, 1995)

Therefore a project scatter factor of 1 is most desired. Hammer and Champy (1993) also stress this by saying a project team has to be a small, multifunctional team: the project scatter factor should be as low as possible.

4.2   Resource Dedication Profile

To realize a small project team, the resources must have what we call the right resource dedication profile. In most R&D organizations, the resources have their own specialization. This knowledge is concentrated on a small piece of work to be done. This greatly influences the project scatter factor. If many people are needed in one project on a part-time basis, a high project scatter factor will be the result, and the project efficiency will be low.

The problems faced in a R&D situation can be solved by changing the resource dedication profile (Fig. 8). Specialists should be transferred to either *all-round project members*, or to *experts*, or to *service employees*.

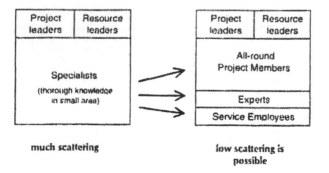

FIGURE 8   Resource dedication profile.

4.2.1   All-Around Project Members

The first group of resources must be at the heart of the project teams. These people must have general knowledge of the whole project and must be flexible within the project. They are the first step toward an efficient and effective well-organized project. The main deflections within the project must be caught by the project members themselves. Above this, allocating people to just one project makes the allocation process far easier.

There are extreme situations and problems that cannot be solved by the project members. For these types of problems, the knowledge of experts with extensive knowledge of a certain discipline will have to be used.

4.2.2   Experts

A small group of people in an R&D organization must have very specific knowledge to use within the projects. Experts can and must be used in problem-solving situations or at project reviews. The project members often don't have the deep knowledge to tackle severe problems. Experts have to provide this knowledge. They give new and extra information to the project.

The experts will be needed in all the projects in the portfolio several times. When they are needed is hard to predict. They cannot be allocated to just one project. They are the coach and main source of information for the project leaders, project members, and group leaders.

The experts have a special place in the allocation process. It isn't possible to predict their efforts in each individual project for a long period (more than 1 or 2 weeks). Therefore, we give the advice to predict the number of experts needed in the long-term resource allocation and give them freedom by not allocating them in the medium-term resource allocation. In the short term resource allocation, they must plan their own work in cooperation with their group leader.

4.2.3 Service Employees

The projects in the portfolio all have unique characteristics, but there are certain activities that must be executed in every project. These are routine activities that can be done by several people of a certain discipline. When this activity is routine, independent of the chosen resource and constant of quality, this activity can be defined as a service. The projects then do not have to worry about these activities. These services can be asked for, internally or externally, when they are needed. The services can be planned independent of people. In the medium-term resource allocation, only a check of the availability versus the need of each kind of service is necessary. By planning services instead of people, the complexity of the medium-term resource allocation process decreases and the work can be organized more efficiently.

4.3 Consequences

Allocation of the resources according to the new resource dedication profiles will substantially influence the performance of an organization. Changing the resources isn't that easy, however. The whole organization must understand the possibilities of the changes. First, discipline leaders must see the need for changing specialists into project members, experts, and service employees. Only a few people are needed as experts. On the other hand, the organization must seek for the services. Defining more services gives better controlled projects, and the resource allocation process is easier to execute. This will greatly influence the career paths of the employees.

5 EXPERIENCES

After having formulated the resource allocation problems, we came to the conclusion that the only viable way to go is in the direction of multiple mono-project situations, despite the initial arguments of discipline leaders that it would be impossible to get all-rounders. The efforts to get efficiency between projects is far less effective than the efficiency that can be gained within each project itself.

Until this study, the five elements of resource allocation were not used explicitly. Now they are placed in the right business process. The long-term resource allocation is placed in the strategic business process. Each year, this resource allocation process is walked through. Directly linked to this process is the medium-term resource allocation. This process is executed each quarter. The day-to-day planning is used within the development and the production process that needs several development resources to optimize the production process. The goals of these three processes were made clear by making the processes explicit in the business process map of the organization. Those involved now better understand the overall need of a resource allocation process.

In the past two quarters, we adapted the medium-term resource allocation process according to our new insights using the project scatter factor and the resource dedication profile. After the introduction of these two indicators, the organization decided to stop striving to find a computer-button, medium-term resource allocation. Maximum effort of the five elements, by linking them and by optimizing each element, does not give as much profit as the usage of the project scatter factor and the resource dedication profile.

The allocation process is now less complex and the throughput time is shorter. Computer planning software, as linked between the medium-term resource allocation and the short-term resource allocation, is not necessary even in an organization with more than 200 people involved on 80 different projects. Medium-term planning is easy to handle and flexible with a spreadsheet and the day-to-day planning can be executed by each individual project leader and the group leader.

6   KEEP IT SIMPLE

Many organizations have a day-to-day planning method in which all detailed tasks are allocated with usage of planning software to individuals. In these organizations, a medium-term resource allocation is not used. However, to couple the day-to-day planning to the strategic business plan, this medium-term resource allocation is absolutely necessary. When using the project scatter factor and the resource dedication profile, a medium-term resource allocation process can be implemented very easily. Moreover, the project results will increase rapidly.

REFERENCES

AS Pillai, AK Tiwari. Enhanced PERT for programme analysis, control and evaluation: PACE. International Journal of Project Management 13(1): 24–29, 1995.

A Platje, H Seidel, S Wadman. Project and portfolio planning cycle: Project-based management for multiproject challenge. International Journal of Project Management 12(2): 100–106, 1994.

M Hammer, J Champy. Reengineering the Corporation, New York: Harper Collins, 1993.

21

The Big Puzzle—Multiproject Management Is Redefining the Way Companies Handle Technology, People, and Vendors to Make All the Pieces Fit

**Clinton Wilder, Bruce Caldwell,
and Martin J. Garvey**

1 INTRODUCTION

Philadelphia Gas and Electric (PG&E) Corporation and vice president (VP)/ chief information officer (CIO) John Keast calls it "the worst of everything": four major information technology (IT) projects, all critical, and all had to be completed within the last 4 months of last year. "Four major projects, and they had to fit together like jigsaw pieces," says Keast. PG&E Energy Services certainly had a business mandate for change—selling gas and electricity in markets about to be deregulated. To do that, PG&E Energy needed to get several systems running at the same time: a financial applications suite from SAP, a back-end billing database from Oracle, and a sales-force automation system and set of pricing tools from Baan's Aurum Software unit, for PG&E Energy's 21 new nationwide sales offices.

Adapted from *InformationWeek*, 1998.

That challenge—the need to handle multiple IT projects in a limited time frame with limited resources—is rolling over long-held methods of prioritization, project management, and technology and human resource deployment at organizations of every stripe. PG&E, United Airlines, Newport News Shipbuilding, Polaroid, Sears Roebuck, Hilton Hotels, and even the CIA are meeting the challenge by shaking IT project management, and often corporate cultures, to the core. The rewards can be dramatic: greater accountability on IT projects, more efficient use of IT talent, better relationships with IT vendors, and better alignment of IT with business goals.

Whether referred to as multiproject management, program management, or simply as the Big Puzzle, the need to handle multiple technology initiatives is increasing. "The growth rate of multiple, parallel projects in need of program management is phenomenal, between 20% and 30% a year," says Hugh Ryan, director of the large, complex systems practice at Andersen Consulting.

That imperative is forcing organizations to rethink how they implement IT projects from the ground up. The first priority, says PG&E's Keast, is a holistic view of common business goals. "If you focus on the big picture first, then you'll have people who can deal with the cross-project situations that inevitably come up," says Keast. "Project teams like that. Too often in the past, they were inwardly facing and lost sight of the whole."

PG&E assigns two or three people to manage cross-project coordination for each project. One is a business line manager, another a technical architecture manager—"someone who can work in the abstract and see the bigger picture," says Keast. Some coordination groups also have a manager of process and information who maps out the business against the application design, figuring out what information is needed at what stage of a particular business process.

That strategy helped PG&E Energy complete its sales and transaction systems late last year, culminating in the SAP financial applications going live January 1. Speed was critical; the SAP implementation took just 4 months. Next up on PG&E's project list are a new billing system and an extranet database of energy usage information.

United Airlines senior VP and CIO Bruce Parker has a similar challenge. United has more than 10 major IT initiatives going on around the world, including systems overhauls in payroll (a mainframe to client-server migration), yield management (running on IBM's SP-2 parallel processor), and UNIX-based accounting systems at regional hubs in London, Miami, and Tokyo. Also keeping United busy are a 30,000-seat TCP/IP network with Java applications to replace dumb terminals and improved data sharing with alliance partners such as Air Canada and Lufthansa for more coordinated frequent-flier rewards systems.

To keep everyone working together, United recently instituted a standardized development process and methodology called Application Development Effectiveness Process Transition (ADEPT). This process mandates a project board, with both business-side sponsors and IT people, for every systems initiative. By keeping methodologies and project management techniques consistent, it's easier for Parker and his staff to keep tabs on lagging projects and to reallocate resources accordingly. "You have to keep a portfolio viewpoint, and project managers have to think beyond the IT part," says Parker.

Also, United has had to rethink deployment strategies for the most important resource of all: people. United seeks to identify specialists in key strategic areas and move them from project to project, as needed. "You'd love to have depth of skills across all the projects, but that's tough to find," says Parker.

Moving limited talent among multiple IT projects has become the modus operandi of the CIA. When one project hits a bump and needs additional resources, all the others are fair game. "First, we look to projects near completion, take the senior talent from those, and assign them to the higher-risk or higher-visibility initiatives," says Michael O'Brachta, an information service officer in the CIA. "If the available pool doesn't work, then we go raid existing projects and make hard decisions about pulling people off to assign them to riskier or more visible projects."

2   SKILLED HELP WANTED

Some skills are in very high demand. Sears is rolling out PeopleSoft human resources applications on Sun Microsystems servers to handle 320,000 employees in 21 business units, including department stores, auto centers, and credit card processing. Sears is handling the load by sharing implementation teams among the units.

"We're trying to leverage economies of scale and skill," says VP of corporate information systems (IS) Ken DeWitt. "Proficiencies with products like PeopleSoft are the new hot skills, and they're in limited supply. If we've done a successful implementation, we need to leverage that skill across the enterprise." So teams are assigned where they're needed most.

Savvy IT managers see the Big Puzzle as an opportunity to complete projects faster while improving the payoff. "It's the only way we can be successful,'' says Joe Durocher, CIO of Hilton Hotels. ''Project teams are working together and everyone is trying to move toward greater integration of all their systems, getting away from the mentality where projects are kept separate from each other.''

Hilton is combining a data warehousing effort with a central reservation system project so that reservations people have access to historical trends data when booking rooms for customers. The hotel chain also is linking a system-wide rollout of Newmarket Software Systems' Delphi sales and catering software package with an effort to build a global sales force automation system.

That will give Hilton's national salespeople better access to account information, the knowledge of what kinds of booking transactions have occurred at different properties, and the ability to see the inventory of available space for meeting rooms as well as guest rooms, says Durocher. Hilton might not have these capabilities if the projects were kept separate, he says.

Then there's speed. ''It's not so much a matter of speeding up the projects once they've started, but putting in a shorter time frame from the beginning,'' says Durocher. ''If we were doing the central reservation project 5 years ago, it probably would have been a 2- to 3-year project. Now, it's closer to 18 months.''

Achieving faster development while assuring interdependency with other new systems may sound paradoxical, but it isn't. Projects managed as part of a whole have more accountability. There's less chance of piling on unnecessary features and obsessing over elegant code when you're part of an interdependent team. ''Gone are the days of development as an art,'' says Bruce Howard, assistant to the director of information management at Polaroid.

Polaroid formed a steering committee of IT and business managers to better coordinate large global projects, such as year 2000 conversion. Under an initiative called Polaroid 2001, the camera maker is trying to model all of its business processes, even IT deployments, after its highly engineered product development processes, says Howard. ''It's not as easy with information management, but it really can be an engineered process,'' he says.

3   THE NEED FOR ALIGNMENT

As Polaroid demonstrates, the foundation for successful multiproject management is airtight alignment between IT and business goals. ''Everyone in IT needs to have a different type of mind-set today,'' says Steve Hassell, CIO of Newport News Shipbuilding. "You have to be much more knowledgeable about how the entire picture is coming together. Everything we're doing emanates from business process change."

Newport News Shipbuilding still does 90% of its work for the Department of Defense, but its business now demands much more sharing of data with the Navy, and even with competitors, during the contract shipbuilding process. "That business change is the fundamental driver behind everything we've done," says Hassell. "We needed to share information with customers, suppliers, and partners. With our legacy systems, it wasn't going to happen."

Along with a transition from an MVS mainframe system to a UNIX and Windows NT environment with 8,000 networked PCs, Newport News is deploying all the manufacturing and financial modules of SAP R/3, an electronic parts catalog from Aspect Development, a supply chain application from i2 Technologies, and a product data management application from Enovia.

Newport News Shipbuilding has put in place an initiative called Shared Data Environment (SDE) as an umbrella over all its major systems projects. Hassell helped formulate SDE when he worked in the company's strategic planning department, reporting to the chief operating officer (COO). Before Hassell became CIO last January, IT reported to the chief financial officer. Not any more. "We moved the entire division to the chief operating officer, rather than move the SDE initiative," says Hassell. "More than anything, that has been the key to success. I have the same boss as the VPs of manufacturing or materials, and that helps break down the walls." More than 60% of the SDE team, Hassell says, is from the business areas.

"That was the only way we could ensure the results we wanted, or that it would be implemented at all," says Tom Schievelbein, Newport News Shipbuilding's executive VP and COO. "Almost all of the processes that SAP touches are operational processes, so you have to have the operations people involved before the system is up and running. I've seen it happen in other companies—you put in a system and it falls by the wayside when operations won't accept it."

The SDE for technology projects is an idea that came from shipbuilding operations, where employees building aircraft carriers and other large craft are used to juggling multiple projects. "Sharing resources among several projects fits right in with our core competencies," says Schievelbein.

It almost goes without saying that solving the Big Puzzle often requires outside management help. "We have too much going on," says Dawn Shattuck, CIO of the state of Michigan's welfare agency, called the Family Independence Agency (FIA). The agency, which is funded with $3 billion in state money and $4 billion in federal money, has large IT projects under way for child support enforcement, child welfare, year 2000 compliance, local office accounting, data warehousing, and an agency-wide deployment of Windows NT clients and Novell servers.

To get a high-level view of all the projects and their various contingencies—for example, which projects will need database administrators at what time—Shattuck hired EDS. EDS brought in 40 consultants and examined FIA's multiple initiatives using Microsoft's Project software and methodology from the Project Management Institute, a professional association of 80,000 project managers that provides training and certification.

"EDS was able to come in and, in short order, meet with project managers and make sure project plans were detailed," Shattuck says. EDS helped FIA develop project-plan details on resources, pricing, testing, and time lines. Of the dozens of FIA's large and small projects in the planning stage, between 10 and 15 are being implemented at any one time. EDS has won contracts to implement at least four of the projects.

PG&E used consultants from Deloitte & Touche to help build its sales and transaction systems. To ensure a close relationship, PG&E opened its internal voice mail and e-mail to the Deloitte & Touche consultants. "Outsiders must get to know the business users," says Keast, "so we treat them like one of the family."

Andersen Consulting began training its professionals in program management, which Andersen calls Business Integration Methodology. The new practice builds on Andersen's 3-year-old application development methodology for large projects, combining it with best practices in project planning, design, implementation, and operation. About one-third of the consulting firm's staff has completed the training.

Brian Keane, copresident of the software services firm, Keane Inc., says program management has its roots in the defense and aerospace industry. Large, complex projects such as manned space missions and missile systems, with dozens of subprojects and myriad interdependencies, required the disciplines of a program management office.

Until a few years ago, Keane says, program management was unheard of in the commercial world. It began to take off in the private sector as companies undertook enterprise-scale projects, such as E-commerce initiatives and outsourcing.

Year 2000 work contributed to the demand for program-management services, but Andersen's Ryan thinks multiproject initiatives will only increase in the future. "Year 2000 slowed down some of the big development, creating a long laundry list of projects that will have to be revisited." Ryan says.

4 VENDORS ON THE HOOK

Solving the puzzle of multiple initiatives also forces fundamental changes in IT's relationships with product vendors. "You have to share the development and implementation load with them," says PG&E's Keast. "We worked Aurum for every piece of work we could. We wanted them to be on the hook."

Suppliers, including Compaq, Hewlett-Packard, IBM, Oracle, PeopleSoft, SAP, and Sun, all offer project or program management and ancillary services to bolt on to their product deployments. "We're in the systems integration business," says Renee Speitel, manager of program management at Compaq. "At any one time, we're managing about 800 projects worldwide. It's the lifeblood of our ability to cement relationships with clients."

PeopleSoft formed a strategy group to focus exclusively on value-added services for large enterprise resource planning deployments. The result is offerings that run the gamut from risk management to technical architecture assessment to executive planning. "We have to offer more than just implementation guidance, and we can't be myopic and think only about our own PeopleSoft products," says Nancy Lyskawa, a national director of customer service. "We have to understand the customer's overall IT and business environment."

IBM majored in program management for many years in its federal sector business, says David Kelly, VP of delivery, operations, and support for IBM Global Services in North America. "Project executives and program managers are key elements of our services, and the new millennium makes that even more so," he says. "There's more to do than most clients can do these days."

That is even more than IBM can handle. To address its own growing needs and those of its clients for project and program management skills, IBM formed a global project management center of excellence 3 years ago that provides employees and clients with training, mentoring, and preparation for certification tests with the Project Management Institute, says Larry Smith, global program director of project management at IBM Global Services. IBM has 8,000 project managers, about half certified by the PMI.

5 GLOBAL KNOWLEDGE

Sun's professional services unit employs global account managers who must keep tabs on all of the projects going on in those accounts—and know how they relate to one another. "There's that moment in time when all projects turn out to be bigger than anyone thought, resources are scarce, and hard decisions must be made to get through it," says Paul Rochester, VP and general manager of Sun professional services. "That's the art of program management."

Hewlett-Packard (HP) is more blunt. "Clients often don't have competent project management," says Kathy Boyd, global services manager with HP's consulting unit. "There's nothing worse than a global project with multiple project managers using different methodologies." HP Consulting's approach, says Boyd, is to manage projects while teaching and training the customer in project management methodologies.

"Problems are accelerated today because of business time frame demands, tight budgets, and very short project deadlines," says Boyd. "Where does any IT project fit in the overall business strategy? That must be known."

Making all the pieces fit is one of the greatest challenges facing today's IT executives, but it's also one of the greatest opportunities. The demand for big-picture program management can catalyze, and then cement, the cherished IT business partnership on which all progressive CIOs insist. "Shared ownership and accountability are always important," says PG&E's Keast, "but they're absolutely critical for multiple projects." Companies that successfully solve the Big Puzzle will be well positioned to make strategic use of IT as the future unfolds.

6 SUMMARY

Elements of successful program (multiproject) management:

- Track performance against program budget, delivery targets, and business objectives; forecast budget and resource requirements.
- Audit project practices to meet quality objectives.
- Coordinate and manage logistics, resources, and infrastructure issues (e.g., personnel, tools, facilities, contractors).
- Maintain a master plan identifying all project interconnections and dependencies and address delays before they affect other projects.
- Make sure there's consistent implementation of methodologies and best practices.
- Monitor changing business requirements; modify project plans and contingency plans as needed.
- Communicate the objectives and progress of the program internally and externally; ensure communication among project teams.

22

The Toyota Benchmark: Multiproject Development Centers

Michael A. Cusumano
and Kentaro Nobeoka

1 INTRODUCTION

For several decades, Toyota has been a leader in adopting new organizational structures and processes in both manufacturing and product development [1]. For firms in many different industries, it has served as a benchmark for performance in these areas. In manufacturing, Toyota's "lean production system," symbolized by the JIT or Just-in-Time techniques, has revolutionized inventory management and manufacturing practices in a variety of industries [2]. In product development, Toyota led the auto industry in establishing project-based management that streamlined product development and effectively coordinated activities in different functional areas [3]. Clark and Fujimoto described Toyota's type of organization as a heavyweight project management system (originally referred to as the *shusa* system in Japanese). This features powerful project managers (shusa) with extensive authority over different functions such as design, manufacturing, and marketing.

Toyota performed remarkably well with its project-centered management system and has set new standards for the auto industry in manufacturing

Adapted from *Thinking Beyond Lean: How Multiproject Management Is Transforming Product Development at Toyota and Other Companies*, 1998.

as well as product development performance [4]. During the past 15 years, the company more than doubled the number of passenger car lines it offers (8 to 18). It also has maintained a 4-year product lifecycle for most of these product lines, shorter than most auto companies in the United States and Europe. In recent years, however, all Japanese manufacturers, including Toyota, have become much more concerned with efficiency in new product development. In most of their major markets, demand has slowed or even declined while their cost competitiveness has decreased because of the appreciation of the yen and improvements by Western competitors.

In this chapter, we discuss how Toyota has again led the auto industry by introducing the most radical changes in its product development organization during the last 30 years. We examine how, during 1992 to 1993, Toyota adopted a strategy and structure specifically for multiproject management of product development. The new organization features three vehicle development centers that group similar projects together, based on common platforms. A fourth center provides common components to the different development centers. This structure differs from Toyota's former project-centered organization, as well as from traditional functional and matrix organizations. We also review the results of this reorganization. Toyota seems to have significantly improved its ability to coordinate across projects as well as to integrate different engineering functions within projects and related sets of projects.

2 PROBLEMS WITH HEAVYWEIGHT PROJECT MANAGEMENT

In 1953, Toyota assigned the first shusa, or heavyweight project manager, to a new vehicle project [5]. When Toyota started product development for the 1955 Crown, Kenya Nakamura became the first shusa to head a project from the beginning. At that time, he was a member of Toyota's engineering management division. Toyota strengthened the shusa organization in February 1965 by formally establishing a product planning division to organize and support shusas. At that time, there were already 10 shusas in the company [6]. Each shusa had five or six staff members, which totaled about 50 members in the division. Toyota did not change the product planning division and shusa system until 1992, when it introduced the center organization. (As a minor change in 1989, instead of shusa, Toyota adopted the term *chief engineer* for its project managers. To avoid any confusion, we use the new term, chief engineer, to refer to this position, rather than shusa or project manager or product manager.)

The changes at Toyota began in 1990. Company executives decided to re-evaluate their entire product and technology development organization.

They were willing to change, if necessary, so that the organization would be better able to compete in the year 2000. Toyota launched an initiative, called the Future Project 21 (FP21), to study any problems in its product development organizational structure and processes. The leader of the project was Yoshiro Kinbara, an executive vice president in charge of product and technology development. A manager at Toyota explained to us that no specific threats triggered this initiative. At that time, Toyota was actually doing better than most of its competitors. Toyota executives recognized, however, that organizations sometimes need review and overhauling to continue to be competitive in a changing environment. A consulting firm, the Nomura Research Institute, which Toyota hired for this project, evaluated Toyota's organization performance as a starting point for the FP21 initiative.

Soon after the FP21 started, the consulting team identified two important problems that led Toyota managers to conclude that they would need to rethink their strategy and structure. First, there appeared to be an organizational problem. In particular, Toyota had become less efficient in internal communications and had come to need more coordination tasks than before to manage new product development. Second, the competitive advantages of Japanese auto makers decreased significantly after around 1990. The rising yen made Japanese products more expensive at the same time that foreign competitors were improving their skills in product development as well as manufacturing. The following sections discuss these two problems in more detail.

2.1 Organizational Problems

Figure 1 shows a simplified version of Toyota's product development organization before its reorganization in 1992. There were, at that time, as many as 16 design or functional engineering divisions and each had a functional manager. There were also about 15 projects proceeding concurrently (the figure depicts only 9 projects). Each project had a chief engineer who belonged to the product planning division and worked under its general manager.

The product development organization was actually a huge matrix that gave roughly similar weights to functional areas and projects. It was not a true project-oriented organization because chief engineers and general managers in the product planning division did not directly oversee the engineering divisions in this structure.

In theory, chief engineers at Toyota had authority over the entire product development process, from concept generation through design and manufacturing. In practice, Toyota's product development organization had become much larger than before, and chief engineers were finding it difficult to control

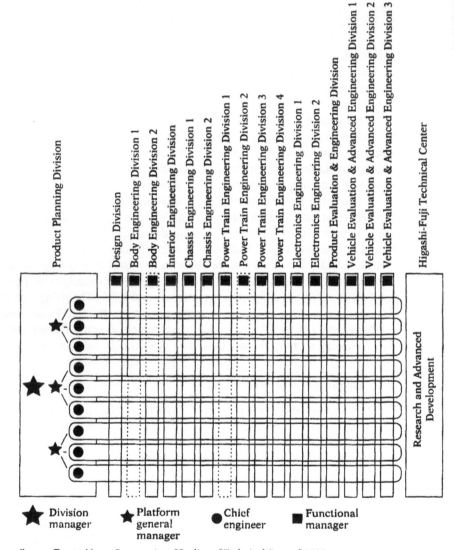

Source: Toyota Motor Corporation, "Outline of Technical Center," 1992.

FIGURE 1 Toyota's product development organization in 1991.

and integrate different functional divisions when developing a new product. In other words, they had difficulty scaling up the matrix approach. As the number of product development projects increased, the number of engineers also increased. At the same time, Toyota's engineers had become more specialized, reflecting the increasing number of different divisions. As of December 1991, there were about 7,000 people in the 16 product development engineering divisions working on the 15 or so concurrent projects. In addition, Toyota had a Research and Advanced Development Group with 2,000 additional people located at the Higashi-Fuji Technical Center [7].

In 1991, a chief engineer had to coordinate people in 48 departments in 12 divisions to launch a new product effort. This estimate comes from Toyota data on frequent participants in project management meetings [8]. In contrast, when there were only 5,000 people in the entire product development organization in 1976, a chief engineer had to coordinate only 23 departments in six divisions. At that time, a chief engineer generally needed to talk with only six division managers to integrate all the design engineering functions. Clearly, during this 15-year period, coordination tasks had become much more complicated for chief engineers.

In addition to this added complexity, another problem made it difficult for some chief engineers to manage new vehicle projects. Relatively young chief engineers did not always get sufficient cooperation from senior functional managers. Originally, only a limited number of charismatic senior managers rose to the position of chief engineer. Toyota people often considered them gods within their projects, and they were able to negotiate successfully with strong engineering managers. In recent years, however, Toyota started assigning relatively junior people to the position of chief engineer, for two reasons. First, the number of chief engineers required to cover all new vehicle projects had increased and not enough qualified senior people were available. Second, Toyota recognized that people needed particular talents to be excellent chief engineers, and their seniority was not as important as their ability.

For their part, functional managers also found it difficult to spend sufficient time on managing the details of so many projects. Most of these managers had to oversee work for about 15 different projects at the same time [9]. Not surprisingly, they usually did not have enough time to deal with complicated issues very well, such as interfaces and interdependencies between multiple projects. Because of the large number of functional divisions and vehicle projects, each chief engineer arranged regular meetings with the relevant functional managers only about once every 2 months.

There was another problem at the engineering level. Because of their narrow specialization, engineers did not have a good "system view" of the entire product. For example, some engineers only knew about a door's inner body structure and did not know much about the outer body because Toyota separated the interior engineering and body engineering divisions. This kind of excessively narrow specialization did not promote the creation of a well-integrated final product. In addition, the narrow specialization caused another problem when Toyota later promoted engineers to become managers in charge of larger engineering tasks, such as developing the entire body. It was difficult to train general engineering managers in the highly specialized organizational structure.

Nor was this organizational structure particularly appropriate for transferring knowledge from one project to another. Because of the narrow specialization and the large number of projects, each engineer frequently had to move among unrelated projects. This practice reduced the sense of commitment to individual products, but managers hoped it would be useful to transfer technical know-how. In reality, however, Toyota found that it could not transfer or use "system knowledge" very effectively simply by transferring engineers frequently from one project to another.

Toyota's rapid growth partially caused these problems. One way to increase the chief engineer's authority and eliminate narrow specialization is to create a pure product-team organization. Chrysler did this for its LH and Neon projects. In product teams, almost all engineers work exclusively for a single project for its entire duration. Toyota executives did not think that the product team organization would suit their needs. This type of organization can work well for firms with a small number of projects and little technical interdependency between multiple products. Toyota has many projects and a limited number of engineers. Therefore, managers do not want to assign engineers to a specific product for the entire duration of a project. The peak period for design work for engineers in an automobile project lasts only about 1.5 to 2 years out of a 4-year cycle. It follows that, when a project task is nearing completion or "outside the peak," engineers should move to other projects to avoid wasting time. In addition, a change in the competitive environment discussed in the next section made the product team approach especially inappropriate. In the new environment, cost reduction and technology sharing among projects has become much more important.

Even the organization at Toyota prior to 1991 had problems with coordination across projects. One of the policies of Toyota's chief engineer system was to encourage the autonomy of chief engineers and to get them to feel like these are *their* projects. General managers in the product planning division above chief engineers, therefore, did not supervise chief engineers in the details of individual projects. In addition, the number of vehicle projects was too large for managers to deal effectively with multiproject issues, such as resource allocation, technology transfer, and component sharing.

Finally, coordination with the Research and Advanced Development (RAD) group located at the Higashi-Fuji Technical Center proved to be a problem [10]. Toyota kept the center relatively independent of specific vehicle projects so that its engineers could focus on research and advanced engineering. Both those involved in vehicle projects and the RAD group felt dissatisfied with this structure, however. Engineers working on vehicle projects did not think that the RAD group developed technologies that were useful for their needs. On the other hand, engineers in the RAD group felt frustrated because vehicle projects did not use technologies that they created. Toyota executives concluded that these two groups needed more integration organizationally.

In summary, Toyota's product development organization had five problems. These caused difficulties both in integrating functions within projects and coordinating across projects:

1. There were too many functional engineering divisions and too narrow a specialization of engineers.
2. There were too many vehicle projects for each functional manager to manage the engineering details of each project as well as coordination across projects.
3. It had become much more complicated and difficult for chief engineers to oversee all the engineering functions.
4. The chief engineer organization did not foster coordination across projects.
5. Management did not sufficiently coordinate the RAD group and individual vehicle projects.

2.2 Changes in the Competitive Environment

The competitive environment surrounding Japanese automobile firms also started changing around 1991. There were two interrelated issues. First, rapid growth in production levels virtually ended. The aggressive product strategy of Japanese automobile firms in the 1980s, such as frequent new product introductions and replacements, in large part reflected their assumption of continuous rapid growth. The new environment required some changes in this strategy as well as in company organization. Second, the importance of cost reduction became even more critical for international competition than before. In addition to the appreciation of the yen, Japanese advantages in development and manufacturing productivity were diminishing. Both factors had a strong negative impact on the cost advantages the Japanese had once enjoyed.

Because of these changes, Toyota executives decided to revise the existing chief engineer system. This system primarily focused on building the best individual products one at a time and encouraged chief engineers to think first about the success of their own projects. For example, a former chief engineer recalled that "each project manager wanted to increase sales of his own product by developing many new proprietary components and by expanding his project's target customer segments into those of other Toyota product lines." He explained that when Toyota's production volume was growing rapidly, these characteristics of Toyota's chief engineer system worked well for the company. Cannibalization of individual product lines was not a major problem. The market in each product segment also expanded, and this growth made it possible for each project to expand its target market.

In addition, in previous years, Toyota often sold more new products than planners had expected. As a result, high development and production costs due to many new proprietary components was not much of a problem. A manager in charge of cost management admitted this:

> Prior to 1991, few new products met an original target cost when it was introduced to the market. The sales volume for each new product, however, usually exceeded its original plan. The large sales volume lowered the actual production cost compared to its original plan through scale economies. In the end, a new product usually reached the production cost that had been originally planned when we fully considered the entire production during its life cycle.

Because of a faster depreciation of manufacturing equipment than in the original plans, production costs also appeared to be lower than expected. Given this common pattern, it made sense for chief engineers to try to develop hit products rather than to try to meet conservative cost targets.

Starting in 1990, however, Toyota's production volume stopped growing, and even declined in some years. Profit from each new product also started decreasing. Under these circumstances, Toyota needed a new strategy and organization, particularly with respect to cost management. Top management considered one aspect of the chief engineer system to be particularly inappropriate in this new environment: The management of individual projects was too independent. Toyota executives concluded that multiple related projects needed more coordination.

In a stagnant market, Toyota executives determined that they needed to position new products more carefully within their portfolio to reduce potential cannibalization. Given a limited total sales volume, one product line could easily take away sales from similar Toyota products. In addition, to reduce production costs, management decided to increase the level of sharing or commonality of components. They could no longer expect sales increases to compensate for high development costs, resulting from the tendency under Toyota's chief engineer system for each project to create too many unique or proprietary components.

In 1997 many symptoms of the old product strategy and organization at Toyota remained. For example, the company still has three distinct platforms for three similar products: the Corona/Carina, the Celica/Carina ED, and the Camry. These exist because the chief engineers for each product wanted to develop their own ideal platforms.

We can understand why Toyota ended up with redundant platforms. At different points in time, no doubt it was important to project managers and engineers to create distinctive new products with new platforms and other innovative technologies. A good engineering organization should be able to do this when necessary for competitive reasons. On the other hand, a good engineering organization should also be able to share technologies and coordinate different projects when efficiency of this sort becomes important. These two objectives—creating well-integrated new products and creating products efficiently by leveraging existing technologies—are, in a sense, contradictory. They require a firm to have strong projects as well as a strong functional orientation to promote sharing. Rather than continuing to struggle with how to balance these two extremes, Toyota decided to reorganize.

3 THE MOVE TO DEVELOPMENT CENTERS

Toyota did not reduce the total number of people working in product development. At the end of 1991, before the reorganization, the company had about 11,500 people in its product engineering organization and the number even rose to about 12,000 in 1993. Rather, Toyota's two major changes specifically targeted the problems discussed in the previous section.

First, in 1992, Toyota divided all of its new product development projects into three development centers, as shown in Figure 2. The center grouping focuses on the similarity in platform design. Center 1 is responsible for rear-wheel-drive platforms and vehicles, Center 2 for front-wheel-drive platforms and vehicles, and Center 3 for utility vehicle/van platforms and vehicles. Each center has between 1,500 and 1,900 people, and works on about 5 new vehicle projects simultaneously. Toyota had considered other grouping schemes, such as by product segment (luxury vs. economy vs. sporty cars, or

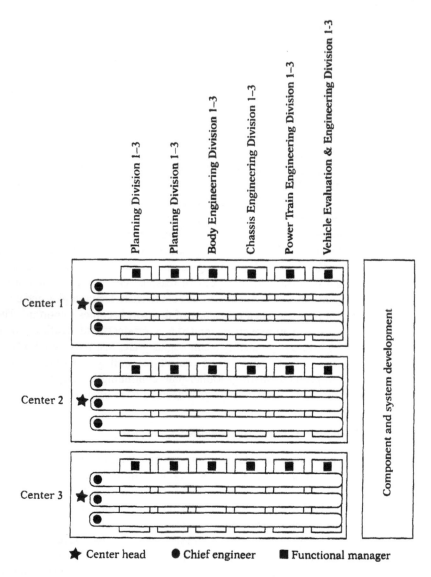

★ Center head   ● Chief engineer   ■ Functional manager

Source: Toyota Motor Corporation, "Outline of Technical Center," 1994.

FIGURE 2   Toyota's product development organization in 1992.

small vs. medium vs. large cars). Toyota management chose platform similarity because this would lead to the highest level of technology sharing among projects within a center. In particular, managers concluded that because new platform development requires such extensive resources, using common platform designs for multiple product lines would save in engineering investments and reduce production costs most effectively.

Second, in 1993, Toyota created Center 4 to develop components and systems for all vehicle projects. It reorganized the the RAD group and assigned most people from this group to Center 4. The RAD group used to work on research and advanced development independently, and Center 4 closely supports vehicle development by providing specific projects with components and subsystems. In addition to engineers in the RAD group, Center 4 added engineers working on some components such as electronics and new engines that did not need daily coordination with a vehicle project.

As discussed earlier, Toyota management had hoped that the center organization would improve coordination and sharing across projects as well as functional integration within projects (such as better coordination of different component groups as well as better coordination of design departments and process engineering). The next section focuses on how key aspects of the reorganization led to improvements in these two areas. Important features of this reorganization include:

- Reduction in the number of functional engineering divisions
- Reduction in the number of projects for each functional manager
- Changes in the roles of the center heads for multiple projects
- Establishment of planning divisions in each center
- Adoption of a hierarchical organization for chief engineers in related projects
- The new role of Center 4.

3.1 Reduction of Functional Engineering Divisions

To decrease the coordination tasks required to build a well-integrated product, Toyota reduced the number of functional divisions for design engineering. We noted earlier that the complexity raised by the large number of functional divisions had made it difficult for chief engineers to manage individual projects. Whereas the old organization had 16 different functional divisions, each new center has only six engineering divisions.

This simplification through the center organization prompted two other changes. First, Toyota lessened the specialization in each functional engineering division. As shown in Figure 3, Toyota used to have two separate

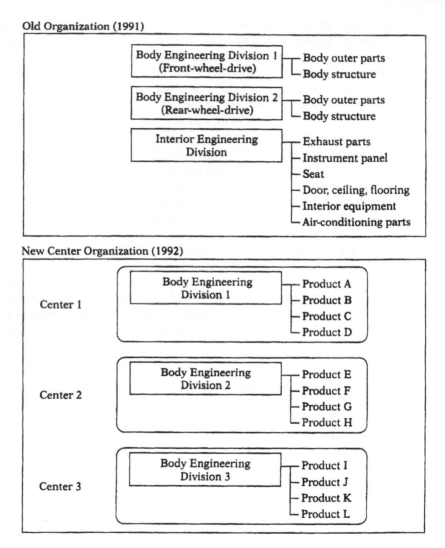

FIGURE 3 Old and new organizations for the body engineering function.

divisions for designing bodies and interior/exterior equipment: the body engineering division and the interior engineering division. In the new organization, the interior engineering division merged with the body engineering division. Another example is the merger of two different chassis engineering divisions, each of which had been separately responsible for suspension systems and brakes. Each design engineering division now has wider design responsibilities. An important point is that this did not enlarge the size of each functional division because each functional division is now responsible for only a limited number of projects within the center.

Second, Toyota reduced the number of functional divisions involved in a specific vehicle project (as opposed to a component project) through Center 4, the component and system development center. This simplified the work of the first three centers because Toyota separated development of some components and subsystems that engineers could manage outside specific vehicle projects.

Toyota considered three factors when determining whether particular engineering functions should be in a vehicle project or in Center 4: (1) Managers decided to keep components that need extensive tailoring for each product within the particular project. (2) They decided to develop within a project components that need careful coordination with other parts of the product design. On the other hand, they concluded that they could develop some components with modular characteristics separately from specific vehicle projects and then insert them into a product design relatively easily. Center 4 should develop these kinds of components and share them with multiple projects. (3) Toyota managers decided to use Center 4 for components that require a lot of new technical knowledge. Such development efforts usually require a group of technical specialists working together. These types of components also sometimes need a long time to develop and may not fit the timeframe of regular vehicle projects.

Following these guidelines, Toyota allocated the development of some components and subsystems to Center 4. For example, the upper-body design directly visible to the customer should be different for each product. Engineers should also carefully coordinate upper-body design with other parts of the product, such as the chassis and interior. Therefore, Toyota decided to manage the upper-body design within a project and to maintain this engineering function within each of the three vehicle centers. On the other hand, components like batteries, audio systems, and air conditioners do not usually need tailoring for each vehicle project. Therefore, Toyota moved the engineering divisions that developed these electronic components to Center 4.

The example of the electronics engineering divisions is actually more complicated and indicates the extensive thought and analysis put into this reorganization. Toyota carefully examined characteristics and interdependencies of each component so that Centers 1–3 would be relatively simple to manage. At the same time, executives wanted the centers to contain all the engineering capabilities needed to develop all the components that required extensive coordination within each project. For example, among the electronics components, the wire harness usually needs tailoring for each vehicle and has considerable interdependency with the body structure. Toyota merged this engineering function into the Centers' body engineering divisions and kept wire harness development within the projects.

Another example of eliminating activities from the vehicle development centers is the design of totally new engines, which Center 4 now does. Many engineering tasks are involved in new engine development that are unrelated to integration tasks within a particular vehicle project. In addition, the timeframe of new engine development does not fit that of specific vehicle projects. New engines usually need 6 to 8 years to develop, which is longer than the 4-year lead time of the average new vehicle project. Each center, however, still has almost 300 power train engineers who work on project integration, because modifying engines for use in particular products requires extensive coordination with each vehicle project. In the old organization, part of Toyota's product development organization took responsibility for both vehicle projects and most component development. This mixture made the former structure complicated and difficult to manage.

In summary, by widening the engineering specialization within each division and by transferring some component development into Center 4, Toyota reduced the number of functional divisions in Centers 1–3. In addition, because Toyota divided each function into three centers, the wider specialization did not require larger functional divisions.

3.2 Reduction of Projects for Each Functional Manager

Each functional manager is responsible for a smaller number of projects in the new center organization. For example, managers in Center 1 now focus only on vehicle projects with rear-wheel-drive platforms. In some functional areas, there were too many projects for functional managers to oversee properly. This is no longer the case.

As shown in Figure 3, the functional manager for interior engineering in the old organization was responsible for all vehicle projects, usually about 15 at any given time. In the center organization, functional managers are only responsible for about five product lines, and these all have technological inter-relationships. Each functional manager now can spend more time on coordination with each chief engineer. In addition, this reduction of the management scope for each functional manager should result in more effective multiproject management in such areas as resource allocation and technology sharing. Each functional division also can focus on fewer types of vehicle technologies. This focus should lead to more efficient development and accumulation of technical knowledge as a division.

3.3 Roles of the Center Head for Multiple Vehicle Projects

Each center head officially supervises all product development operations and personnel, including chief engineers and design engineering functions within the center. Equivalents to the center heads in the old organization were three deputy general managers who supervised chief engineers in the single product planning division. The three deputy general managers used to be in charge of small cars, large cars, and trucks/vans. They reported to the general manager of the product planning division. However, they officially managed only chief engineers, not functional managers and engineers, as seen earlier in Figure 1. Functional engineering division managers reported to another executive. Toyota did not want general managers above the chief engineers to manage the details of each project. In the old structure, it was not clear which general managers—those above chief engineers or those above the functional managers—had more authority.

In the center organization, each of the three center heads now has time to manage more of the technical details for multiple vehicle projects within one center. Therefore, whereas the old organization was officially a matrix both at the chief engineer level and at the general manager level, Toyota has reorganized primarily around projects. Moreover, top management wants the center heads to balance two important roles.

First, management expects a center head to help each chief engineer integrate different engineering functions. One of the key elements of Toyota's former chief engineer system had been the strong leadership of chief engineers. As discussed earlier, however, chief engineers found it difficult to coordinate the growing number of functional managers. In the center organization, chief engineers usually can rely on the center head's support to deal with the different functional divisions. Second, the center heads are responsible for coordinating all the different vehicle projects within the center. Their responsibilities include supervising the functional engineering divisions. Because both projects and functional divisions report to one manager, this structure should reduce conflict. The separate planning division in each center, discussed next, also exists to help the center heads coordinate projects.

3.4 Planning Divisions in Each Center

Each center has a planning division of 170 to 200 people. These people provide executive support for the center head and staff three departments: the administration department, the cost planning department, and the product audit department. The administration department is particularly important. This department takes charge of personnel management, resource allocation, and long-term product portfolio planning for the center. It also conducts advanced concept studies for individual product proposals before these become formal projects with an assigned chief engineer. The management support and portfolio planning that these planning divisions provide are critical to the effective operation of the center organization.

We noted that Toyota previously had a single product planning division for its entire product development organization, and chief engineers used to belong to this single division. Most staff members in the product planning division also worked directly for individual chief engineers. For example, Toyota used to divide most cost management staff in the division by vehicle project and had them report to individual chief engineers. In the new organization, cost management staff are more independent of chief engineers and report to the center's planning division manager and the center head, although they continue to work closely with chief engineers. This reflects one of the central concerns at Toyota, which is that each center needs to reduce costs by more efficiently leveraging resources and components across multiple projects.

The management scope used to be so large in the old organization that Toyota found project portfolio planning and resource allocation too complicated to manage well. Now the center planning divisions can consider technology sharing and resource allocation among multiple projects more carefully because they can focus on a small number of closely related products.

3.5 Hierarchical Organization of Chief Engineers

Another feature of Toyota's center organization is the hierarchical chief engineer structure for managing product families, as shown in Figure 4. This structure also helps strengthen the multiproject perspective of the center organization. For example, there used to be two separate chief engineers for the ES 300 and the Supra projects. Now, there are still two chief engineers, but one supervises both the ES 300 and the Supra projects and primarily manages the

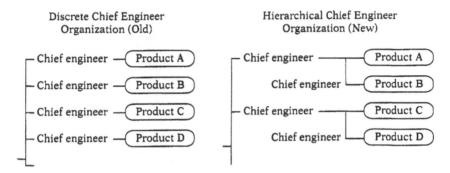

Discrete Chief Engineer Organization (Old)

Hierarchical Chief Engineer Organization (New)

FIGURE 4   Hierarchical chief engineer organization for multiproject management.

ES 300 project. The other chief engineer manages the Supra project and reports to the chief engineer of the ES 300. Toyota also made the same kind of change for another pair of projects: the Tercel and the Starlet. Although Toyota does not adopt this type of structure for all projects, the company appears to be moving the organization in this direction.

Each pair of projects shares almost identical platform and drive-train designs, even though these two projects target completely different customer segments and have separate product concepts. For example, the ES 300 is a luxury sedan and the Supra is a sports car. Therefore, it is important to manage the two projects separately so that each project develops a distinctive product that fits with its own target market. A planning division manager at Toyota related that it is difficult for a chief engineer to develop two widely different products and give the same level of commitment to each. At the same time, however, because these two projects share the same platform design, they need extensive coordination. Therefore, the projects have to achieve differentiation in product characteristics and integration in product development simultaneously. The hierarchical chief engineer organization is one way to pursue these two goals in parallel.

3.6 New Role of Center 4

As we explained earlier, Toyota based Center 4 primarily on the RAD group in the old organization. As shown in Figure 5, the company has not significantly changed the basic structure of the organization and technical areas. Technical areas of both the old and new organizations include vehicle (body and chassis), engine and drive-train, electronics, and materials. There was, however, one

Old Organization: Research and Advanced Development Group (RAD group)

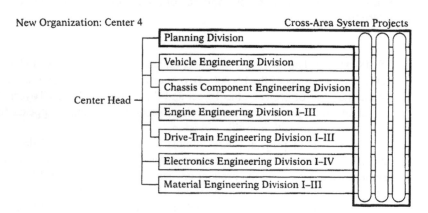

FIGURE 5   Center 4 and its original organization.

important change in mission. Center 4 focuses on developing components and subsystems for vehicle projects. In contrast, the RAD group was more oriented toward research. The relationship between the RAD group and vehicle projects resembled that between upstream and downstream organizations. Now Center 4 has become a part of the vehicle development organization and is responsible for subsystem components that Toyota can better develop outside specific vehicle projects.

   The RAD group had about 2,000 people, whereas Center 4 has about 4,000. As discussed earlier, companies can develop some components or subsystems like electronics and new engines outside specific vehicle projects. Centers 1–3 can now focus on creating well-integrated and distinctive products.

One of the most significant improvements regarding Center 4 was the introduction of a new organizational mechanism called the "cross-area system project." Developing some subsystems requires new technical knowledge in multiple areas. To create such new components, Toyota forms project teams containing engineers and researchers from multiple technical areas. Toyota temporarily locates these projects in Center 4's planning division, and the head of Center 4 selects and assigns their leaders. In the old RAD group, different technical areas usually worked separately, and there was not enough coordination to deal easily with this type of project.

For example, Center 4 recently developed a new low-cost antilock brake system (ABS). In this case, Toyota was able to use similar systems for all its new vehicle projects. It would not be efficient for an individual vehicle project or a product development center to develop new technology that required innovations in the chassis, electronics, and materials. Toyota thus formed a project team including people from these technical areas to develop the new ABS.

The head of Center 4 is also in a good position to integrate the different technical areas. In the old organization, division managers of the different technical areas were relatively independent. The old RAD group also gave top priority to inventing new technologies. As a result, top management gave each division relatively strong autonomy with respect to research agendas and time frames. The introduction of the cross-area system projects represents the new orientation of Center 4 as well as the new important role of this center head.

Toyota did not completely discard its basic research functions. Toyota Central Research & Development Laboratories, Inc., which has about 1,000 researchers, continues to work on basic research as a separate R&D unit. In addition, because Center 4 became less oriented toward research, Toyota established a new internal research division and assigned about 500 researchers to this unit, primarily from the old RAD group.

3.7 Summary of Organizational Changes

Figure 6 summarizes the changes in Toyota's vehicle development organization. This evolved from the old product development group to Centers 1–3. Meanwhile, the component and subsystem development organization evolved from the RAD group to Center 4.

As we have seen, the new center organization simplified product development in two ways. First, it excluded some areas of component development to allow projects to focus on the integration of product development activities, rather than component development. This change reduced the number of

Change in Coverage of Product Development Organization

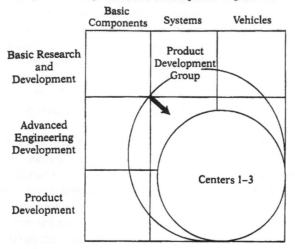

Change in Coverage of Component Development Organization

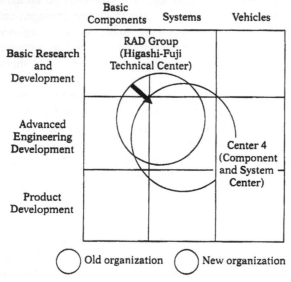

○ Old organization   ○ New organization

Source: Based on "Outline of Toyota Technical Center," Toyota Motor Corp., 1991 and 1993.

FIGURE 6 Changes in the vehicle and component development organizations.

people in the core development organization from about 7,000 to 5,000. Second, Toyota divided the entire product development organization into three centers. As a result, each center only has about 1,500 to 1,900 people. This is a drastic change with respect to management scope, compared with the 7,000 people in the earlier product development organization. In component development, Toyota shifted the orientation from research to subsystem development. Because Center 4 is responsible for developing more components and subsystems than the RAD group, the number of people increased from about 2,000 to 4,000.

4 OUTCOMES OF THE ORGANIZATIONAL CHANGES

After introducing the center organization, Toyota claims to have achieved significant improvements in several areas.

4.1 Project Integration Through a Streamlined Structure

Figure 7 summarizes the impact of the reorganization on reducing coordination tasks for chief engineers as they manage different functional groups. As discussed earlier, before the reorganization each chief engineer had to coordinate, on average, 48 departments in 12 divisions to develop a new vehicle. Primarily because of the reduction in the number of functional divisions and

Number of Divisions/Departments

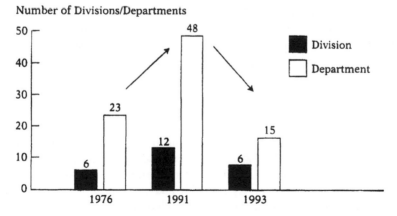

Source: Based on "Activities and Achievements of FP21," Toyota internal document, 1994.

FIGURE 7   Changes in the number of divisions coordinated.

departments, a chief engineer in the new organization has to manage only 15 departments in six divisions. Toyota also compared these numbers with those back in 1976, when there were only about 5,000 people working in product development. At that time, each chief engineer had to communicate with 23 departments in six divisions. The change into the new organization reduced the communication complexity down to the level of 1976, when the shusa organization still worked relatively effectively.

Each functional manager and engineer now covers a wider portion of the automobile design. Because of this, cross-functional coordination tasks have decreased among chief engineers as well as engineers, which directly affects the effectiveness and the efficiency of project integration. In addition, it has become relatively easy for functional managers and engineers to see the entire picture of a vehicle project. This change also solved some other problems in the old organization. Engineers can prepare on the job for the time when the company promotes them to managers, because they can now learn about a broader scope of component engineering. Engineers also now seem to have more of a sense of achievement and ownership regarding specific products. This should improve their level of commitment and job satisfaction. Because each functional manager is responsible for fewer vehicle projects than before, it also has become easier for a chief engineer to communicate frequently with functional managers. Chief engineers used to meet with all their functional managers only about once every 2 months. Now, chief engineers and the six functional managers, as well as the center head, have weekly meetings, called the Center Management Meeting.

The appointment of Center heads also greatly improved project and product integrity—how well pieces fit together to get a high-quality outcome. Chief engineers, as in the old organization, still have not assumed formal authority over functional managers. On the other hand, Center heads oversee all product development projects, including the work of functional managers. The Center heads can work directly on integrating different engineering functions. Using their positions, they can support chief engineers if problems arise in coordinating different functions. For example, when chief engineers encounter difficulties in negotiating with a strong functional manager, they can discuss the issue in the Center Management Meeting and seek the support of the Center head. This makes it easier for the Center management to arrive at decisions and implement them relatively smoothly and quickly. In this sense, with the backing of the Center head, chief engineers have regained more of the authority that the original shusas used to enjoy.

Table 1 summarizes progress on some important performance measurements [11]. According to Toyota sources, the new organization helped reduce

TABLE 1 Outcomes of the Center System Reorganization

	Performance Change	Major Factors
Development cost (average project)	30%	• Reduction of prototypes • Increase in component sharing
Number of prototypes (average project)	40%	• Intensive coordination between different engineering and testing functions • Increase in CAE usage
Lead time (average project)	Shortened by a few months	• Reduction of prototypes • More extensive simultaneous engineering

Source: Based on "Activities and Achievements of FP21," Toyota internal document, 1994.
Abbreviation: CAE, computer-aided engineering.

development costs on the average project by 30% and the number of testing prototypes by 40%. The drop in prototypes was a primary reason for the reduction in development costs. Fewer testing prototypes reflects, in part, more effective communication and coordination. To test many different items in one prototype, projects need intensive coordination among different design divisions and testing divisions. For example, without good communication, it would be difficult to combine the testing items for interior equipment and the chassis into a single prototype. Good coordination within a center also enables technically related projects to share some test data, such as basic platform characteristics regarding handling. In addition, simplified communication and project coordination have enabled Toyota to increase the extent of simultaneous engineering. This has helped cut project lead time by a few months. Stronger project management supported by the Center head also may have contributed to quicker decision-making and faster progress in development.

5 MULTIPROJECT INTEGRATION WITHIN A CENTER

The new organization strengthened the multiproject perspective because of the leadership of the Center heads and support from the Center planning divisions. We noted that, before 1992, the large number of vehicle projects made it difficult to manage Toyota's entire project portfolio and interproject coordination. Now, participants at the weekly Center Management Meetings discuss the details of multiproject management. In addition, each Center has its own building so that all Center members can be co-located. Co-location at Toyota emphasizes the geographical integration of the center members, rather than just the members of an individual project, which is becoming common in the United States.

To achieve better integration within a Center, each also now defines its own vision and theme for product development. Sharing a basic vision that focuses projects within the Center helps members effectively coordinate engineering activities. As of the mid-1990s, the development theme or focus of each center was as follows:

Center 1: Development of luxury and high-quality vehicles
Center 2: Development of innovative low-cost vehicles
Center 3: Development of recreational vehicles that create new markets

We can see another example of change in cost management activities. Toyota used to set and monitor targets for development and total product costs at the individual project level, led by individual chief engineers. Most cost management staff members worked directly for chief engineers, and their orientation was the cost performance of individual projects. In the new organization, in addition to cost management at the project level, each Center sets and monitors the cost targets for all the projects within the Center, led by the Center head. Cost management staff members now belong to the planning division in each Center and report to the planning division manager as well as to the Center head. The new cost management activities and Center structure, thus, have increased the concern with multiproject management. Specifically, each Center has incentives to increase component sharing among multiple vehicle projects, which is one of the best ways to reduce product costs. Project-centered management and "one-at-a-time" thinking cannot do this.

With respect to component sharing, one critical issue each Center is now working on is to reduce the number of basic platforms used among different products. For example, Center 2, as of the mid-1990s, offered five distinct platforms:

1. Celica/Carina ED/Caren
2. Camry/Vista
3. Corona/Carina
4. Corolla/Sprinter
5. Tercel/Corsa/Starlet

The planning division manager in Center 2 believes that five platforms for compact-size, front-wheel-drive models is too many. The center planned to significantly reduce the number of the platform designs over the next several years. In the past, Toyota managers tended to justify so many distinct designs by economies of scale because they manufactured more than 200,000 units per year of each of the five platforms. It is true that there are scale economies with the different dies needed to make the platform designs. At that level of production, a company does fully use each die for its entire useful lifecycle. There are many other areas that could benefit from a reduction of platform designs, such as prototype design, production and testing, and component development and handling.

This manager concluded our interview by admitting that a major challenge for his center was to develop products that use as many common components as possible but still provide customers with differentiated functions and value. The focus of each Center's planning division on a limited number of technically related projects appears to have facilitated this objective through more careful project portfolio management.

For parts smaller than the platform, Toyota also has started a sharing program that monitors component and subsystem usage in individual projects. Toyota chose 290 different components or subsystems for this initiative, ranging from instrument panel subassemblies to small parts such as door regulators. A Center makes a list of a limited number of variations for each component group. New product development projects then choose components from the list. When engineers from a vehicle project want to invest in a new component, they must come up with a new design that has a better cost-value ratio than existing components on the list. When a new component design meets the requirement, it replaces one of the components on the list, so that the total number of variations will not increase within the firm. Because of the Center organization, management of this program has become practical and effective. In the old organization, because of the large management scope, Toyota did not pursue this type of sharing very systematically.

Another sign of better integration among Center members is a growing sense of intercenter competition. The three Centers now compete with each other to reduce costs, using products developed before the reorganization as benchmarks. Of course, this type of competition could have a negative impact on organizational learning if each Center tried to hide its good processes and technical discoveries. At Toyota, however, this does not seem to be the case. Senior executives and the Center heads strongly encourage engineers to learn as much as they can from the other Centers and to share innovations. For example, each Center has its own engineering functional divisions, such as body engineering and chassis engineering. Three engineering divisions for the same type of technologies and components compete with each other. When one body engineering division comes up with an idea for cost reduction, engineers from the other two divisions commonly learn the new technique at least for the next project so they will not fall too far behind best practice.

Other activities have started within each Center to strengthen their integration, which directly or indirectly helps multiproject coordination within the center. For example, Center 1 held a design and engineering competition in which groups of young designers and engineers competed with innovative car designs for a public motor show. Center 3 has started an initiative called the "Let's Challenge Program" to encourage center members to submit interesting and useful ideas for new models. Each center also publishes its own newsletter.

6 COMMENTS

Addressed below are some potential problems of the Center system, which came up during our interviews.

First, Toyota has found it difficult to balance the autonomy of the chief engineers with the authority of the Center head and the objective of improving Center integration. Extensive guidelines for chief engineers imposed by Center managers would not boost the motivation and commitment of chief engineers or the people who work for them. Nor do Toyota executives want chief engineers to work only on what the Center managers want. Therefore, Toyota has encouraged the Center managers to provide only basic guidelines and to allow the chief engineers to retain as much authority as possible. Executives also have carefully chosen the Center management teams. For example, six people play a critical role in Center management: three Center heads and three planning division managers. Except for the planning division manager of Center 3, who used to be an engine design manager, five of the six used to be chief engineers. This personnel assignment may help avoid any misunderstandings between the Center managers and chief engineers.

Second, Toyota has experienced some problems coordinating across the Centers. The Centers' managers combine projects based on technology and design relatedness and try to minimize intercenter coordination requirements. Compared with other grouping schemes, such as around market similarities, Toyota's Center organization should increase component sharing *and* produce distinct products. There are still difficulties, however. For example, when sports-utility vehicles became a hot segment, all three Centers wanted to introduce one of these models. Because Toyota did not need to develop three sports-utility vehicles at the same time, executives had to step in and coordinate the plans of the three Centers. How to solve this problem was not so clear, however. Either Center 1 or 2, which are responsible for basic sedans, or Center 3, which develops sports-utility vehicles, could have been logical choices to create a sports-utility vehicle based on a sedan platform. Toyota executives eventually decided that only Center 1 or 2 should develop this kind of vehicle to take advantage of the sedan platforms. Improving coordination across the Centers could become the subject of another reorganization in the future. At the moment, however, the advantages of relatively autonomous development centers seem to outweigh the disadvantages by a large margin.

7 NOTES

1. This chapter is based mainly on interviews at Toyota with three general managers, four product managers, 15 engineers, and three cost management planners between 1992 and 1994. We also visited the company several times between 1995 and 1997.

2. Schonberger, 1982; Cusumano, 1985; Womack, Jones, and Roos, 1990.

3. Ikari, 1985; Womack, Jones, and Roos, 1990.

4. See Womack, Jones, and Roos, 1990; and Womack and Jones, 1996, as well as Cusumano, 1985.

5. We used Ikari, 1985, as a reference for the shusa organization during the 1950s and 1960s.

6. Each of the 10 shusas was responsible for the Crown, Mark II, Publica, Century, Celica/Carina, Toyota 200GT, Corona, Corolla/Sprinter, Toyoace, and Mini-Ace.

7. The 7,000 people in the 16 engineering divisions and the 2,000 people in the RAD group added up to 9,000. There were, in total, about 11,500 people working on product development. The rest of the people were engaged in support activities such as patent management, certification process management, CAD system development, and prototype development.

8. Even though there were 16 engineering divisions, a chief engineer for a particular project did not necessarily need to manage all of these. These data were based on Toyota's internal measurements. The company did not explain in detail its methodology for determining these metrics, however.

9. There were a few exceptions. For example, as of 1991, there were already two separate body engineering divisions, each of which was responsible for front-wheel-drive and rear-wheel-drive vehicles, respectively. Therefore, each functional manager was in charge of about half of all the vehicle projects.

10. Because the Research and Advanced Development group was

mainly located in the Higashi-Fuji Technical Center, these two names often are used interchangeably. Higashi-Fuji is located about 150 miles east of Toyota headquarters, where most product development engineers are located. This chapter uses a shorter name, the RAD group, which is not used at Toyota.

11. We rely on data from an internal Toyota document. The manager who provided us with this document claimed that these numbers are based on a comparison of similar projects, although we did not receive a more detailed explanation of the measurement methodology. The numbers in this table include direct outcomes of the change in the organization structure as well as those of accompanying process changes. In addition, some factors not directly related to the reorganization, such as an increase in the use of computer-aided engineering (CAE) tools, are also included.

REFERENCES

MA Cusumano. The Japanese Automobile Industry: Technology and Management at Nissan and Toyota. Cambridge: Harvard University Press, 1985.

Y Ikari. Toyota tai Nissan: Shinsha Kaihatsu No Saizensen [Toyota versus Nissan: The Front Line of New Car Development]. Tokyo: Diamond, 1985.

R Schonberger. Japanese Manufacturing Techniques. New York: Free Press, 1982.

J Womack, D Jones. Lean Thinking, New York: Simon & Schuster, 1982.

J Womack, D Jones, D Roos. The Machine That Changed the World. New York: Rawson Associates, 1990.

23

Multiple Projects, Limited Resources: Implementing Effective Project Management

Bradley K. Alston

1 INTRODUCTION

There comes a time in an organization's existence when someone will ask, "Isn't there a better way to do this?" Until that point in time, a common form of managing projects is the "whatever" method. This method uses whatever knowledge and means a project manager has to manage a project. By following the "whatever" approach, individual project success is highly dependent on the individual project manager's ability. If we were to ask the question, "How do you manage your projects?" of an organization that uses the "whatever" approach, the answers will vary greatly. However, the answers would, most likely, depend on the level of skill and understanding of each particular project manager. The techniques, tools, and methods used by the project managers would follow the same dependency.

Methods used will range from "gut feel" to a more formalized method with defined process steps. Tools will range from none, or paper and pencil, to automated planning, estimating, and scheduling systems specifically designed

Adapted from the *Proceedings of the Project Management Institute 1998 Seminars and Symposium.*

for project management use. All of the project management efforts will commonly be performed independent of each other. Therefore, any successes are not communicated to other project managers.

Faced with the task of implementing a more structured approach to project management, where do you start?

2 A GENERALIZED PROJECT MANAGEMENT SOLUTION

For the most part, organizations begin establishing a more formalized project management method based on a grass-roots effort. This phenomenon occurs because that is where most of the "pain" is being felt, and management has yet to realize that better project management is what is needed. The anticipated benefits of increasing the level of project management maturity is that the organization will see more projects being completed on time, within budget and with the desired quality of deliverables.

Sometimes the anticipated benefits of better project management fail to materialize. The desire to provide a robust and extensive project management system can lead an organization into project management overkill. The sequence of events for the improvement of project management within an organization will probably follow the steps outlined below.

1. A team is formed to address the issues surrounding the organization's project management situation.
2. The project management team makes a list of tools and vendors that will address the needs of the organization.
3. Tools are evaluated.
4. A recommendation is made to management as to which tool(s) should be purchased.
5. Approval is given, along with the recommendation that a project management coordinator be appointed to direct the implementation efforts.
6. During the implementation, the project management methodology is developed. The methodology contains a rather comprehensive set of organization-specific standards and guidelines.

3M HIS Experience: After following the steps above, our organization chose ABT Corporation's Project Workbench (PMW) as the preferred tool. One of the capabilities of PMW was that it could handle multiple projects.

3 INITIAL IMPLEMENTATION

Once your project managers get back into the "real world," it won't take long to find out how effective the training and implementation was. In fact, there will be project managers volunteering such statements as, "I can't use this!" "Our project is too different to use this," and "I don't think I'm the right person to do this." Upon closer inspection, you find that the root cause of these types of statements is that the project managers are trying to fill a dual role. From an information technology (IT) perspective, project management is commonly a "second job" that technical team leaders, lead analysts, or other technical team members are asked to fill. Unfortunately, software projects have a tendency to involve project managers more directly than we would like. They end up not having enough time to apply proper project management techniques and tools to their project(s). When time constraints are tight (and when aren't they on a software project?), the technical tasks are performed while the project management tasks take a back seat.

It is difficult in this type of situation to expect proper project management to take place for those dealing with only a single project at a time. The difficulties and frustrations are compounded in a multiple project environment.

That is not to say that there haven't been successes. In fact, you will find that there are varying degrees of successful application of project management techniques on each project. You will also find that those who had a lower degree of success will be the ones who are fairly vocal about it. Some of the more common statements heard are "I can't use this!" "Our project is too different to use this," and "I don't think I'm the right person to be doing this."

3M HIS Experience: It became apparent that those who do relatively well are those who have either a higher degree of interest in or have some affinity for project management. A lot of feedback we received concerning the project management effort was interpreted as "we need this stuff, but we don't have time to do it!"

One interesting phenomenon we noticed was that the success, or failure, of applying good project management practices to our projects did not have much to do with the actual tool being used.

4 NEXT STEPS

It is extremely difficult to provide a project manager with more time to perform his work. However, what can be provided are ways to make the project management effort less time consuming. This is a "first aid" approach to project management systems; that is, apply appropriate first aid to the area(s) with the most need.

A tactic used frequently in sports when things are not going very well is to go back to practicing the fundamentals. This tactic can work for project management implementations as well! It really doesn't matter where you are in your implementation or what your project environment is. Fundamentals are always in style. After all, aren't the fundamentals what we need before we get more sophisticated as time goes on? If we can get a handle on the application of fundamentals to single projects, creating a multiple project environment will be more tolerable. So, what are the fundamentals of project management? The answer to that question should be something close to scope, schedule, costs, and resources. Without timely and accurate information on these project elements, management of that project will be extremely difficult. If managing a single project were difficult, a multiple project environment would quickly become overwhelming.

3M HIS Experience: Two areas of our project management system needed to be addressed: methodology and tools. A decision was made to look at ways of simplifying our defined project management methodology and the use of tools to support that methodology.

4.1 A "New" Methodology

As might be expected from implementing a comprehensive project management system, it can be difficult and overwhelming for those involved in applying the methodology and tools.

3M HIS Experience: We were being less than successful after the initial implementation of our "do all, end all" methodology. It was decided that a better approach would be to provide a set of simple guidelines to our project managers, asking only for the fundamentals. It was hoped that doing so would increase the understandability of how to apply project management in our "unique" environment.

The perception of "uniqueness" was that our project managers were also development team members who had to fill dual roles in a software development environment.

The implementation strategy now follows the steps outlined below.

1. *Develop a clear and concise guideline for a particular piece of the project management system.*
2. *Implement the piece developed in step 1, above.*
3. *Allow some "field testing" time to elapse.*
4. *Review the effectiveness of the implemented piece.*
5. *If the results of step 4 are favorable, select another piece of the project management system and repeat the steps above.*
6. *If the results of step 4 are not favorable, modify the guidelines to better meet the needs of the project managers.*
7. *Repeat the process until all desired pieces of the project management system are in place.*

After a time, all of the fundamental components of a project management methodology will be in place. The success of implementation will be a matter of continuous monitoring and improvement. By focusing on needed fundamentals, our methodology went from a 60- to 70-page document to a 20-page document.

A parallel effort to reduce the size and complexity of our original methodology was the modification of use of PMW. We also introduced new tools that we felt would further reduce the time necessary to apply good project management techniques to our projects.

4.2 The How-Tos

First, remember what the goal of providing project information will bring. For single projects, goals will be focused on being able to better control the project. In a multiple project environment, goals will be more along the lines of making more informed resource allocation decisions (human and capital) and managing the project portfolio. Having information goals will provide guidance as you address the questions of "What do I need to provide the necessary information?" and "How do I get what I need to provide the necessary information?"

Second, using "What do I need to provide the necessary information?," develop a set of questions that addresses the required "what's." The following is a partial list of "what" questions that show up frequently when addressing an organization's informational needs.

- What has been done?
- What is planned to be done?
- What resources are needed?
- What does the project look like?
- What corrections need to be made?

Asking project stakeholders to develop a list of "what" questions will save you the time and effort of coming up with what you think they need. After all, the stakeholders are the ones who require the information in the first place! Analysis of the stakeholder's questions will generally show two trends:

1. The data required by the stakeholders is relatively basic.
2. Each category of stakeholder (e.g., functional management, customer, and sponsor) will require slightly different presentations of the same data.

Third, decide how you are going to get the data necessary to answer the stakeholder's "what" questions. Most of the data can be found in your current

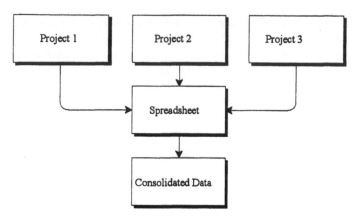

FIGURE 1 Project consolidation.

project management tool(s). A number of tools are available to address the needs of single projects. However, if you are trying to consolidate data across multiple projects, the single project tools quickly reach the limit of their effectiveness. You can consolidate project data by extracting the single project data and using a spreadsheet, or other tool, for the consolidation activity (Figure 1).

Without the capability of storing data to a single repository, generation of cross-project information becomes tedious and time consuming. A repository-based solution is a must for multiple project environments (Figure 2)! The remainder of this chapter will present what 3M HIS has done to improve its project management system through simplification.

Tools and Users

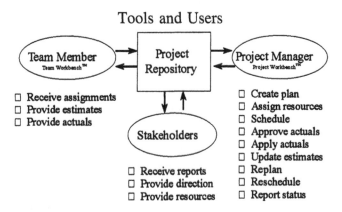

FIGURE 2 Project management system.

Activity	Time Saved (hrs)
Time Sheet Reconciliation	0.5
Code Lookup	0.2
Paper Handling	0.3
Total	1.0

FIGURE 3 Team member time savings.

5 PROJECT MANAGEMENT AT 3M HIS

Our organization selected ABT Corporation's Project Repository (PR) as part of our project management solution. What the repository did for us was to provide a central facility for data collection. This data can then be viewed from different perspectives as required by different project stakeholders. In addition, one of the "bottlenecks" in our project management effort was the administrative burden associated with time tracking. We used a manual system. Therefore, in addition to the repository product, we added ABT Corporation's Team Workbench (TWB) product as one of our project management tools. Team Workbench allowed us to reduce much of the administrative burdens associated with reporting time by project team members. Team members would no longer have to figure out which project codes to use on their timesheets or pass paper among themselves and their project manager. Project managers would be able to receive "up to the minute" status of effort on tasks.

A view of our project management system's tools and users and the roles each of the users play is shown in Figure 3.

When asked what the actual time savings was, one of our project's team members provided the figures shown in Exhibit 3.

The total time saved is not immediately very impressive. However, multiply this figure by the number of resources using TWB and the result can be astounding, especially if you translate it into a dollar amount! One of our functional managers estimated that approximately 70% of their administrative time was saved during the timesheet review and approve cycle every month by using TWB. We are still in the process of improving the time reporting procedures and anticipate an even greater reduction in administrative time and cost.

The prerequisite for project team members using TWB effectively is the creation of a project work breakdown structure (WBS). Instead of imposing a formalized project template with a mandatory structure, we trained the project managers on a few basic concepts behind creating a WBS and let them develop

Project A

Assigned Resources	Availability
Resource 1 Name	50%
Resource 2 Name	75%
Resource 3 Name	30%

FIGURE 4   Resource assignment.

it according to their particular project's needs. Additionally, the project WBS was subject to review. These reviews were informal one-on-one sessions in which suggestions were made for improving the usefulness of the WBS.

In the repository-based environment, each project was initiated within the repository. Initiation involves creating an empty WBS, the assignment of team members, and allocation of team member's time as a percentage of their availability (Figure 4).

The benefit of being able to centrally specify the availability of a resource to a project or projects is that total allocation of each resource can be monitored. What that means in a multiple project environment is that as resources are assigned, requested availability is validated so as not to allow overallocation. Issues concerning the assignment and allocation of project resources can be addressed by the functional manager responsible. Using resource information provided from the repository, functional managers could more clearly see the potential effects of reassignments or reallocation of resources.

Information regarding resource effort by time codes, percentage of time spent on a given project, and direct versus indirect time spent (project vs overhead) is provided during the course of the project. Once the project is underway, data are being collected daily; that is, team members are providing the effort being expended on project tasks through the time tracking tool, TWB. These data are used to provide the necessary information for objective resource management decisions.

Outside of functional management, other project stakeholders are more interested in the scope and schedule aspects of the project. However, by focusing on the basic measures of these aspects, all the informational needs of the stakeholders are met. Below is a list of data points included in our effort to better control projects. We are trying to provide information necessary for objective decision-making, not data for heavy statistical analysis.

Resource 1

Assigned Projects	Allocated Time
Project A	50%
Project B	20%
Total Allocated	70%

FIGURE 5   Resource allocation.

Using periodic reports, these data points are compared to previous measurements to determine trends, both good and bad.

Project Area	Measure
Scope	• Total number of tasks and their status (not started, started, and completed)
Schedule	• Total number of hours (actuals and estimates) • Project end date • Milestone dates

Measuring critical project areas increases our ability to control that project. Applying the same methods and techniques across multiple projects gives a more clear understanding of our project portfolio as well as project interdependencies. This leads to increased ability to set project priorities and make resource adjustments (Figure 5).

6   SUMMARY

Difficulties managing a single project will be intensified in a multiple project environment. Therefore, it is critical to establish practices and tools that enhance the opportunity for project success on a project by project basis. Any incremental gains on a single project will provide substantial cumulative gains in a multiple project environment.

Don't get lost in the intricacies and complexities that project management can, and usually does, provide. Remember the primary objectives for having project management in the first place—planning, tracking, and controlling project scope, schedule, cost, and resources. In other words, don't forget the fundamentals. Simplify your methodology and tool usage. When you find something that works, transfer that knowledge to other projects and include it in your methodology. Build your tool usage and methodology over time, using the successes from previous tries. The amount of time needed to develop an adequate and effective project management system will depend on organizational maturity, which includes management support, available budget, interested people, and the like.

There are no substitutes for education and training. Be prepared to provide recurrent training, mentoring, and consulting to those asked to follow methodology and use the tools you have developed. Do not leave out the necessary management training! It is especially important to help management understand the role of project management in the organization and the benefits received from following the methodology and using the tools. All of this effort will cost money; the more of a business case you make of it, the more management will understand why it is being done.

Don't ever expect a "silver bullet" approach to solving your project management needs. A solid foundation with evolutionary growth will reward you with a more robust and practical project management system than if you were to try the "big bang" theory of project management implementation.

By implementing an effective project management system, you can satisfy statements such as "do more with less," "do it right the first time," and "work smarter, not harder." Better project management will result in better business performance. Now all that is needed is to make it happen!

Bibliography

Anonymous. Critical chain concepts. Scitor Corporation, www.scitor.com, 2000.

Anonymous. 2000. Leveraging Microsoft Project in a multi-project environment. Artemis Management Systems, www.artemispm.com, 2000.

Anonymous. 2000. Multi-project scheduling and Open Plan. Welcom, www.welcom. com, 2000.

Anonymous. 2000. Programme Management Definitions. The Programme Management Web Site. www.e-programme.com, 2000.

Abba, WF. How earned value got to primetime: A short look back and glance ahead. Proceedings of the Annual Project Management Institute Seminars & Symposium, 2000.

Abdel-Hamid, TK. A multi-project perspective of single project dynamics. Journal of Systems & Software 22(3):151–165, 1993.

Agarwal, R, L Roberge, M Tanniru. MIS planning: A methodology for systems prioritization. Information Management 27(5):261–274, 1994.

Aguilh, F. Understanding software release management. Proceedings of the Annual Project Management Institute Seminars & Symposium, 2000.

Akiyama, Y, T Ohki, T Ohkubo. A practical and quantitative approach to improve program management for service and outsourcing. Proceedings of the Annual Project Management Institute Seminars & Symposium, 2000.

Alston, BK. Multiple projects, limited resources: Implementing effective project management. Proceedings of the Annual Project Management Institute Seminars & Symposium, 1998.

Archibald, RD. Managing High Technology Programs and Projects. New York: John Wiley & Sons, 1992.

Ash, R, DE Smith-Daniels. The effects of learning, forgetting, and relearning on decision rule performance in multiproject scheduling. Decision Sciences 30(1):47–82, 1999.

Balachandra, R. Critical signals for making the go/no go decisions in new product development. Journal of Product Innovation Management 2:92–100, 1984.

Bartolomeo, TL. Program management in a multiple IPT environment. Proceedings of the Annual Project Management Institute Seminars & Symposium, 2000.

Batavia, R. How to maximize project success with the right contracting strategy. Proceedings of the Annual Project Management Institute Seminars & Symposium, 2000.

Becker, M. Project or program management. PM Network 13(10):78–79, 1999.

Berkey, W. Where in the schedule is your budget? Proceedings of the Annual Project Management Institute Seminars & Symposium, 2000.

Bernstein, LS, DJ Lazicki. MIS for implementing multi-project programs. Proceedings of the Infrastructure Planning and Management Conference, 357–361, 1993.

Berry, DB. Planning and managing multiple projects. PM Network (November):49–53, 1999.

Bowers, M, R Groom, K Morris. A practical application of a multi-project scheduling heuristic. Production & Inventory Management Journal 37(4):19–25, 1996.

Bock, D, JH Patterson. A comparison of due date setting, resource assignment, and job preempting heuristics for the multiproject scheduling problem. Decision Sciences 21(3):387–402, 1990.

Burgess, JS. Program management: Modernization help for LHAs. Journal of Housing 50(5):200, 1993.

Bunnik, EC, GA Garrett. Creating a world-class PM organization: A success story. PM Network 14(9):52–55, 2000.

Buttrick, R. The Interactive Project Workout. 2nd ed. London: Financial Times/Prentice Hall, 2000.

Calogero, B, LE Metcalf III. Global program management: Solutions for the next generation of programs. PM Network 14(6):40–44, 2000.

Carter, A. As program management function evolves, benefits increase. Engineering and Management 142(3):26–29, 1995.

Chen, V. A 0–1 goal programming model for scheduling multiple maintenance projects in a copper mine. European Journal of Operational Research 76 (July), 1994.

Clark, CW. Software packages don't management projects—people do! Proceedings of the Annual Project Management Institute Seminars & Symposium, 2000.

Coffin, MA, BW Taylor III. Multiple criteria R&D project selection and scheduling using fuzzy logic. Computers & Operations Research 23:14, 1996.

Combe, MW, GD Githens. Managing popcorn priorities: How portfolios and programs align projects with strategies. Proceedings of the Annual Project Management Institute Seminars & Symposium, 1999.

Cooke Davies, T. Leading change programmes. Project Manager Today, June, 1998.

Cooper, RG, SJ Edgett, EJ Kleinschmidt. New problems, new solutions: Making portfolio management more effective. Research Technology Management 43(2):18–33, 2000.

Coulter, C III. Multiproject management and control. Cost Engineering 32(10), 1990.

Cusumano, MA, K Nobeoko. Thinking Beyond Lean: How Multi-Project Management Is Transforming Toyota and Other Companies. New York: Simon and Schuster, 1998.

Davies, C, A Demb, R Espejo. Organization for Program Management. New York: John Wiley & Sons, 1979.

Davis, EW, GE Heidorn. Optimal project scheduling under multiple resource constraints. Management Science 17(12):803–816, 1971.

Daw, C. Managing multiple projects is much like raising teenagers . . . managing resources over multiple projects. Proceedings of the Annual Project Management Institute Seminars & Symposium, 1999.

Dawood, R. Quarto pyramid model of the project. Proceedings of the Annual Project Management Institute Seminars & Symposium 1–8, 1996.

Dean, BV, DR Denzler, JJ Watkins. Multiproject staff scheduling with variable resource constraints. IEEE Transactions on Engineering Management 39(1):59–72, 1992.

Deckro, RF. A decomposition approach to multi-project scheduling. European Journal of Operational Research 51(1):110–118, 1991.

DeMaio, A, R Verganti, M Corso. A multi-project management framework for new product development. European Journal of Operational Research 78(2):178–191, 1994.

Diab, ME. Teaming in the virtual world . . . getting beyond location. Proceedings of the Annual Project Management Institute Seminars & Symposium, 2000.

Dinsmore, PC. An executive game plan for managing enterprises by projects. Proceedings of the Annual Project Management Institute Seminars & Symposium, 1999.

Dinsmore, PC, T Treneman. Enterprisewide project management: Getting off to a solid start. Proceedings of the Annual Project Management Institute Seminars & Symposium, 2000.

Dinsmore, PC, EY Mozes. Corporate project management: Leading the global management transition to the 21st century. Proceedings of the Annual Project Management Institute Seminars & Symposium, 1999.

Dirik, A. Program management excellence: Simple approaches for complex product development. Proceedings of the Annual Project Management Institute Seminars & Symposium, 1999.

Dobson, MS. The Juggler's Guide to Managing Multiple Projects. Project Management Institute, 1999.

Dumond, EJ, J Dumond. An examination of resourcing for the multi-resource problem. International Journal of Operations and Production Management 13(5): 54, 1993.

Dye, LD, JS Pennypacker. Project portfolio management and managing multiple projects: Two sides of the same coin? Proceedings of the Annual Project Management Institute Seminars & Symposium, 2000.

Ejigiri, DD. A generic framework for programme management: The cases of Robert Moses and Miles Mahoney in the U.S. International Journal of Public Sector Management 7(1), 1994.

Elkins, T. Resource management on an ecommerce project. Proceedings of the Annual Project Management Institute Seminars & Symposium, 2000.

Enrick, NL. Value analysis for priority setting and resource allocation. Industrial Management (September-October), 1980.

Eskerod, P. Meaning and action in a multi-project environment. Understanding a multi-project environment by means of metaphors and basic assumptions. International Journal of Project Management 14(2):61–65, 1996.

Evaristo, R, PC van Fenema. A typology of project management: Emergence and evolution of new forms, International Journal of Project Management 17(5):275–281.

Farrelly, E. The next generation of project management rides the information super highway. Proceedings of the Annual Project Management Institute Seminars & Symposium, 1998.

Ferns, DC. Developments in programme management. International Journal of Project Management, August, 1991.

Frumerman, R, D Cicero, C Baetens. R&D programs with multiple related projects. Research Management 30(5), 1987.

Furaus, JP, et al. Communicating in a multi-project environment with a single-sheet project plan. Proceedings of the Annual Project Management Institute Seminars & Symposium, 1995.

Gareis, R. Program management and project portfolio management: New competencies in project-oriented organizations. Proceedings of the Annual Project Management Institute Seminars & Symposium, 2000.

Gentry, M, C Leibensberger, R Manalo. Be the big gorilla, track 15 projects and keep the monkeys off your back. Proceedings of the Annual Project Management Institute Seminars & Symposium, 1999.

Gildea, D. Transitioning from trust to understanding: Introduction of project management initiatives into a legacy program. Proceedings of the Annual Project Management Institute Seminars & Symposium, 1999.

Githens, GD. Programs, portfolios, and pipelines: How to anticipate executives' strategic questions. Proceedings of the Annual Project Management Institute Seminars & Symposium, 1998.

Gokhale, H, ML Bhatia. A project planning and monitoring system for research projects. International Journal of Project Management 15(3):159–163, 1997.

Gordon, J, A Tulip. Resource scheduling. International Journal of Project Management 15(6):359–370, 1997.

Gray, RJ. Alternative approaches to programme management. International Journal of Project Management 15(1):5–9, 1997.

Gray, RJ, PJ Bamford. Issues in programme integration. International Journal of Project Management 17(6):361–366, 1999.

Grove, NE, R Salcedo. Project management of a biopharmaceuticals improvement project in a team-based organization. Proceedings of the Annual Project Management Institute Seminars & Symposium, 1998.

Haas, T. Managing multiple IT projects: Process re-engineering. Artemis Management Systems, www.artemispm.com, 1999.

Harris, JR, JC McKay. Optimizing product development through pipeline management. In: MD Rosenau, Jr. et al. The PDMA Handbook of New Product Development. John Wiley & Sons, 1996.

Hartmann, S, A Sprecher. Hierarchical models for multi-project planning and scheduling. European Journal of Operational Research 94, 1996.

Hartmann, S, A Sprecher. A note on "hierarchical models for multi-project planning and scheduling." European Journal of Operational Research 94(2):377–384, 1996.

Hecker, ML. Setting up and managing integrated product teams. Proceedings of the Annual Project Management Institute Seminars & Symposium, 2000.

Heinrich, P, M Leghorn. 1998. A new class of software application integrated product development management tools. Proceedings of the Annual Project Management Institute Seminars & Symposium, 1998.

Hendriks, MHA, B Voeten, L Kroep. Human resource allocation in a multi-project R&D environment. Resource capacity allocation and project portfolio planning in practice. International Journal of Project Management 17(3):181–188, 1999.

Hennings, CM. Proposing a program office for a service organization. Proceedings of the Annual Project Management Institute Seminars & Symposium, 1999.

Hoffmann, E, J Moore, LV Suda. An enterprise-wide project management approach: Developing systems-wide thinking through training at NASA. Proceedings of the Annual Project Management Institute Seminars & Symposium, 1998.

Howard, PA. Megaproject management using program management techniques. Proceedings of the Annual Project Management Institute Seminars & Symposium, 1998.

Howell, RA. Multiproject control. Harvard Business Review 46(2), 1968.

Ireland, LR. Managing multiple projects in the twenty-first century. Proceedings of the Annual Project Management Institute Seminars & Symposium, 1997.

Jones, K, J Weiskittel. Program management: A key for integrated healthcare delivery systems. Proceedings of the Annual Project Management Institute Seminars & Symposium, 1997.

Joshi, VS, T Cook, R Bonner. Project management approach for small capital projects. Proceedings of the Annual Project Management Institute Seminars & Symposium, 2000.

Juhre, F. Managing international and cross-cultural projects. Proceedings of the Annual Project Management Institute Seminars & Symposium, 2000.

Keefer, DL. Allocation planning for R&D with uncertainty and multiple objectives. IEEE Transactions on Engineering Management 25(1):8–14, 1978.

Kempf, R. Selecting and working with a project management partner. Proceedings of the Annual Project Management Institute Seminars & Symposium, 2000.

Keys, LK. Programs/projects management and integrated product/process development in high technology electronic products industries. IEEE Transactions on Components, Hybrids and Manufacturing Technology 14(3):602–612, 1991.

Khamooshi, H. Dynamic priority-dynamic programming scheduling method (DP)2SM:

A dynamic approach to resource constraint project scheduling. International Journal of Project Management 17(6):383–391, 1999.

Khorramshahgol, R, JP Ignizio. Single and multiple decision making in a multiple objective environment. Advances in Management Studies 3:181–192, 1984.

Kimm, VJ. Program management in a period of strategic realignment: A practitioner's perspective. International Symposium on Technology and Society, 1996.

Klijn, E, L Kroep, H van Mal. Managing cost and time of engineering activities in a multiproject organization. Proceedings of the Annual Project Management Institute Seminars & Symposium, 1998.

Klinger, DJ, CI Saraidaridis, KS Vanderbei. Reliability program management: Today and tomorrow. Proceedings of the Annual Reliability and Maintainability Symposium, 1992.

Kobylarz, K. Establishing a Department of Defense program management body of knowledge. Project Management Journal 23(1):5–7, 1992.

Knutson, J. Managing multiple projects in a matrixed organization. Proceedings of the Annual Project Management Institute Seminars & Symposium, 1994.

Kulbis, RR. Achieving agility with large programs of change. Proceedings of the Annual Project Management Institute Seminars & Symposium, 1997.

Kurstedt, HA, EJ Gardner, TB Hindman. Design and use of a flat structure in a multiproject research organisation. International Journal of Project Management, November, 1991.

Kurtulus, IS. Multiproject scheduling: Analysis of scheduling strategies under unequal delay penalties. Journal of Operations Management 5(3):291–307, 1985.

Kurtulus, IS, EW Davis. Multi-project scheduling: Categorization of heuristic rules performance. Management Science 28:161–172, 1982.

Kurtulus, IS, SC Narula. Multiproject scheduling: Analysis of project performance. IIE Transactions 17(1):58–66, 1985.

LaGassey, GC. Laying track from the cowcatcher of the bullet train. Proceedings of the Annual Project Management Institute Seminars & Symposium, 2000.

Lawler, TP III, K Dieterle. Leveraging project management for process improvement. Proceedings of the Annual Project Management Institute Seminars & Symposium, 1999.

Leach, LP. Developing the enterprise multiproject critical chain plan. In: LP Leach. Critical Project Management. Boston: Artech House, 2000.

Levene, RJ, A Braganza. Controlling the work scope in organisational transformation: A programme management approach. International Journal of Project Management 14(6):331–339, 1996.

Levine, HA. The truth about multiproject scheduling: Now it can be told. PM Network, January: 22–26, 1993.

Levy, N, S Globerson. Improving multiproject management by using a queuing theory approach. Project Management Journal 28(4):40–46, 1997.

Litterer, JA. Program management: Organizing for stability and flexibility. Personnel 44(9): 1963.

Lonergan, K. Programme management. Project—The Journal of the Association of Project Managers, July, 1994.

Lonergan, K, M Dixon. Managing control systems in a programme environment. Project—The Journal of the Association of Project Managers, October, 1994.

Lorenzoni, AB, RE Westney. Control of small projects. AACE Transactions, 1980.

Maltzman, R. Coordinating the coordinators: Thoughts on providing leadership for project managers. Proceedings of the Annual Project Management Institute Seminars & Symposium, 1998.

Mandell, MP. Managing interdependencies through program structures: A revised paradigm. American Review of Public Administration 24(1), 1994.

Matsuura, N. Monitoring and rewarding multiple projects using a weighted performance index in a performance-based contract. Proceedings of the Annual Project Management Institute Seminars & Symposium, 1997.

May, RD. Program management in a changing contractual environment. Proceedings of the Annual Project Management Institute Seminars & Symposium, 1998.

McCauley, M, A Bundy, W Seidman. Effective resource management—debunking the myths. Proceedings of the Annual Project Management Institute Seminars & Symposium, 1999.

McCracken, CJ, PJ Auger, JH Baratta. Program scheduling: Not exactly = project scheduling. AACE International Transactions, 1995.

McElroy, W. Implementing strategic change through projects. International Journal of Project Management 14(6):325–329, 1996.

Meredith, JR, SJ Mantel Jr. Multiproject scheduling and resource allocation. In: Project Management: A Managerial Approach. New York: John Wiley & Sons, 1995.

Mohanty, RP, MK Siddiq. Multiple projects—multiple resources scheduling: A multi-objective analysis. Engineering and Production Economics, October, 1989.

Moore, TJ. An evolving program management maturity model: Integrating program and project management. Proceedings of the Annual Project Management Institute Seminars & Symposium, 2000.

Nelson, B, B Gill, S Spring. Building on the stage/gate: An enterprise-wide architecture for new product development. Proceedings of the Annual Project Management Institute Seminars & Symposium, 1997.

Nkasu, MM. COMSARS: A computer-sequencing approach to multi-resource constrained scheduling. International Journal of Project Management, August, 1994.

Nobeoka, K, MA Cusumano. Multiproject strategy, design transfer, and project performance: A survey of automobile development projects in the US and Japan. IEEE Transactions on Engineering Management 42(4):397–409, 1995.

Nobeoka, K, MA Cusumano. Multiproject strategy and sales growth: The benefits of rapid design transfer in new product development. Strategic Management Journal 18(3):169–186, 1997.

Odum, RF. Program management process on F/A-18E/F—new directions. Proceedings of the Annual Project Management Institute Seminars & Symposium, 1998.

O'Hara, S, G Levin. Using metrics to demonstrate the value of project management. Proceedings of the Annual Project Management Institute Seminars & Symposium, 2000.

Ohmae, Y, S Hasegawa, M Okuda. Multi-project scheduling. Journal of Information Processing 15(2):267–279, 1992.

Olford, WJ. Why is multiple-project management hard and how can we make it easier? Proceedings of the Annual Project Management Institute Seminars & Symposium, 1994.

Oliva, LM. Program management is always team management. Proceedings, International Engineering Management Conference, 1990.

Orr, AJ, P McKenzie. Programme and project management in BT. British Telecommunications Engineering 10(4), 1992.

Padgham, HF. Choosing the right program management organization. Project Management Journal 20 (2), 1989.

Palmer, B. Programme management in the public sector. Project—The Journal of the Association of Project Managers, September, 1994.

Palmer, B. Practical programme management. Project Manager Today, January, 1995.

Paparoni, MN. ALFIL: Multi-project planning and information system. Proceedings of the Annual Project Management Institute Seminars & Symposium, 1994.

Parth, FR. Categorization of small projects. Proceedings of the Annual Project Management Institute Seminars & Symposium, 1998.

Patrick, FS. Program management—turning many projects into few priorities with TOC. Proceedings of the Annual Project Management Institute Seminars & Symposium, 1999.

Payne, JH. Management of multiple simultaneous projects: A state-of-the-art review. International Journal of Project Management 13(3):163–168, 1995.

Payne, JH, JR Turner. Company-wide project management: The planning and control of programmes of projects of different type. International Journal of Project Management 17(1):55–59, 1998.

Pellegrinelli, S. Programme management: Organising project-based change. International Journal of Project Management 15(3):141–149, 1997.

Pells, DL. Program management plans: Effective tools for managing multiple projects. Proceedings of the Annual Project Management Institute Seminars & Symposium, 1998.

Phillai, A, H Seidel, S Wadman. Project and portfolio planning cycle, project-based management for multiproject challenge. International Journal of Project Management 12(2):100–106, 1994.

Pillai, AS, AK Tiwari. Enhanced PERT for programme analysis, and control and evaluation: Pace. International Journal of Project Management 13(1):39–43, 1995.

Platje, A, H Seidel. Breakthrough in multiproject management: How to escape the viscious circle of planning and control. International Journal of Project Management, November, 1993.

Platje, A, H Seidel, S Wadman. Project and portfolio planning cycle: Project based management for the multi-project challenge. International Journal of Project Management, May, 1994.

Platje, A, S Wadman. From Plan-Do-Check-Action to PIDCAM: The further evolution of the Deming wheel. International Journal of Project Management 16(4):201–208, 1998.

Porubeck, D. Program management tools: Additions to the toolkit. Pharmaceutical Technology 24(2):72–80, 2000.

Posner, DA, T Carney. Beyond APQP: A simplified integrated project management system for automotive suppliers. Proceedings of the Annual Project Management Institute Seminars & Symposium, 1998.

Posner, DA, J Kurtz. Utilizing an expert system for development of an integrated project management system for CROs. Proceedings of the Annual Project Management Institute Seminars & Symposium, 1999.

Rakos, J. Automated multi-project planning and control system. Proceedings of the Annual Project Management Institute Seminars & Symposium, 1996.

Ramo, S. Management of government programs. Harvard Business Review 43 (July–August), 1965.

Reiss, G. Programme management, part 1. Project Manager Today, May, 1994.

Reiss, G. Programme management, part 2. Project Manager Today, June, 1994.

Reiss, G. Multi-project scheduling and management. World Congress on Project Management, June, 1996.

Reiss, G. The role of the programme and project office. Project Manager Today, November, 1994.

Reiss, G. Multi-project scheduling and management. Project—The Magazine of the UK Association for Project Management, December-January, 1996.

Reiss, G. Multi-project scheduling & management. The Programme Management Web Site, www.e-programme.com, 2000.

Ricciuti, M. Project management: Easy ways to manage multiple IS projects. Datamation 37(22), 1991.

Rizzo, T. Operational measurements for product development organizations—part 2. PM Network 13(12):31–35, 1999.

Russett, R. Developing and documenting your company program management process. Proceedings of the Annual Project Management Institute Seminars & Symposium, 1997.

Scheinberg, MV. Planning a portfolio of projects. International Journal of Project Management, June, 1992.

Scheinberg, MV. Multiproject planning: Tuning portfolio indices. International Journal of Project Management 12(2):107–114, 1994.

Scheinberg, M, A Stretton. Multiproject planning. International Journal of Project Management 12(2), 1994.

Shankar, V, R Nagi. Overview of a flexible optimization approach to multi-resource, multi-project planning and scheduling. Industrial Engineering Research Conference Proceedings, 1996.

Shapiro, V, N Shutt. Project management meets the year 2000 challenge. Proceedings of the Annual Project Management Institute Seminars & Symposium, 1997.

Sharad, D. ABCs of a multi-project control system. AACE Transactions, 1997.

Sipos, A. Multiproject scheduling. Cost Engineering 32(11), 1990.

Smith, JA. Changing corporate culture—a breakthrough approach. Proceedings of the Annual Project Management Institute Seminars & Symposium, 1999.

Speranza, MG, C Vercellis. Hierarchical models for multi-project planning and scheduling. European Journal of Operational Research 64(2):312–325, 1993.

Stevens, SN. A six-step change process for project management in high-tech organizations. Proceedings of the Annual Project Management Institute Seminars & Symposium, 1998.

Stinson, JP, EW Davis, SM Khumawala. Multiple resource contrained scheduling using branch and bound. AIIE Transactions 10(3):252–259, 1978.

Strange, G. Examination of linkage concepts in programme management. International Journal of Programme Management 15 (March, April, May), 1995.

Strevell, M, S Subramanian, P Cantu. Project portfolio management: Case study— implementation in a microprocessor design center. Proceedings of the Annual Project Management Institute Seminars & Symposium, 2000.

Swanston, WJ, GT Biggar. Developing a framework for establishing cross-functional integration within a product development project. Proceedings of the Annual Project Management Institute Seminars & Symposium, 2000.

Talentino, J, J Sletten. Closing the gap: A multi-project management challenge. Cost Engineering, November, 1990.

Thiry, M. A learning loop for success program management. Proceedings of the Annual Project Management Institute Seminars & Symposium, 2000.

Tonne, CL, R Bauhaus. Wisdom of wizards: Creating the framework for successful new product development—the HP way. Proceedings of the Annual Project Management Institute Seminars & Symposium, 1999.

Tsubakitani, S, RF Deckro. A heuristic for multi-project scheduling with limited resources in the housing industry. European Journal of Operational Research 49: 80–91, 1990.

Tullett, AD. The thinking style of the managers of multiple projects: Implications for problem solving when managing change. International Journal of Project Management 14(5):281–287, 1996.

Turner, JR, A Speiser. Programme management and its information systems requirements. International Journal of Project Management 10(4), 1992.

Turner, R. Programme management: The software challenge. Project Manager Today, March, 1994.

Urbaniak, DF. Integrated program management support system is key to automotive future. Project Management Journal 22(3), 1991.

van der Merwe, A. Program management demystified. International Journal of Project Management 16(1):65–65, 1998.

van der Merwe, AP. Multi-project management—organizational structure and control. International Journal of Project Management 15(4):223–233, 1997.

Vandersluis, C. Multi-project management's conundrum. Computing Canada 21, (26 April), 1995.

Vercellis, C. Constrained multi-project planning problems: A Lagrangian decomposition approach. European Journal of Operational Research 78(2):9, 1994.

Warburton, RE. Business processes for managing multiple projects. PM Network, February, 7–8, 1995.

Waters, JK. Juggling act. Software Magazine 20(2):34, 2000.

Watto, R, P Newman, J Brown. Multi-project management: Tools and techniques. Project Manager Today, March, 1992.

Webb, S, S Lane, M Oliver. Evolving the program management office for e-projects. Proceedings of the Annual Project Management Institute Seminars & Symposium, 2000.

Westney, RE. Effective control of multiple small projects. AACE Transactions, 1989.

White, Cheryl. Theory to practice: SEI CMM L3 rapid attainment techniques. Proceedings of the Annual Project Management Institute Seminars & Symposium, 2000.

White, DE, JR Patton. Metrics and CSFs for your MOBP process. Proceedings of the Annual Project Management Institute Seminars & Symposium, 1998.

Whiteman, C. Is programme management a matter of corporate survival? Project Manager Today, June, 1998.

Whitson, BA. Managing many projects the easy way. Facilities Design & Management, June, 1992.

Whitten, N. Organizing for multiple projects. In: EnterPrize Organization. Newtown Square, PA: Project Management Institute, 2000.

Wiegand, FM. Managing multiple capital projects in the electric utility industry. Project Management Journal 21(3):13–17, 1990.

Wilder, C, B Caldwell, MJ Garvey. Trends: The big puzzle—multiproject management is redefining the way companies handle technology, people, and vendors to make all the pieces fit. InformationWeek (August 3):36–41, 1998.

Wiley, VD, RF Deckro, JA Jackson. Optimization analysis for design and planning of multi-project programs. European Journal of Operational Research 107(2):492–506, 1998.

Wirth, I, A Hibshoosh. Decision support system for multiproject scheduling of resources in blood collection programmes. International Journal of Project Management, November, 1988.

Woodward, CP. Micro to mainframe multiproject scheduling. AACE Transactions, 1988.

Wysocki, RK, R Beck Jr, DB Crane. Extensions to multiple projects. In: Effective Project Management. New York: John Wiley & Sons, pp 268–277, 1995.

Yager, S. Managing multiple projects in large IS organizations. Proceedings of the Annual Project Management Institute Seminars & Symposium, 1997.

Young, TS, JE Pacotti Jr. A new scheduling paradigm: Finite capacity planning for managing the multi-project, resource matrix organization. Proceedings of the Annual Project Management Institute Seminars & Symposium, 1994.

Yuen, M, D Dodds. Object-oriented technology for managing multiple projects. AACE
    International Transactions, 1995.
Zapalac, R, K Kuemmler, T Malagon. Establishing management information systems
    for multiproject programs. Journal of Management in Engineering 10(1): 1994.
Zimmermann, T, S Yohe, J Defarge. Dante: Getting out of the inferno! Proceedings
    of the Annual Project Management Institute Seminars & Symposium, 2000.

Index